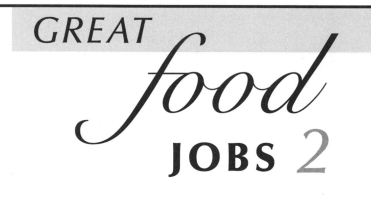

GREAT *food* JOBS 2

PRAISE

"Irena Chalmers is a culinary individualist and food publishing leader who continuously thinks outside the box. Inventing, owning, and running businesses, she questions standards, digs for facts and figures, explores new territory. Which is why this second volume of *Food Jobs* is chockablock with ever more inventive ideas for navigating a career in the food field—and she probably has volume three up her sleeve!"

—PAMELA MITCHELL, FOOD ENTREPRENEUR (AND FORMER EDITOR AT *EVERY DAY WITH RACHAEL RAY*, *SAVEUR*, *EVERYDAY FOOD*, AND *FOOD & WINE* MAGAZINES)

"Irena Chalmer is the ultimate food jobs "matchmaker." Chalmer's marvelous book is a must-have for anyone thinking about a job in the culinary field as it is an excellent resource, brimming with wisdom and information. The reader is encouraged to follow their passion while using creativity and thought to land a dream job. With Chalmers' wit and humor the book makes for incredible reading as she delves into traditional food jobs as well as more rare occupations. *Great Food Jobs 2* will inspire anyone to find the perfect culinary niche."

—STELLA FONG, WINE AND FOOD EDUCATOR, WRITER, FORMER CHAIRPERSON OF IACP COOKBOOK AWARDS

"Irena Chalmers's informative book is a masterful drawing of the curtain to reveal more food-related jobs than you ever imagined possible. Her joy in "matchmaking" people's interest in food with their other passions is genuine, and her light and engaging style makes for a fascinating and enjoyable read. A must-have for anyone contemplating a career in the food world."

— RICHARD GRAUSMAN, FOUNDER & PRESIDENT, THE CAREERS THROUGH CULINARY ARTS PROGRAM (C-CAP)

"Open wide: Irena Chalmers' serves up more appetizing options for a life in food. If I'd had this book years ago, I would have made food my first career (instead of switching to it later). But as this book shows, it's never too late. It's inspiring to see people making a living from food – in so many new, creative ways. A must-read for anyone wanting to meld food-passion with work. Even if you don't work in the food industry now, this book may inspire you to make that long-dreamed of career-change – or not. A comprehensive overview like this is a great tool for gauging what's right for you. *Great Food Jobs 2* is like having a food-career counselor in the palm of your hands. No one knows more than Irena Chalmers about the working world of food, and she spotlights both traditional and new opportunities for raising food passion to a professional level. Brava!"

— Kate Heyhoe, Executive Editor, Global Gourmet

"This is a book that allows you to dream and makes the brilliant Irena Chalmers your fairy godmother. As executive director of Culinary Command, a program for retraining veterans for careers in food and hospitality, we have added *[Great] Food Jobs 2* to our curriculum. It brings hope, wonder and just plain fun to answering the question, "Where exactly do I fit in?"

—Chef David James Robinson, Founder/Executive Director, Culinary Command

"If food is your passion but you want to make it your profession, this is the book you've been looking for. An extraordinary resource jam-packed with creative options and honest advice."

—Kathleen Flinn, author of the *New York Times* bestseller, *The Sharper Your Knife, the Less You Cry*

GREAT *food* JOBS 2

IDEAS AND INSPIRATIONS
FOR YOUR JOB HUNT

IRENA CHALMERS

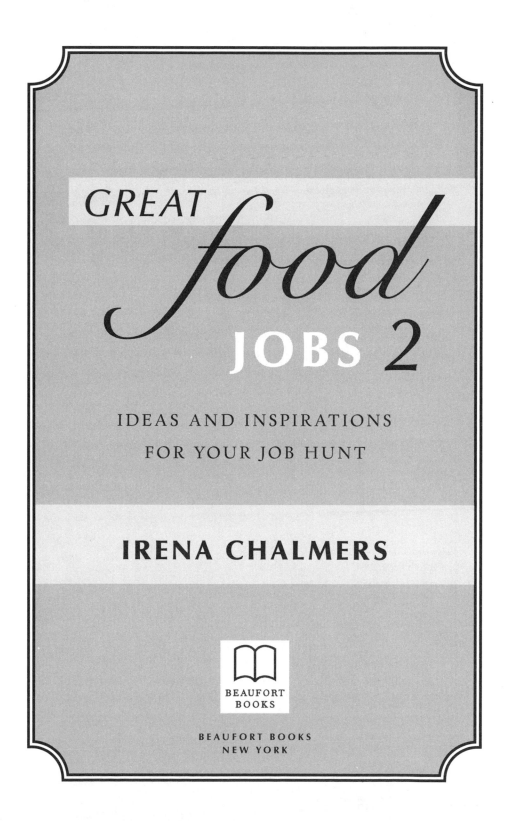

BEAUFORT BOOKS
NEW YORK

FIRST EDITION

Library of Congress Cataloging-in-Publication Data
Chalmers, Irena.
Great food jobs 2 : ideas and inspirations for your job hunt / by Irena Chalmers. -- First edition.
pages cm
Includes index.
ISBN 978-0-8253-0692-1 (pbk. : alk. paper)
1. Food service--Vocational guidance. 2. Cooking--Vocational guidance. 3. Food trade--Vocational guidance. I. Title.
TX911.3.V62C422 2013
647.95023--dc23
2013024829

For inquiries about volume orders, please contact:

Beaufort Books
27 West 20th
Street, Suite 1102
New York, NY 10011
sales@beaufortbooks.com

Published in the United States by Beaufort Books
www.beaufortbooks.com

Distributed by Midpoint Trade Books
www.midpointtrade.com

Printed in the United States of America

Interior design by Jamie Kerry of Belle Étoile Studios

Cover design by Howard Grossman

Contents

No matter what our physical surroundings or our religious and cultural beliefs, we all have many things in common. We all experience the emotions of sorrow and joy, rage and repentance, love and hate, fear and, occasionally, courage.

And everywhere, throughout every part of the world, we gather together to eat and drink at the end of the day. It is this sharing of food that defines us as family and unites us as members of the human family.

Food is the common thread that unites us all. It is love made tangible.

I'd rather entertain and hope that people learn, than teach and hope that people are entertained.

—WALT DISNEY

For Dr. Tim Ryan, president of the Culinary Institute of America; for my many friends on the faculty; and for all the cherished students, past, present, and future.

acknowledgments

LARRY ASHMEAD, THE editor of my *Great American Food Almanac*, was my inspiration. He delighted in gathering information from the most improbable sources, ranging from *Funeral Home and Cemetery News* to *Mr. Popper's Penguins*. I too love stumbling across little-known food facts from anywhere and everywhere, whether from the Academy of General Dentistry, *World Watch* magazine, or *American Demographics*.

This publication expands upon my previous book, *Food Jobs: 150 Great Jobs for Culinary Students, Career Changers, and Food Lovers*. In that companion book, I called on my lovely network of friends in the food world to describe the work they do. This publication, too, owes a debt to the expertise of my colleagues and includes musings and material from my Food Jobs class at the Culinary Institute of America, where I very happily serve as teacher and mentor.

Megan Trank is the editor every writer hopes for but few are fortunate enough to experience. She read and read and reread the manuscript and organized my thoughts into a coherent body of work. I am deeply indebted to her for her wisdom, patience, and dedication.

The design is the invitation to the reader to open the book and turn the pages. It is the designer who provides the soul of a book. I am also profoundly grateful to Jamie Kerry of Belle Étoile Studios, whose many hours of careful work are a fine example of creativity and sensitivity.

And if Megan and Jamie provide the body and soul, it is Felicia Minerva who gives wings to the manuscript. My appreciation envelops them all and include Eric Kampmann, friend and brilliant founder/CEO of Beaufort Books.

Finally, to the Culinary Institute of America's dean of liberal arts and business-management education, Dr. Kathy Merget, and to Associate Dean for Liberal Arts, Dr. Denise Bauer, I express my deepest affection and admiration.

introduction

"Everyone has an internal compass. Some find it and it points the way to go. Others find it but choose to ignore it. Yet others don't know it is there. They may trudge along on well-worn paths that lead nowhere."

—Ann Patchett, author *State of Wonder*

AMONG MY GREATEST joys in life is teaching a course at the Culinary Institute of America in Hyde Park, NY. It is devoted to love affairs.

I am the matchmaker.

My class is entitled Food Jobs. Students tell me what they love to do in their spare time (like riding a bike or playing the guitar or going shopping), and I try my best to find or invent a food job for them. The cyclist is now writing a food column for a cycling magazine, the guitar player has been hired as a personal chef for a rock group, and the student who likes to go shopping locates props for a food photographer.

They use their culinary knowledge and combine it with a passion to do something that will make them happy.

The key word here is "passion." When you talk to anyone who has been successful, "passion" is the word that always crops up.

I am always pleased when I receive a call from a food lover who is thinking about embarking on a new career in the food world or changing from his or her current job and entering a new corner of the vast food universe. Sometimes together we can figure out a new path that hasn't previously been glimpsed.

DECISIONS, DECISIONS

If you want to work in restaurants, you must love restaurants—and many of us do—but you might also consider employment at a health spa, a museum café, or a kitchen in a hospital. You could work at a country club, where perks might include access to the golf course, tennis courts, swimming pool, or sailing. Perhaps you would prefer to be a corporate chef or a private chef. If you worked in a kitchen at a college, this might allow you to audit classes—tuition-free.

It is important to try to form a link between at least two things that you are good at. If you love drinking beer and can cook, consider opening a brewpub at which small meals are served. But not any old brewpub, a distinctive one. Brew your own beer. Find a farmer willing to grow special hops for you. Make yours the only place to be for the in-crowd.

Deciding what to do is incredibly difficult, because there are so many choices. There is no star to point the way and no map to guide each person's unique journey. The decision to embark upon a career or apply for a new job involves—or should involve—a lot of serious thinking. *Right now.* If not now . . . when? Wait and you'll miss the bus.

▶▶ FOOD FOR THOUGHT ◀◀

Any business will be more successful if it is well designed. There are three components to ensuring a thriving restaurant: 1) good food, 2) good service, 3) great value. First impressions set up the expectations.

OPTIONS ON THE HORIZON

Many students dedicate enormous sums of money toward earning a degree from a culinary school. Countless hours are spent in classrooms. A phenomenal amount of physical and emotional effort is spent pursuing a degree, yet when graduation day arrives, too little time is devoted to thinking about and planning for what comes next. Too often, the first job offer is accepted because it is the only one on the table. Fortunately (though I fear I sound like Pollyanna), there are indeed many opportunities waiting to be discovered.

SAILING THE OCEAN BLUE

There is nothing more satisfying than charting your own journey and sailing through the storm to your personal port. Having a sense of direction is infinitely less scary than being lost at sea. You have many destinations from which to choose.

You could be a private chef and travel with an international superstar or diplomat or with an athlete who is competing on the world stage. Have you considered cooking on a small luxury yacht? You'd be responsible for preparing three meals a day, but you wouldn't need to worry about car payments or the rent for an apartment. Nor would you have to pay taxes on your income whenever you were at least three miles off shore.

Many major restaurants, fast food chains, and catering companies—including Aramark and Sodexo—have branches in several countries, as do hotels and food-processing companies. Look into employment at Kimpton Hotels, W Hotels, and other worldwide boutique and resort hospitality companies, as well as the familiar names. Is it possible there might be a job for you at Sundance, Robert Redford's environmentally sensitive property in Utah and home of the famed film festival?

Employment in the United States can lead to many travel opportunities abroad. Supermarkets and food-processing companies engage experts to travel the world in search of coffee, tea, cheese, chocolate, olive oil, pasta, cookies, and other prepared foods and raw ingredients.

Would you like to design vegan wedding cakes (for such clients as Chelsea Clinton) or to create sculptures of butter or ice? Locate your hero and beg for an internship opportunity. With any luck, you may ascend to a permanent position.

Would you prefer to be a career counselor or an event planner? A food scientist or the owner of a bed & breakfast? A TV star or a food cartoonist? A literary agent or a restaurant designer? A recipe tester or a flavor maker? The curator of food exhibits or a culinary librarian?

Are you interested in humanitarian causes? Have you thought about developing hunger relief programs or helping write sustainable agricultural or fishing policy? Perhaps you would consider working for a food-related foundation or charitable cause. Or you may want to work for a local soup kitchen or a national organization like Share our Strength or Meals on Wheels, providing food for the frail and elderly. Investigate FoodCorps.org.

It's admirable to volunteer, but there are many surprisingly well-paid positions to be found creating programs to counter cooking illiteracy.

Clearly these are all vastly different career paths. But if you are able to narrow your options, it becomes considerably easier to focus your research. If you are interested in science and technology, you may be able to strike art and design from your list. If you want to cook, explore the dozens of opportunities open to you in restaurants and food service. Similarly (or oppositely), if you yearn to become a writer, you may need to seek employment wherever a check can be found.

What Else Can I Do?

- Pastry chefs can make a living reproducing clients' houses, cars, or boats in the form of special-occasion cakes or well-tempered chocolate sculptures.
- Gingerbread-house designers can auction their "buildings" and give the money to worthy causes. It is great advertising and good public relations too. If you are seeking inspiration, look no further than Martha Stewart's famous gingerbread houses as a starting point.

Would you consider taking a highlighter and marking every one of the jobs mentioned so far with a "Nah," a "Huh?," or a "Wow! I could do that!"?

If you find yourself out of breath or confused by these many options, be comforted to know that they are only a few among many more delicious choices. Just remember, if you are doing anything you don't want to do, you are WYMBAT: wasting your money, brains, and time!

CHANGING COURSE: FROM FOOD LOVER TO CAREER CHANGER

You are taking a huge risk if you are thinking about starting a new career. Simply reading these words is a measure of your bravery, your sense of adventure, and your willingness to take charge of your life.

But whether we know it or not, we are all taking risks all the time. Even if we are classified as full-time employees, we are really freelancers. The sword hangs over our heads by a slender thread. The greatest asset we have is our ability to transform our knowledge and experience into stepping-stones to the next opportunity. Knowledge and experience are worth far more than money in the bank (though having money in the bank is very good too)!

Rather that thinking about permanence and security, we should all be anticipating—indeed, hoping for—change. Change is the only constant in the continuum of our lives.

One third of culinary students are career changers in their mid- to late thirties, and some are even older. They come from all walks of life. They are former airline pilots, lawyers, advertising executives, engineers, scientists, nurses, figure skaters, opera singers, and sales reps. They have previously worked in offices, schools, hospitals, and even in prisons. Some have served in the military or civil service. Many have already worked in restaurants and have determined that an in-depth education from a cooking school will advance their careers. *What they all share is a passion for food (though not necessarily for cooking).*

Once you decide to go to culinary school, you almost immediately have to decide whether to specialize in culinary programs or in baking and pastry arts. Be sure to examine the options available at several schools before choosing one over another.

▸▸ FOOD FOR THOUGHT ◂◂

I received a call out of the blue from someone I didn't know. He wanted some advice about his career, so I asked him to tell me about himself. His answer was, "I want to be rich." He went on to announce that he planned to open a restaurant. At this, I recalled a sheep rancher in Colorado who said, "The way to make a small fortune in this business is to start out with a large one." The same can apply in the restaurant business. I didn't relay this information to my caller.

RESTAURANT WORK IS NOT ALWAYS HOSPITABLE

Working in a restaurant (or owning one) is a dream job for many people, but it ranks among the most notoriously stressful things that you can do. It can be as grueling working in a restaurant on Friday or Saturday evening as it is being a member of the surgical team in a hospital operating room, even one engaged in brain surgery. I know, because I have tried both. (Once, after a seven-hour operation, our surgical team—known affectionately as The Nutcracker Suite—hastened to the staff dining room. On the menu was Brains in Black Butter. Aghast, we all went out for fish and chips!)

The good news is that the hospitality industry is the second largest employer nationwide, providing work for more than thirteen million people. Here's more good news: there *is* a job for you. You just have to find it. Think of how many different dates we all go through before we find the one true keeper.

Thinking Ahead

Deciding to change your career, to embark on a new venture, or even to just change jobs are all major undertakings. Doing so means thinking ahead and anticipating where you want to be in the short term, not the long term. This is because you will probably change your mind *and* change jobs several times. Most people do.

Remember: you're in charge.

You exchange your time for someone's money, but you are not an indentured servant.

To quote Robert Kennedy, "All of us might wish at times that we lived in a more tranquil world, but we don't. And if our times are difficult and perplexing, so are they challenging and filled with opportunity."

WHAT IS SUCCESS?

I was seated next to a stranger at a luncheon. Searching for a topic of conversation, I asked him for his view on the subject of success. "My son is a success," he volunteered without a moment's hesitation. Inwardly I groaned. "Crumbs, now I'm in for it," I thought. I resigned myself to hearing about my companion's wildly successful hedge-fund manager son and his adorable grandchildren. Having no means of escape, I said, "Do tell me about your son."

So he did.

He said that his son had been a rotten kid from the day he was born. By the time he was twelve, he had already been in trouble with the law. By seventeen, the boy had dropped out of school and become a drug dealer. He made so much money that he was able to buy himself a hugely powerful and expensive motorbike. Three days later, he lost control of the bike and hit a tree. In an instant, he became a paraplegic. He would spend the rest of his life in a wheelchair.

Since his accident, the son has invented several valuable tools designed to help people with disabilities. He has testified before Congress on behalf of handicapped people. And yes, he is married and has three adorable children.

My luncheon friend said his son had achieved success in his journey through life.

I agree. Success comes in many guises.

FINDING YOUR NICHE, NOW

The urgent need to find a job is at the top of many minds. Even the crème de la crème are worried. We all have friends who are either actively looking for work or fear that they soon will be. But as has been said, "Out of crisis comes opportunity."

Maybe we should all actively dream about what we secretly *want* to do and cast aside all those horrid, nagging fears about what we think we *have* or *ought* to do to make ends meet. When I am asked to give advice, the most important suggestion I can offer is: If you don't ask for what you want, there is close to zero percent possibility that someone will come along and offer it to you.

Your monumental task is to figure out what it is that you want. Keep an open mind. If your goal is set, figure out who can help you to achieve your objective. Everyone has dark days. Only you can brush away the inevitable doubts that will cloud the horizon and keep going.

The reason an athlete wins a tennis championship is because he has prepared his body and his mind—and hit ten million balls—before winning the final match. Along the way, he loses a few games too. Everyone does. (When an avid supporter declared that a certain politician could walk on water, the cynic replied, "Sure, but can he swim too?") Even saints suffer.

A ONE-WAY TICKET

I very much enjoy my role as a mentor. Sometimes complete strangers call me. They sound agonized. They don't know what they want to do next. One day, a young woman made an appointment to visit me. She arrived in my office and slumped into a chair. She looked really miserable.

"I hate my job" were her first angry words. Pause. "I hate the commute." Sniffle. "I hate the restaurant where I'm working. I hate the people I am working with. I hate the weather here. I *really* hate my boyfriend." I waited a moment. She looked up and said tearfully, "I want to go to Florida."

"Aha," said I.

"It's my grandmother," she volunteered, "She throws a fit every time I say I want to go to Florida." I asked her grandmother's age: sixty-three. I then made a little calculation. Her grandmother could live thirty or thirty-five more years.

I had the answer to her problem. I suggested that either she could stay with her grandmother and throw away the next thirty years of her life, *or* she could buy a one-way ticket to Miami, find a job, and invite her grandmother to come and visit her for a vacation.

Three days later, she threw open my door waving the boarding pass for her flight to Miami. She was beaming. Her grandmother had hugged her and was already planning a vacation to Florida. Ta-dah!

FIRST THINGS FIRST

In Adam Gopnik's book *The Table Comes First: Family, France, and the Meaning of Food*, Fergus Henderson, the creative genius of the London restaurant St. John, complained, "I don't understand how a young couple can begin life by buying a sofa or a television. Don't they know the table comes first? The table comes first. The table comes first, before the meal and even before the kitchen where it's made. It precedes everything in remaining the one plausible hearth of family life, the raft to ride down the river of our existence even in the hardest times." *New Yorker* writer Adam Gopnik agreed with Chef Fergus Henderson and used the concept as the title of his excellent book.

Recommended Books

What Now? by Ann Patchett

Beaten, Seared, and Sauced: On Becoming a Chef at The Culinary Institute of America by Jonathan Dixon

The Sorcerer's Apprentices by Lisa Abend

Blood, Bones, and Butter: The Inadvertent Education of a Reluctant Chef by Gabrielle Hamilton

The Making of a Chef by Michael Ruhlman

The Pleasures of Slow Food by Corby Kummer

Fast Food Nation by Eric Schlosser

Now vee may perhaps have begun.

—PHILIP ROTH, THE LAST LINE OF *PORTNOY'S COMPLAINT*

CHAPTER 1

restaurants and foodservice

Restaurants are not about food; they are about power banking, real estate … and ego.

—ANONYMOUS

Airport Chef
Antarctica Chef
Assistant to Celebrity Chef
Baby Food Chef
Bacon Smoker
Bagel Baker
Barista
Bistro Owner
Bread Baker
Brunch Chef to the Bereaved
Butler
Calorie Counter
Caterer
Cruise-Ship Chef
Dinner & Movie Chef
Dinner-Party Chef
Dishwasher
Embassy Chef
Food Engineer
Food Financial Analyst
Food Geographer
Food Truck Owner
Fine-Dining Restaurateur
Fish Chef
Franchiser
Health Inspector
Hospital Chef
Kiosk Chef
Military Chef
Monastery Chef
Museum Chef
Picnic Preparer
Pizza Chef
Prison Chef
Personal Chef
Recipe Tester
Research Chef
Sandwich Maker
Spa Chef
Specialty-Diet Chef
Table-Manners Trainer
Tabletop Consultant
Vegetarian Chef
Vineyard Chef
Waiter/Server
Water Sommelier
Wedding Food Planner
Zoo Chef

CHANGING TIMES

THERE HAVE BEEN monumental changes in the food industry during the last thirty years. We are experiencing one of the greatest food revolutions of any time in our culinary history. It is as though an enormous tidal wave has swept over the land and left, in its wake, fertile fields ready to be planted with new seeds, new ideas. We have traveled in time and technology, from being intimidated by the haughty maître d's of fine-dining restaurants, to trying to figure out how to eat "food" presented to us on pillows and twigs. As Juliette Rossant, editor of *Super Chef* magazine, explains:

> Major technology changes have enabled chefs to expand their empires: through improved methods of transportation communications, refrigeration, packaging, and education. In the world of food, the "global village" had two levels of impact. On the first, the ingredients of regional cuisines became physically accessible everywhere. On the second, and in contrast, a chef no longer needed to be present physically in any specific restaurant thanks to mobile telephony and the Internet.
>
> Another essential ingredient that made Super Chefs possible was money. The American economic climate of the 1980s and 1990s meant not only that capital was available for such risky ventures as fine dining restaurants but also that more and more people had income to dispose of on the delights of dining in expensive restaurants.

A future historian who wished to look back on the customs of the past would do well to concentrate on our restaurants, because they are reflections of our popular culture. In kind, the leading voices of our own past were Carême and Escoffier. They set the table for cuisine minceur, a rarified cuisine that was introduced in 1974 by Michel Guérard at Les Prés et Les Sources Eugénie. Gael Greene, restaurant critic at *New York* magazine described the singular food philosophy of Guérard's Cuisine Minceur at that time:

> Lunch is quite frankly, breathtaking: a perfect poached egg crowned with tomato coulis, snips of chive, and bits of minced chicken riding a crisp al dente artichoke heart in a cool, pale green sea of subtle cucumber purée—a concerto of texture, color, and taste. What a glorious lunch. But wait. There is more. A second giant plate appears, wearing a serious statement in beige: thinnest slices of duck in a rich pepper-studded sauce (nothing but white cheese—"zero calories," as Guérard puts it—duck stock, and water whirred in a blender) with petals of apples. Dessert is another still life: a trembling fluted mound of delicate coffee custard capped with a crunch of espresso ice, ribboned with candied orange peel and a punctuation of ripe currants.

Gael Green is still writing about restaurants at insatiablecritic.com. She is the co-founder and guardian angel extraordinaire of Citymeals-on-Wheels.

FUTURE SHOCKS ARRIVING IN THE DINING ROOM

Writing in *Leite's Culinaria, Inc.* in 2008, Jess Thomson describes the sixth course at Alinea restaurant in Chicago:

> Ordering the sparkling water requires an interview: "Would you like hard bubbles or soft bubbles? Wineglass or water glass?"

The waiters return, this time bearing big, square pillows, and I'm momentarily thrilled about the prospect of naptime. As they get closer, an unmistakable lavender aroma envelopes our space, and I think how wonderful it would be if one of these pillows arrived in the middle of a trans Pacific airline flight, instead of on my dinner table where I think my plate should be.

But there will be no nap. A duck course alights on each pillow, and we're instructed to eat, quickly. Each time I cut into the tender duck, the plate rocks under my knife, and invisible puffs of lavender escape from the pillow, flavoring the meat through my nose.

I'm delighted but my dining companion disagrees. She sniffs: "This is like eating my underwear drawer."

Reprinted with permission from Leite's Culinaria (leitesculinaria.com)

RESTAURANTS

What Is a Restaurant?

The very word "restaurant" is huge; it embraces every dining experience. As we push open the door, we know just what to expect from a diner, a coffee shop, a fast food restaurant, a pizza parlor, a deli, an ice cream parlor, or the dining car on an Amtrak train. The word "restaurant" encompasses bistro, brasserie, café, cafeteria, grill, tavern, osteria, and trattoria. Each has its own ambiance, and we anticipate that we will receive food that is clean, fast, safe, well-priced, and convenient.

The name of every successful contemporary chef becomes synonymous with the name of his or her restaurant (except at such places as the Four Seasons, Le Cirque, and Disney World, where the name of Mickey Mouse or the brand supercedes the transient names of passing chefs, who tend to leave and launch their own empires).

Hospitality is an all-inclusive concept. It is made of many moving parts and integrates many skills, including those pertaining to art and architecture, design, lighting, and the control of room noise, as well as those skills having to do directly with food. The proprietor strives to create the maximum comfort level, even the correct temperature of the room—the smallest details aim to culminate in an evening of pleasure.

The Food Revolution Begins

Frank Bruni wrote the following in his *New York Times* series, Critic's Notebook:

> In October 1985, Danny Meyer, age 27, turned a corner in the restaurant business and launched a hungry-for-change world with the opening of the Union Square Café. First the publishers, and then the world, beat a path to his always welcoming open door.
>
> A fascination with classic French cooking was forever more trumped by an insistence on something lighter, more flexible, and less hidebound. The trickle of a simpler sensibility from California became a tide. The glories of the Greenmarket took ineradicable root.
>
> That same year Alfred Portale opened Gotham Bar and Grill. And, Drew Nieporent introduced us to Montrachet and his wonderful galaxy of restaurants. Jean-Georges created fusion French/Asian cuisine. Gradually service became less formal and more friendly. Dress codes were relaxed.

FOOD JOB: *Fine-Dining Restaurateur*

Staging, pronounced "starging," is an abbreviated form of a traditional apprenticeship. There is no better way to learn. Study a restaurant you admire and apply for a position to stage there. This is usually an unpaid honor following a successful interview with a senior chef. You will not be paid in dollars but you will gain invaluable experience. Many restaurants will accept an enthusiastic application to stage for a day or longer. During this time, you can decide if this is truly the destination of your dreams. Even if you spend the day peeling carrots, you will be able to make a close observation of the atmosphere and working conditions. A formal letter of application accompanied with a résumé sets the process in motion. If you are unsure of how to address your letter, just call the restaurant and ask for guidance. Easy! This is a time to draw on your network and mention the name of a mutual acquaintance, a teacher, or a brief meeting you may have had with a current or previous employee of the restaurant.

White Tablecloths Are Gone with the Wind

In an effort to reduce monstrously huge bills for laundering white tablecloths, leading-edge chefs are serving their food on bare tables made of (wipe-clean) exotic woods. Restaurant owners are also focusing their attention on less formal service. They are reducing prices and offering shorter menus and simpler foods.

►► FOOD FOR THOUGHT ◄◄

According to Dr. Tim Ryan of the Culinary Institute of America, fine-dining restaurants represent only one-third of 1 percent of all restaurants in the United States.

FOOD JOB: *Bagel Baker*

One of the most interesting breads known to man is the bagel. In America, bagels have their greatest appeal in cities with significant Jewish populations as they were traditionally a Jewish food.

American Demographics magazine reported that gay women buy more honey-wheat bagels than the rest of the population. No one knows why. Nor can we fathom why businessmen in suits buy plain bagels during the week and choose funky varieties at the weekend when they are wearing casual clothing.

We can understand why athletes buy salt bagels and why chewing on a plain bagel comforts teething babies, but why professors prefer poppyseed bagels is anyone's guess.

And how do the demographic researchers know the line of work or sexual preference of those who buy bagels, anyway? Is there an all-seeing identification camera at the counter? Or are the researchers just guessing?

▸▸ FOOD FOR THOUGHT ◂◂

- Bruegger's is the only national bagel chain. It bakes and sells nearly ninety million bagels a year (Bruegger's Press Release, 2012).
- Lender's Bagels, now owned by the Pinnacle Foods Group, had revenues of $40.9 million last year from the sale of 23.4 million six-bagel packages (Symphony IRI Group).
- Ben & Jerry's was originally going to be a bagel company, that is, until Ben Cohen and Jerry Greenfield found out how expensive it would be to buy all the necessary equipment to start their business. They decided it would be cooler to concentrate on ice cream.
- In *The Joys of Yiddish*, author Leo Rosen notes that the first printed mention of the word *bagel* is found in the Community Regulation of Kraków, Poland, in 1610. It states: "Bagels were given as a gift

to any woman in childbirth." Rosen adds that the word is derived from the German word *beugel,* meaning "a round loaf of bread." But those who would dispute this claim that the word is derived from the Middle High German word *bugel,* meaning "a twisted or curved bracelet or ring."

FOOD JOB: *Bread Baker*

Bread, like rice, has transcendent symbolic value in the countries that depend on it for their basic sustenance.

> *Bread knows no boundaries. It is a valued part of almost every culture and religion. Lack of bread can, and often does, result in revolution. History has shown that those without bread hunger for blood. In the distant past, the breaking of bread with friends and family, and even strangers symbolized friendship. Guests would not be harmed but protected in the presence of the host.*
>
> —Unknown

Yes. We Have No Bread

At four p.m. on September 7, 1940, 348 German bombers escorted by 617 fighters began intense air raids on London. Two hours later, guided by the fires set by the first assault, a second group of raiders launched a relentless attack that lasted until four thirty the following morning. An eyewitness recalls that this was the beginning of the blitz. For the next fifty-seven consecutive days, London was bombed day and night. Fires consumed huge areas of the city. Residents sought safety wherever they could find it. Many fled to the Underground subway stations, which sheltered as many as 177,000 people during the nights. The offensive rapidly spread to other cities throughout the country.

German submarines in the Atlantic attacked British supply ships, cutting off the importation of wheat from Canada.

When, in 1946, the government imposed bread rationing, Winston Churchill vehemently opposed the measure. He called it "one of the gravest announcements that I have ever heard made in the House of Commons," and the *Daily Mail* called it "the most hated measure ever to have been presented to the people of [that] country."

During the war, adults in Britain had a weekly ration of two ounces of tea, two ounces of butter, two ounces of cheese, and *one* fresh egg. When they were purchased, these foods were crossed off in the government-issued ration books. The system succeeded in ensuring fairness; everyone was forced to go on an austerity diet. There were no bananas.

How fortunate we are now. We have an abundance of marvellous breads.

The English poet Robert Browning (1812–1889) spoke words of wisdom when he declared, "If thou tastest a crust of bread, thou tastest all the stars and all the heavens."

Recommended Books

The Bread Bible: 300 Favorite Recipes by Beth Hensperger

The Bread Bible by Rose Levy Beranbaum

Bakery Names

Nice Buns	Blue Duck Bakery
Crumbs	Ponies & Unicorns
Sweetie Pies	Sweet Somethings
Take the Cake	

In 2011, Crumbs Bake Shop, the country's largest cupcake chain, went public in a $66 million reverse merger with an investment firm. The company posted an estimated $31 million in revenue from sales of about thirteen million cupcakes at roughly $3.75 per delicacy. One year later, the sprinkles have begun to drop from this rosy delight.

There are no tools that can duplicate the hands of a baker.

—David Braverman

▸▸ FOOD FOR THOUGHT ◂◂

In Portland, Oregon, Ken Forkish bakes a special rye bread. Among his ingredients are grains that have been used by a local brewery to brew beer.

FOOD JOB: *Bistro Owner*

There has never been a better time to open a bistro. In 1986, I wrote *American Bistro* with contemporary recipes, menus, and tales of restaurateurs in the pursuit of dreams. At that time, I thought we were still at the evolutionary stage of the marvelously intriguing adventure trying to sample everything and all at once.

The menu offered sautéed breast of duck with fresh foie gras and golden caviar, as well as cornmeal pancakes with fried chicken and mashed potatoes and gravy. I recall that we had a wonderful time shouting applause and encouragement to the chefs and spurring them on to new creations with which to delight us.

The late restaurateur George Lang and his wife Jenifer were owners of Café des Artistes. For my book, he wrote this recipe:

Yield: One Good-Sized Bistro

The Cooking Utensils

About 4,000 square feet of space near a paved road.

One very long lease, which is like the girdle on a fat lady—maybe it's tight, but it lets her breathe.

Ingredients

For the Dough:

Several sackfuls of money, preferably not yours, and without strings attached.

For Flavoring:

A well-seasoned chef, male or female (between 120 and 200 pounds), preferably one whose ego has to be fed only once a day.

1 *bouquet garni* of assorted cooks and key personnel. Average age should be 30 years old with a minimum of 20 years of experience.

1 bartender with four hands and no pockets.

A medium-sized, all-purpose kitchen planner.

Yeast:

1 fully-grown manager who will make the bistro rise without too much kneading.

For the Sauce:

1 fully ripened interior designer (do not remove backbone).

1 fine-grained graphic designer and one uniform designer (optional).

For the Topping:

1 public relations person, whipped until a froth has formed.

Method

Before combining the ingredients, undertake dozens of market research studies. Then ignore them and go with your own instincts.

A gut instinct is not a reliable economic indicator.

▸▸ FOOD FOR THOUGHT ◂◂

In the United States, American cuisine has surpassed the cuisines of France, Italy, Germany, and pretty much the rest of the universe in popularity. The First Symposium on American Cuisine was convened by Phillip S. Cooke and Daniel Maye in Louisville, Kentucky, in 1982.

• •

My Word: Sushi is the New Pizza

Experts tell us that we can trace sushi's origin back to the fourth century B.C. in Southeast Asia, where salted fish was an important source of protein. The fish was cleaned and packed in rice, where the natural fermentation of the rice helped preserve it. This "sushi" was taken from storage after a couple of months. Only the fish was eaten. The rice was discarded.

Over time, the concept of sushi spread throughout China and, eventually, was introduced into Japan. There, the sushi was consumed when the fish was still partly raw and the rice had not yet lost its flavor. Later yet, during the Edo era (1603–1867), "chefs" began making variations on sushi as a way to eat both rice and fish. During this period, rice was mixed with vinegar and combined not only with fish, but also with various vegetables and dried foods. The new dishes were unique to Japanese culture.

Slowly, slowly, sushi evolved from a way of preserving fish into a distinctive cuisine emphasizing sparklingly fresh ingredients. Today, each region of Japan still maintains its own unique taste by utilizing local products to compose different kinds of sushi.

• •

Sushi Schools

The Sushi Chef Institute (SushiSchool.net) is a culinary school for people who want to learn the essence of sushi-making techniques and their background in Japanese culture. The California Sushi Academy (Sushi-Academy.com) offers one-day, five-day, and twelve-week intensive courses in sushi making.

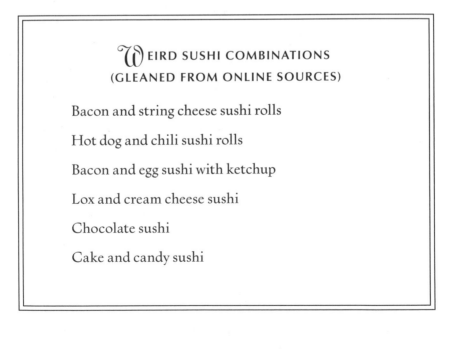

WEIRD SUSHI COMBINATIONS (GLEANED FROM ONLINE SOURCES)

Bacon and string cheese sushi rolls

Hot dog and chili sushi rolls

Bacon and egg sushi with ketchup

Lox and cream cheese sushi

Chocolate sushi

Cake and candy sushi

▶▶ FOOD FOR THOUGHT ◀◀

- Robots can make beautiful sushi with super-human speed.
- In Tokyo a huge tuna was sold at auction for $736,000. That's a mighty big heap of sushi.

FOOD JOB: *Barista*

The term "barista" is derived from the Italian word for bartender, and bartending it is, though the drinks are based on coffee. The job requires the ability to remain calm as customers debate whether to have this or that as a long impatient line forms behind them. Even after the order is placed, the customer must face another quandry: if she leaves a tip in the prominently placed paper cup on the counter while the barista's back is turned, does her generosity actually count?

▶▶ FOOD FOR THOUGHT ◀◀

It takes at least two weeks to learn how to be a barista at the Coffee Bean & Tea Leaf in Los Angeles, California. That includes four days in an actual classroom to "learn the culture" of the company, followed by seven days of in-store work said Jackie Cox, the franchise's training manager.

BECOMING BARISTAS

By Michael Osborne

What is it that transforms a career civil engineer and a nursing-home nutritionist into a pair of highly regarded baristas and the co-owners of a thriving small business? For Ken and Janet Kraft, proprietors of the Crafted Kup in Poughkeepsie, New York, this transformation was not born from an innate passion for coffee beans. The path that led the couple to start this popular coffee shop on the northern edge of Vassar College instead involved checking off boxes on a wish list. As Ken neared retirement, he and Janet began searching for a business opportunity that they could pursue together. Since he was tired of decades of lengthy commutes, finding something to do close to home was one of Ken's top priorities. Both Ken and Janet are people persons, so whatever they did also needed to involve the public in general and young people in particular. Ken is a track-and-field official on the side and really enjoys being around the younger crowd

Out on a couples date in Beacon, New York, Ken and Janet found themselves in a cozy, locally owned coffee house. The community vibe was palpable. Ken says, "That's when it hit me. I can do this." The next piece of the puzzle was to find the right location. This turned out to be no problem at all. A former sushi shop had been vacant for several months, and it was easy to transition the place into a laid-back comfort zone full of soft armchairs, antique end tables, and vintage lamps. Because of its proximity to Vassar, students would make up about 30 percent of the clientele and almost all of the Crafted Kup's labor force.

Next, the Krafts undertook a crash course in coffee. "Coffee," Ken says, "is all about the beans and the water." They did an extensive analysis of Poughkeepsie's water, sent the results to some coffee experts, and determined that a filtration system was imperative. But the analysis didn't stop there. Ken and Janet both had highly technical backgrounds, so they carefully thought through every step that brought them closer to opening. They joined professional organizations, attended conventions, went to barista competitions, sought advice from industry leaders, and invested in top-notch equipment. Ken bought a copy of the *FabJob Guide to Become [sic] a Coffee House Owner* by Tom Hennessy, and he followed the author's instructions to the letter.

Behind the bar, through repetition and by learning from early mistakes, the couple mastered the techniques that produce great coffee drinks. "It's about knowing your customers, and making the drinks the way they like best," Ken says. Assuredly, the details matter. Keeping the equipment clean and properly maintained, knowing the right temperatures, and being able to muster the thirty pounds of pressure required for a quality espresso pull are all just as important as the provenance of the beans and the exactitude of the local roaster. "It's also about really caring about what you do and taking pride in your work," Ken says.

Five years later, the Crafted Kup is clearly doing things right. The business generates enough cash flow to pay the Krafts' salaries and has shown a track record of steady growth. For two years running, *Hudson Valley* magazine has cited the Crafted Kup for the best latte in its large and diverse culinary area.

Ken and Janet warn against the pitfall of starting a business without adequate capitalization and further advise keeping the concept simple. "Our brain trust is one of our most valuable assets." Advice from local restaurateurs, an attorney friend, and from Michael Grant of the Black Cow Coffee Company has helped the couple avoid costly mistakes. "It's been a hard climb," Janet asserts, "but I started without preconceived notions. Everything just kind of fell into place, and I must admit, I've been pleasantly surprised."

Ken and Janet have successfully created a locally owned coffeehouse that competes well against convenience stores and giants like Starbucks and Dunkin' Donuts. It is a place where students and locals alike come to hang out, which is just what Ken envisioned. The recipe is basic: Be consistent with the store hours, the quality of the ingredients, and the dedication to customer satisfaction. It really is that simple.

Michael Osborne is a writer, artist, and CIA-trained chef with Southern roots and an abiding fondness for New York—especially the Hudson Valley

BEHIND EVERY SUCCESSFUL RESTAURANT IS A GREAT STAFF

Owning and running a restaurant are far from the only food service jobs available. Many people start at the bottom of the ladder and gradually ascend to superstar status.

FOOD JOB: *Dishwasher*

A philosopher could argue that the job of the dishwasher is just as important as every other station in a restaurant. There can be no service without clean plates. A remarkable number of successful people started their professional lives as dishwashers in restaurants. Qualifications: must possess a cheerful disposition.

Masa restaurant in New York City seats only twenty-six guests. Each has a twenty-nine-course dinner. The dishwasher must therefore wash 26 × 29 = 754 plates every evening. Fortunately, there are relatively few pots and pans to scrub.

> *The best-paid job should be the dishwasher: the proliferation of little plates results in much more work.*
>
> —Michael R. McCarty, Restaurateur

RARE FOOD JOB: *Food Engineer*

Ed Fountain builds food-tossing devices for advertisers. He has constructed such contraptions as a machine for the Long John Silver's chain that causes shrimp to collide in midair.

FOOD JOB: *Food Geographer*

No, this isn't what you think it is. A food geographer studies traffic patterns, real estate purchases, school enrollment, and other factors within a defined geographic region, even a given zip code, and advises restaurants as to which street corner will be the most advantageous for business.

FOOD JOB: *Waiter/Server*

At the first Symposium on American Cuisine in 1982, the audience was invited to come up with a new, gender-neutral title for a person who brings food and takes away plates. After much introspection, it was determined that this person is a "mommy." The idea didn't catch on though. The preferred term for a waiter is now *server.*

Lost Job

Servers who suddenly find themselves out of work can usually rethink their options. First, though, time is needed to lick wounds: Gone will be the shared family meals (even though the food is often horrible). Gone will be the tips. Gone will be that "couple of beers" with coworkers at the end of the evening.

▶▶ FOOD FOR THOUGHT ◀◀

The poorest-paid "servers" are the guys on bikes who deliver pizzas, Chinese food, and other food items. On a fifteen-dollar order, such a driver might receive as little as a two-dollar tip and some mumbled thanks for his hazardous ride, which may often take him through a cold, wet night.

> *Could anything be worse for an actor, who earns his living as a waiter. He finally gets a part—as a waiter.*
>
> —Henry Morales

New Opportunities for Servers

A lost job is an opportunity to see what is around the corner. It can provide the needed incentive to move to Hawaii or Italy or Spain or Australia. There are embassies in every major city in the world. All of them invite guests to parties. All need servers.

Servers have many prospects lying at their feet. They just have to choose one and bend down to pick it up.

Caterers are always looking for attentive servers who know how to place (not drop) a plate on the table. Some specialize in catering weddings and receptions for politicians and stars of the stage and screen. Work can be found in hunting and fishing lodges, in small boutique hotels, large resorts, and, indeed, wherever food is served. If you can match your hobby, your passion, or your special interests to your talents as a professional server, you'll never look back. You will wonder why you didn't make the move voluntarily.

Benefits of Being a Server

Established businesses may offer some or all of these benefits:

Flexible hours

Salaries paid every week

Additional payment for working on national holidays

Paid vacations

Full or partial medical insurance

Contributions to 401K plans

Life insurance and retirement plans (though not often)

Dining room discounts

Servers' Salaries

Servers at luxury restaurants in Las Vegas can make $150,000 a year and even more, thanks to the electrifying arrival of high rollers renowned as "the whales."

A server working in the banquet department of a luxury hotel or fine-dining restaurant can anticipate an hourly rate of $7.40–$15.00. Add hourly tips ranging up to $16.38. Add overtime of $8.19 to $24.33. Add (hopefully) a bonus of $1,500 to $3,000. Total pay $16,649–$38,710.

Of course, these figures vary from country to country, from city to town, and from business to business.

Note: A server in a diner or small independently owned restaurant earns less than minimum wage. The take-home pay is almost entirely dependent on tips.

My tip: Explore all your options and all the possibilities just waiting for you to take the first step.

My Word: Waiters Must Learn When to Wait

Future servers may recite the nutrient content of each dish and offer a free blood test and weigh out at the end of the meal. There is a rumor that restaurants, not content with the institution of smoke-free areas, will, in the future, designate cholesterol-free, salt-free, and trans-fat-free zones.

Maybe they will also designate "adult" districts, where hedonistic holdouts from the cult of militant health worship may cheerfully drink martinis, eat steak with béarnaise sauce, slather hollandaise sauce on their asparagus, dollop sour cream and butter on their baked potatoes, and generally behave with delicious abandon. Raised eyebrows will be forbidden, as will any unsolicited forecasts on the probable outcome of such wanton self-indulgence.

Guests demand service that is smooth without being stuffy or intimidating. They are looking for big flavors, generous servings, prompt attention and value for their money.

—Restaurant critic

The Rules of the Server

By Sir Wilfred Gowers-Round (1855–1945)

1. A waiter's job is to serve, and never to interpose himself.
2. The ultimate goal of waiting is inconspicuous service.
3. Waiters must be clean and smart, and should never wear cologne.
4. Under no circumstances should a waiter ever touch a diner.
5. Unasked for advice should never be proffered.
6. Unless asked, no plates should be removed until all have finished dining.
7. Women diners should be afforded respect equal to men.
8. The bill should be placed on the table without ceremony.

My Word: Wait a Minute

A lot of people think that servers are transient folk who would much prefer to be occupying themselves with more desirable work, but as the status of the chef has become more elevated, the role of the server has begun to change too. It may be disheartening to toilers in the hot kitchen to discover that more people go to restaurants because the service is good than because the food is fabulous. Guests want to be served, not merely fed.

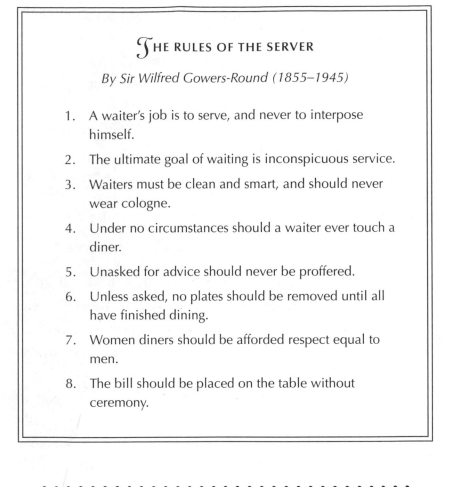

Every now and again there is anguished talk about elevating the public's perception of servers by including the gratuities in the check and offering a decent salary with benefits and paid vacations. A sensible as this proposal seems on the surface, it continues to face implacable opposition from almost everyone.

• •

Management Says "No"

Managers claim that if gratuity were added to checks, the public would be shocked (shocked!), at their total bills. This way of thinking seems to suggest that you *can* fool all the people all the time and that the notion of the expectation of a server's eager anticipation of a tip will always come as a complete surprise. You might think that the restaurant industry, a cornerstone of the American economy, could figure a way out of this quagmire.

Servers Say "No"

Many servers don't want to change the system. Minimum wage is $7.25 an hour for everyone else, but although many weary servers make only $2.13 per hour in wages, in some exalted palaces of gastronomy—particularly those with grand banquet facilities—they can count on very large gratuities indeed.

Guests say "No"

There is a notion, too, that guests like to exert their power by grading server performance and deciding whether to leave a gratuity of the customary twenty percent. The total is rarely more. Sometimes it amounts to considerably less. Research has shown that men tip more if the server is female and that women tip more if the server is male.

Rural servers in the South take home less money than those working in northern cities.

A single guest usually leaves a tip of twenty percent. At a table of five or more, when the check is split, the tip is usually close to 13.2 percent. The larger the party, the greater the likelihood of a reduced tip unless the amount has been agreed to in advance.

Some Tips about Tips

Apparently, it makes little difference whether a server advises the guest to select the baby-back ribs or the scallops, whether he provides his name or grovels or vanishes inappropriately or asks, with his thumb on the plate, "Who gets the lobster?" It makes little difference if he addresses Grandmother as "Señorita" or interrupts the conversation to inquire, "How's everything, folks?" But as sure as can be, a tip will be significantly reduced if a server kneels to take an order, touches a guest, or decorates the check with a smiley face.

A Cornell University study revealed that professional conduct and prompt attention do little to guarantee a big tip from the vast majority of restaurant goers. Instead, the tip is influenced more by the size of the check and a fear of disappointing the server than by the quality of service. If this shocking news is true, then it follows that the notion of managers that tips incentivize good service is invalid. In most other civilized countries, France included, service is included in the check so that no one need engage in arithmetical speculation.

Basically, the notion of the server is not compatible with the American view of equality. Service is given and accepted more comfortably at a gas station. In a restaurant, the role of the guest in relation to the server is less certain, and the prestige of female servers is even more ambiguous.

My Word: Words of Caution

An alert server recognizes when trouble is brewing. An employer who invites an employee out to lunch simply in order to fire him shows extremely bad taste, as do couples arriving late, drunk, or nursing thunderously bad tempers. The server seats such guests side by side on a banquet rather than on opposite sides of the table so that there is less temptation for the terminated employee or the jilted lover to deliver a sharp blow to the nose of his or her antagonist.

Unlike other businesses, restaurants don't usually expand their empires by gobbling up others; they create new ones.

The reason we don't like French restaurants anymore is because they don't serve Italian food.

The reason we go to a restaurant for the first time is not the same reason we go back.

According to recent figures from the US Bureau of Labor Statistics, the culinary industry represents one of the fastest-growing occupational categories in the nation. There are more than 900,000 restaurant locations in the United States, and the industry provides jobs for more than 12.2 million employees. Projected annual sales are increasing at a rate of nearly 5 percent per year and have a total economic impact of over $1.2 trillion.

It is quality of service that sets great restaurants apart from good ones. At a great restaurant, the workers at each level—from the managers, to the servers, to the runners and bussers—know how to come together to perform an intricate ensemble dance.

MESSAGE TO WAITSTAFF

By Joe Baum, Restaurateur

A great restaurant is theatrical and full of energy. At the same time, it is accessible and comfortable. We are in the business of delivering value and an unobtrusive extension of reality. We must sincerely convey the aspiration that everything we do, is for the pleasure and sensual delight of our guests. Our service must be anticipatory, professional, friendly, and leavened with good humor. If this sounds romantic, we must work hard at being romantic, because even classics do not survive unchallenged; they are challenged every night by the relentless American appetite for change. Our commitment is to understand the expectancy of our guests, and our hope is that they will come back often, and that every time they do, they will pause, and smile, and say, "I have always loved this place."

We are in the business of pleasure and every threat to pleasure is a threat to business.

If there is a complaint I want to turn it to my advantage. I want the guests to tell everyone how well I treated them.

Whoever wrote the rules that food tastes better because it's more expensive, more formal, and served with more pretense is wrong.

—Danny Meyer, Celebrated Restaurateur

When Gramercy Tavern opened its doors in 1994, they demonstrated that success can be achieved by using local ingredients when it made sense to do so, and by borrowing and adapting cooking techniques from around the world to create a new style of dining that explodes with excitement and sophistication. They set the standard for a restaurant that is elegant without being intimidating and service that is friendly without being intrusive. The food has big flavors, generous servings and the atmosphere is similar to being welcomed into a big, happy party.

—a Restaurant critic

FOOD JOB: *Water Sommelier*

The post of "water sommelier" turned out not to be the pseudo-job that *Time* magazine's Joel Stein expected it to be, that is, after he lunched with bottled-water specialist Michael Mascha, a former wine sommelier and the author of a book about specialty waters. After preemptively declaring that water has no smell, little taste, and costs too much in most restaurants, Mr. Stein's skepticism was quickly allayed. Mr. Mascha insists that "high-quality bottled waters have unique mouth feels that can affect a fine-dining experience." We learn something new every day!

Behind-the-Scenes Food-Service Jobs

Do not worry if you are not a star in the kitchen or if serving in a restaurant scares you, there are innumerable foodservice opportunities that lie beyond the boundaries of the traditional restaurant.

WHY A BAKED POTATO MAY COST TEN DOLLARS

An industry analyst explains:

When a guest requests the check, he is in reality paying the restaurant's rent. The less costly the real estate, and the shorter time the table is occupied, the lower will be the price of the meal. This is not the only factor that is figured into each menu item by a long shot. The physical space occupied by the table and the chairs—and also included in is the square footage clearance for pulling the chair away from the table to allow the guest to be seated. A percentage of the cost of the initial architectural design, legal fees, insurance, and other setup costs are assigned to that potato. So is the insurance, the investment in china, glasses and silverware and vacuum cleaners, administration costs, salaries, staff uniforms, laundry, flowers, stocking the bar, and the coat hangers for the cloakroom. When you ask for a half portion, you will readily understand the reason(s) half the size doesn't cost the restaurant half its real cost. The longer the time the guest occupies a table, the more money is being burned by the owner.

FOOD JOB: *Food Financial Analyst*

A computer-savvy consultant can find work helping restaurateurs and entrepreneurs gain greater online visibility. Analysts are able to study menu choices made by guests in restaurants and to subtly increase the profitability of the business by redesigning the menu in such a way that it guides the diner to make more profitable food choices.

Porterhouse executive chef and managing partner Michael Lomonaco said the following: "Restaurant food costs should be estimated at 28–32 percent, while labor and related costs should be between 30 and 35 percent of total sales, liquor included. Operating expenses should range from 12 to 15 percent of total sales, and rent, less than eight percent of the total."

A steakhouse has the burden of the high cost of the meat but the relatively small labor cost of tossing the steak under the grill and retrieving a baked potato from the oven.

FOOD JOB: *Health Inspector*

Foodborne illness costs the American economy $152 billion a year. Twenty-five percent of illnesses can be traced to contaminated fruits and vegetables. Doctors tell patients with impaired immune systems to avoid eating any raw foods—everything must be cooked in order to minimize possible contamination. If you ever yearned to become a detective, you could think about becoming a sleuth who searches for the source of an outbreak of foodborne disease. Food inspectors do this same kind of work but under less pressure, so long as an outbreak of *E. coli*, *Salmonella*, or *Listeria* has not actually occurred.

FOOD JOB: *Recipe Tester*

What can I earn if I decide to be a recipe tester?

Recipe testers must cook and write the preparation details of five or more recipes a day. This is sometimes freelance work, and may be billed at $75–$125 per recipe, plus the cost of ingredients. Note that it may be necessary to test a recipe three or even four or more times. A tester working on a cookbook is more likely to be offered a project fee.

▶▶ FOOD FOR THOUGHT ◀◀

The first edition of *The Alice B. Toklas Cook Book* included a recipe for fudge. One of the ingredients was cannabis, a hard-to-find ingredient in

Paris at the time. Apparently (you probably already knew this), the heat of the oven would release the pot's essence and quite light up the taster. It's discovery in the cookbook resulted in its omission from subsequent printings.

As you probably know, pot has been legalized in some states... the idea of potluck suppers has taken on an entirely new meaning!

▶▶ FOOD FOR THOUGHT ◀◀

There are two ways to write a recipe: one is negative, the other is positive. For example, "If you put the cookie dough on a hot cookie sheet, it will spread, and the edges will burn." Or, "If you put chilled cookie dough on a cold cookie sheet, it will keep its shape and bake evenly."

FOOD JOB: *Tabletop Consultant*

A tabletop consultant makes an appointment with the executive chef or restaurant owner and shows pictures of plates, glasses, and silverware (or better yet, a comprehensive collection of real-life samples borrowed from showrooms). After making his selection, the consultant returns all the rejects to the showrooms. This job involves a lot of schlepping.

Restaurant architects and graphic designers work with tabletop and clothing consultants. Seek employment with these specialists and explore fashion and design courses at schools like the Rhode Island School of Design or the Fashion Institute of Technology.

Fashion designers present photographs of innovative concepts for uniforms for cooks and waitstaff. Professional uniform designers hire attractive actors to strut their stuff. The objective is for everyone to look their best.

• •

My Word: Losing Your Shirt

Deciding what to wear when dining at a topless bar may not be the most vexing problem of the day, but the topic of dress codes in restaurants is an issue that gets a lot of people hot under the collar. If you have seen the glorious fashion parade in the film *My Fair Lady*, you will know exactly what do when Her Royal Highness invites you to Ascot to bet on the horses. The rules are clearly spelled out: "A hat must be worn to cover the crown of the head and shoulders must be covered. Trouser suits are permitted, but must be of matching material. Gentlemen are required to be attired in black or grey morning dress with a top hat. Service dress may also be worn. Overseas visitors are welcome to wear the national dress of their country."

Similarly when a fine-dining restaurant says that you can "come as you are," it most definitely does not mean that, if you have a job at UPS, you can expect the welcome mat should you arrive in your brown work togs.

Uniforms identify police and firefighters, nurses and surgeons, astronauts and train conductors, airline pilots and beekeepers, mechanics and cheerleaders, criminals and judges, bathing beauties and baseball players, gowned academics, bikers, ballerinas, and even, ever so briefly, brides, by their wedding gowns.

It is rare for any of these people to show up at a smart restaurant clad in such clothes and say, "Four for dinner, please." Jaws would drop. Conversation would cease.

Restaurant guests are not encouraged to wear anything "funny" on their heads. Except in Texas, it is not considered good manners to wear a cowboy hat indoors—though some seem to think it stylish to wear cowboy boots everywhere they go. Reversed caps advertising a feedlot or oil company are uncouth. Even queens leave their tiaras in the closet when they go out to eat. It is not socially acceptable behavior to wear jewels on your head, but it is perfectly respectable to flash diamonds on your fingers.

Body piercing is permitted if limited to the ears, but only if costly baubles dangle from them. Rings through the nose and tongue are upsetting. Permanent tattoos are frowned upon in some places, though in others, transiently painted faces are highly desirable.

Shirts should never be worn as reading material. Numbered, orange-colored, one-piece prison jumpsuits would be distracting for other diners.

Breathtakingly plunging necklines and skirts slit all the way up to the howdy doody are only to be worn on formal occasions, when there are more than five glasses at each place setting and the gentlemen are wearing tuxedos and bow ties.

A jacket is required to eat lobster if it has already been pried out of its shell. A bib is worn to eat a whole lobster.

Most of us understand all these rules, whether or not they are stated.

• •

CHEFS, CHEFS EVERYWHERE

Chefs can find employment cooking in cafeterias, executive suites, sports arenas, dining rooms, concert halls, luxury retirement villages, dinner-and-a-movie establishments, and for congregations that meet and greet one another at the conclusion of religious services.

▶▶ FOOD FOR THOUGHT ◀◀

A Census Bureau report reveals that the percentage of unmarried Americans in their early thirties has more than doubled during the last decade. Many within this group are expected (by the folk at the Census Bureau, though not necessarily by those in question) to remain single throughout eternity. Restaurants, noting this state of affairs, are increasing the size of their bars so singles can sit beside each other (though not necessarily together) and eat tapas or other little meals.

Recommended Book

Little Meals: A Great New Way to Eat and Cook by Rozanne Gold

FOOD JOB: *Airport Chef (Height Haute)*

Restaurant Smart Brief reports the following: "Airport restaurants run much like traditional eateries, with a few additional challenges: they benefit from delays and flight cancellations but all too often the seats are filled with hungry, grumpy passengers who are unwilling guests. It is not surprising that among the many rules and regulations is the requirement for sharp kitchen knives to be tethered at all times. Metal knives on restaurant tables are not permitted."

In addition to this, all food deliveries are carefully scrutinized for lethal bugs of all kinds. Every new employee must first undergo security clearance. Servers are required to have the patience of a saint. So this is an occupation that has to cope with more than the customary challenges.

Even so, there are several entirely different kinds of work in this sector of the hospitality industry. Food jobs range from menu planning, recipe development, and recipe testing to financial management and waitstaff jobs.

Private plane chefs have a slightly easier time than those who work at busy airports—they can supply elegant snacks or partially cooked food that is reheated aloft in the microwave. The chef must bear in mind that the sense of taste is greatly diminished when cruising at 30,000 feet. (This is the reason airlines often serve food that tastes of mostly nothing at all.)

If there is a small, private airport near you, write a business plan, bring samples, offer your services as an official caterer. Check every airline individually for employment opportunities.

> *We don't have airport restaurants; we have restaurants in airports and must maintain the same standards in each place that bears our name.*
>
> —Airline Food Consultant

▸▸ FOOD FOR THOUGHT ◂◂

- Airline food is now eaten before boarding the plane. There is no more pie in the sky.
- Smart hotels are now offering "picnics" as parting gifts. The meal is designed to be eaten with one hand while flying in a cramped airline seat or driving.
- Resident chefs are offering club-class passengers such goodies as smoked salmon pizza.

★ RARE FOOD JOB: *Antarctica Chef*

If you look at a map of the world, it really isn't that far from New Zealand to Antarctica. But the distance between working as a pastry chef at a posh New Zealand resort to working as a baker at the remote McMurdo Research Station in Antarctica is enormous.

Enter Gemma Tarlach, the Culinary Institute of America '07 graduate and intrepid baker and chef who found this continent—inhospitable to human life, save for the technology that makes it possible—among her favorite places on earth. After trying out McMurdo for a summer as a production baker (when the research facility has a population of one thousand and the temperature hovers at a balmy negative five to negative thirty-five degrees Fahrenheit), Gemma decided to "winter over." That means living through Antarctica's darkest, windiest, and coldest months, when temperatures range from between negative forty-nine and negative ninety-four degrees Fahrenheit. It takes a special kind of person to winter over, and only two hundred people remain at McMurdo during these months. Everyone who takes on the challenge of wintering over must pass a psychological evaluation before being accepted.

Gemma loves the Antarctic's barren landscape, the interaction with the station's scientists, the quirkiness of her colleagues, the challenge of creating good food with limited ingredients, and, of course, the ever-present emperor penguins.

Supply flights are so few that Gemma's culinary challenges can be as dramatic as the weather she faces. But having previously worked at both a huge Las Vegas casino preparing banquets for fifteen thousand and a super-exclusive resort catering to only twenty-four patrons at a time, nothing really ruffles her. She's gone from having organic flour and exotic fruits at her fingertips whenever she wants them to relying on the summer plane from New Zealand for fresh dairy products. When fresh ingredients run out, Gemma works with powdered dairy products and other stores from a massive yearly delivery of food, materials, and scientific equipment known as the "vessel evolution."

For the next several months, not even planes can get in or out, so Gemma has learned to be creative in an entirely new way. Tinkering with recipes to get them to work when she has run out of bread, flour, sugar, or molasses can be both fun and maddening, but she loves the challenge.

Originally printed in mise en place *magazine, a publication of the Culinary Institute of America (June 2011)*

FOOD JOB: *Baby-Food Chef*

Sales of organic baby food produced by small-scale entrepreneurs continue to soar into the stratosphere. Frozen and jarred foods for tiny tots sell for a premium, at least four times more than mass-produced varieties. This sector is forecasted to expand, even if the birth rate declines or remains unchanged. In the minds of many moms, the word *organic* is equated with purity.

FOOD JOB: *Bacon Smoker*

The smoking of various foods is becoming increasingly popular. Small, artisanal entrepreneurs are smoking everything from bacon and pork to fish and shellfish. Everyone has an opinion about the right equipment, the correct wood, and the perfect time and temperature to use. To get started, order several different kinds of bacon online. Taste critically. Judge the degree of smokiness that most appeals to you and try to replicate it. Put Benton's hickory-smoked bacon at the top of your list. Seek advice from experts. Create a website and use social media to find customers for your products. Splurge on packaging. It is important that your food look as sublime as it tastes.

FOOD JOB: *Brunch Chef*

When I ask culinary students whether they enjoy the role of brunch chef, almost all of them reply with an emphatic "NO!" So my conscience doesn't allow me to recommend this job.

Woody Allen reports that at a brunch in memory of his father, the departed was depicted in a lifelike (or almost lifelike) bust of chopped liver. There wasn't a dry eye among the mourners.

• •

My Word: What's for Brunch?

It's good to keep things simple. Breakfast on the Concorde on a flight from Paris to New York was simple. The only thing on the menu was a bowl of berries with a silver spoon and more than enough champagne to chase away any lingering fear of flying. Breaking the sound barrier (twice) is not conducive to elaborate fare.

Health spas, too, have a hard time coming up with edible brunch-buffet offerings. There is not a lot you can do, even under the best circumstances, to coax an egg white into tasting like anything good, especially when it has been stuffed with the kind of weeds that grow wild in cracks in the pavement. The undeniable truth is that the words "healthy" and "breakfast" don't go together with the same blissful harmony as does the made-in-heaven marriage of bacon and eggs.

In my opinion, we are confronted with far too many choices on the brunch-buffet table. First thing in the morning, it is taxing to decide whether to have the grapefruit juice, orange juice, apple juice, or cranberry juice; the fried eggs, poached eggs, scrambled eggs, or steak and eggs. Shall I have hash browns or grits? Whole wheat or white? Bagels or muffins? Scones or biscuits? Waffles or pancakes? Danish pastries, French toast, or English muffins? Butter or margarine? Tea or coffee? Regular or decaf? Milk and sugar? Large, medium, or small? On and on it goes.

There are far too many descriptive adjectives to plough through as well: crunchy (granola), crispy (bacon), sizzling (sausage links), house-smoked (lox).

"Assorted" is another word that crops up on a lot on brunch menus: assorted seasonal fruits, assorted pastries, assorted cereals with 2 percent, skim, or regular milk.

"Your choice" is another favorite line. It is a subtle way of suggesting that it would be polite to select only one—either/or but not both. We are invited to sample an establishment's "very own, homemade, fresh-baked, farm-fresh, country-fresh, new-laid (or is it -lain?), freshly-brewed selections."

It would save everyone a heap of trouble if brunch chefs would just pare everything down to tea and toast or coffee and a croissant. And the Sunday morning newspaper. A Do Not Disturb sign would be good too.

• •

FOOD JOB: *Brunch Chef to the Bereaved*

I've noticed that a bunch of people have been dying lately. This presents a great opportunity for chefs.

We should remember that funerals are for the living. The most honored survivors walk slowly, with bowed heads, and mourn from a lectern. Grieving friends who are held in high esteem are invited to shoulder the casket, from out of doors to the indoors and then back out again.

Others simply sob.

All this heavy-duty emotion is sure to build a hearty appetite. Brunch for the bereaved is a niche market that is assured of growth as the population ages and as the inevitable becomes, well, unavoidable.

►► FOOD FOR THOUGHT ◄◄

As the creator of Maxwell's Plum, the operator of Tavern on the Green, and the restorer of the Russian Tea Room, Warner LeRoy was a larger-than-life restaurateur. At his memorial service, one of his friends wryly noted: Warner "always yearned to be awarded another star from the restaurant critic of *The New York Times*, and now, when you look up at the night sky, you can see him shining brighter than all the millions of others." Warner always was a shameless competitor.

FOOD JOB: *Cruise-Ship Chef*

Catering on a cruise ship can be an exciting and challenging job. CruiseJobLine.com supplies the prospective chef with the following qualifications to consider before jumping aboard:

- I like to travel internationally.
- I enjoy working with teammates from around the world.
- I don't mind working seven days a week during intense, four-to-eight-month stretches of time.
- I can adjust to sharing a small-sized cruise cabin.
- I can handle unpredictable sailing conditions and participation in cruise staff safety procedures. Check Cruise Lines International Association for job listings and search the Web sites of specific cruise lines.

You never know: perhaps it would be prudent to take swimming classes before applying.

FOOD JOB: *Specialty-Diet Chef*

Developing your skills as a chef knowledgeable of specialty diets, whether vegan, vegetarian, diabetic, low cholesterol, low fat, gluten-free, salt-free, or kosher, will open many doors, whether in corporate settings or as a personal or private chef.

FOOD JOB: *Assistant to Celebrity Chef*

There is a particular pleasure to be obtained by simply being in the company of like-minded people. A food lover will be in the center of the action as a personal assistant to a celebrity chef.

The job requires the ability to write well. It is necessary to communicate with the staff and the media, help with speech writing, make travel arrangements, and organize literally every facet of the boss's life. To get a good idea of the ever-expanding role of a trusted personal assistant, check out this terrific Web site, MyVeryOwnAssistant.com/special-events.html. Dinner reservations are (sometimes) among the perks.

FOOD JOB: *Celebrity Chef*

How do *you* become a celebrity chef like Rachael Ray, the EVOO (extra virgin olive oil) media hottie? At thirty-seven, Rachel signed a $6 million book contract. In her spare time, she launched a magazine called *Everyday with Rachael Ray* while her talk show bubbled on the front burner. *Chowhound* pegged Rachael's annual earnings in the multimillion-dollar range a few years ago.

Rachael began making real money even though she isn't a chef and didn't earn a degree from a cooking school. Nevertheless, she is a celebrity.

Paula Deen isn't a chef either, though she is the star of three TV food shows. Her estimated net worth hovers in the stratosphere—$24 to $28 million. Her speaking fees, along with those of several other food celebrities, run from between $75,000 to $100,000 per talk. Culinary stars are also provided with first-class transportation, luxurious lodging, and complimentary "incidentals" like breakfast and booze.

Wolfgang Puck *is* a chef with several stars to his credit. He is also an entrepreneur and the originator of many branded consumer products. His annual take-home pay soars around $16 million. His launching pad was pizza. Since opening his first restaurant, Spago, in West Hollywood in 1982, Wolfgang Puck has opened a total of twelve fine-dining establishments and thirty-four casual restaurants. He is a force of nature and even opened a restaurant in London. The James Beard Foundation honored him with a Lifetime Achievement Award in 2012.

It is such great entertainment to count other people's money, though invariably, we are quite wrong.

Recipe for Success: Anthony Bourdain

Anthony Bourdain observed, "Few things are more beautiful to me than a bunch of thuggish, heavily tattooed line cooks moving around each other like ballerinas on a busy Saturday night. Seeing two guys who'd just as soon cut each other's throats in their off hours moving in unison with grace and ease can be as uplifting as any chemical stimulant or organized religion."

Anthony Bourdain, who attended Vassar College and the Culinary Institute of America, wrote an article that appeared in the *New Yorker* in 1999 entitled "Don't Eat Before Reading." This led to his first book, *Kitchen Confidential*, which has been translated into seventeen languages. He has likewise been a star of several TV series. *Get Jiro*, his first food-themed graphic novel, is ruthlessly and comically violent and speaks to the cultlike obsessions of the foodie elite.

The Influence of Celebrity Chefs

As an admired group, celebrity chefs exert an ethical influence over a large sector of the food universe that is quite disproportionate to their relatively small numbers. They forge alliances with local farmers, who supply them with superior ingredients. The chefs become betrothed to the food media, who in return adore them and provide them with favorable press coverage and shower them with awards. This powerful triumvirate—chef, farmer, and the media—influences the opinions and purchasing decisions of millions of consumers.

Paul Bocuse: The Most Celebrated of Celebrity Chefs

It was a big, big weekend at the Culinary Institute of America when a final round of the Bocuse d'Or USA Competition was staged there. Everything was in readiness. The students were giddy with excitement. The teams of competitors for the award were given five hours to prepare and half an hour to plate both a meat dish and a fish dish, along with an array of garnishes. The meat and fish to be used had been announced in advance. A galaxy of multistarred judges waited to scrutinize the contestants' results.

A stunning amount of practice and effort would lead up to the American team's final five-and-a-half hour marathon in Lyon, France, following this qualifying round at the CIA. Five hundred thousand dollars had been raised for the team. Part of this money was used to build a rehearsal space—an exact replica of the Bocuse kitchen at the Greenbrier in Lyon—inside the very same Cold War cafeteria bunker in which Congress would have been served in the event of a nuclear war.

The Culinary Olympics

The former director of the German Chefs initiated the Culinary Olympics in Frankfurt in 1900. This biggest and most traditional of culinary competitions takes place every four years and has become a Mecca for cooks and *pâtissiers*, with contestants arriving from forty-five different nations. Several chefs from the Culinary Institute of

America, including its current president, are gold-medal winners of this arduous contest.

Michelle Obama Holds Hands with the Naked Chef

Chefs are holding hands with advocacy organizations and community leaders. Under the banner of Alice Waters (the saint), Jamie Oliver (the naked one), and Michelle (the Obama), they are teaching little children how to grow and cook their own food. They are doing well by doing good. Astute politicians have long known that this kind of activity carries a lot of weight with teachers, parents, and grandparents, all of whom vote. Naturally, chefs too have become admired in doing this work. Jasper White, chef-owner of Summer Shack in Boston, Massachusetts, is working to clean up Boston Harbor. He is among many who support good works in their local communities. The roles of chefs become both evolutionary and revolutionary as they combine science with conscience and teaching with learning.

First Lady Says: Let's Move!

First Lady Michelle Obama launched the Let's Move! Initiative before a gathering of 800 invited chefs in the Rose Garden of the White House. She said, "This is an initiative to reverse the devastating long-term consequences of childhood obesity and to improve the quality of the food served in public schools." She encouraged all invited guests to join in the challenge by saying, "You are all at the heart of this initiative ... You know more about food than almost anyone—other than grandmas—and you've got the visibility and the enthusiasm to match that knowledge."

FOOD JOB: *Dinner-Party Chef*

A skilled chef can find fame and fortune cooking for dinner parties for clients in their homes—whether in preparing simple foods or cassoulets, coulibiacs, and other elaborate dishes. To get started, offer to cook and serve a meal on a trial basis, charging only the cost of the ingredients. Word of mouth will sing your praises, and you will rapidly fill your engagement calendar. Note that the law requires that all cooking be done in the client's kitchen, not in your apartment and transported in a taxi or your family station wagon. Make sure that you have a signed contract, a deposit, and a clear understanding of the client's needs before you start cooking. The higher the fee you propose, the more will be expected of you. And remember, you are not entitled to take home the leftovers. Do everything possible to make sure you will be invited back. Smile a lot.

The Ultimate Dinner Party

A memorial dinner was held for Pierre Franey in the Crystal Room of the Tavern on the Green in 1996. There were five hundred official guests and a few gate crashers. Everyone, simply everyone, was there. Each table was set for twelve guests, with colorful, summery floral tablecloths, a dozen bottles of wine, and huge, three-foot-tall vases of flowers. At the end of this jubilant meal, Pierre's wife, Betty, handed out copies of the French national anthem. The band struck up, and the inebriated celebrants tottered unsteadily to their feet. Never before was there such a lusty, full-throated rendering of "La Marsellaise," which was sung to a sudden bursting forth of hundreds of fireworks, rocketing from every vase.

Restaurants are made for moments like these. I cannot begin to imagine I will ever again experience a menu such as this. It was written in exquisite calligraphy by the hand of the late artist-restaurateur George Lang.

The assemblage of celebrity chefs was not unusual, but the elaborate menu and stunning wine selections will not soon be replicated. The astronomical cost of this memorable meal is close to incalculable, though I can't remember having paid for it. Maybe I was the guest of someone to whom I still owe a belated thanks.

I thought you might enjoy tasting the meal in the palate of your mind:

THE MEMORIAL DINNER FOR PIERRE FRANEY

Tavern On The Green

HORS D'OEUVRES

Perrier-Jouët Fleur De Champagne, 1989

DAVID BURKE

Le saumon, confit au sel marin et aneth
(Salmon Pastrami)

La cuisse de faisand farcie
(Barbecue pheasant dumpling)

PATRICK CLARK

Medallion D'agneau Avec Ratatouille Et Croutons
(Seared Loin Of Lamb On Ratatouille Croutons)

Les Raviolis De Canard Et Shiitake
(Crispy Duck And Shiitake Dumpling)

JEAN LOUIS PALLARDIN

La Nage À La Chair D'oursins
(Sea Urchin Nage)

La Friture D'huitres De Belons
(Fried Belon Oysters)

Paul Prudhomme

Le Beouf Á La Basile
(Beef Basil Baskets, Southern Biscuits And Molasses Muffins)

Les Crevettes À La Biere, Sauce À L'orange Et Raifort
(Beer Battered Shrimp With Orange-Horseradish Sauce)

Jean-Jacques Rachou

Salade De Caille En Chemise Lucullus
(Quail Lucullus With Baby Greens)

Jean-George Vongerichten

Roulade De Thon À La Japonaise Et Coulis Et Raifort
(Tuna Spring Roll With Soybean Coulis)

La Tarte De Bolets Aux Saveurs D'onions Et Noix
(Porcini Tart With Onion And Walnut Spray)

LA SOUPE

Gerard Boyer And Gotha Khumm

Le Consommé Aux Ravioles De Foie Gras Et Truffle Noires
(Consommé With Foie Gras Ravioli And Black Truffles)

LE PREMIER POISSON

Andre Soltner And Georges Perrier

Le Bouillon D'homard Fumé À La Mousse De
St. Jacques Et Brunoise De Legumes
(Scallop Mousse With Brunoise Of Vegetable And
Lobster And Smoked Lobster Bouillon)

LE DEUZIÈME POISSON IN HONOR OF PIERRE FRANEY

Le Coulibac De Saumon
(Coulibiac Of Salmon)

Trimbach Riesling 1994

LA VOLAILLE

Paul Bocuse And David Bouley

Le Pigeon rôti en croute d'herbes organiques,
legumes de printemps glacés
(Pigeon baked with organic herb crust, glazed spring vegetables, Périgord truffles and fingerling potato puree)

Louis Jadot Chassagne Montrachet Blanc 1990

LA VIANDE

Alain Ducasse

Agneau De Lait Legumes De Saison En
Beaux Morceaux, Jus De Rôti
(Roasted Baby Lamb, Spring Vegetables, Pan Juices With Black Truffles And Fingerling Potato Puree)

Château Grande Larose, 1988

LES DESSERTS

Daniel Boulud, Francois Payard, Dieter Schorner, Jacques Torres And Andre Renard

La tornade de desserts
(ice creams and frozen desserts)

Le Café ou Moka ou Thé
(Coffee, mocha, or tea)

Friandises
(table delicacies)

Perrier-Jouët Fleur de Champagne 1989

Just to give you an idea of the complexity of just a single one of the dishes on the menu, here is a description of one of Pierre Franey's favorite foods, coulibiac. This *is* an out-of-this-world creation to be served on a very special occasion. It is prepared with layers of crêpes covered with poached wild salmon and mushroom *duxelles*, all enveloped in a piquant white-wine sauce and flavored with dill and cayenne pepper. The salmon filling is spread evenly between layers of chopped hard-boiled eggs combined with fragrant rice. The whole thing is then wrapped cozily in a soft brioche dough and is garnished with more strips of brioche and gently brushed with egg yolks stirred with heavy cream. It is brushed again and again so that it will achieve a glorious golden glaze when it's done. While baking, it's force-fed with gallons of sweet butter poured through little parchment paper chimneys inserted through the brioche so that the salmon and all the other precious constituent parts inside will stay moist. To call this dish divine would be an understatement.

FOOD JOB: *Dinner-and-a-Movie Chef*

Movie houses, especially small art-house theaters, are moving into the dining business. Patrons may be supplied with a boxed picnic to accompany the film or may be seated at a table before or after the film for a more formal meal.

Entrepreneurs are introducing film festivals, morning movies for mom and the kids, midnight cult movies for serious fans, and are even catering special events for the community and corporate functions.

Art shows are so much more satisfying when accompanied with creative snacks.

Taken a step further, innovative chefs could offer a special *Nutcracker Suite* meal after the performance of the ballet. The foods could be matched to the dances; for example, sugar plums, Turkish delight, Chinese fortune cookies. As an added surprise, the chef could engage little girl ballerinas to pass baskets of bread to the diners.

Menus could also reflect the themes of the movies they were paired with. For example, there could be a re-creation of the meal served to the restaurant critic in the scene from *Ratatouille* or a literal interpretation of the feast from *Babette's Feast*. There could be a tasting of the typical British boarding-school food—including toad in the hole, bubble and squeak and spotted dick—that Harry Potter might have eaten. A truly ambitious team of chefs might re-create the final meal served on the *Titanic*.

FOOD JOB: *Embassy Chef*

A Korean student was graduating from culinary school without a single job prospect lined up. He was a really nice guy and a truly fabulous cook. The difficulty was that he could barely make himself understood in English.

He found a job as a sous-chef at the Korean embassy in Washington, DC. There, they spoke his language, and he happily prepared the food that he loved to cook and that his employers loved to eat. It was a match made in diplomatic heaven.

There are plenty of job opportunities out there even when English is not your first language. If you look beyond the embassies and consulates in many cities in the United States and around the world, you'll find further opportunities. I'll stick with Korea for this example, and mention that Korean Airlines employs chefs for their hospitality suites.

Likewise, if you check the Korean Chamber of Commerce, you'll find that it lists over three hundred Korean businesses in the United States alone. Many would surely welcome a Korean catering service.

▶▶ FOOD FOR THOUGHT ◀◀

Executive chefs are employed in embassies and consulates in every capital city, from London and Paris to Sydney and Singapore.

Traveling to faraway places while officially in government service will enable you to bypass all the customary red tape that is required when applying to work in another country, such as the need to obtain a visa and work permit.

FOOD JOB: *Fish Chef*

David will graduate from a professional cooking school in six weeks' time. He's getting worried. He still doesn't know what he wants to do next. He definitely doesn't want to be a line cook. He is a career changer and is among the oldest students in his class.

"So," say I, "if you could do anything in the world, what would it be?"

"Don't know...," he answers, "I just don't know. I like to be outdoors." He looks anxious. And sad.

"What do you like to eat?"

"Everything."

"What was your favorite class?"

"Fish, I really like fish." (Now we are getting somewhere.)

"What do you like about fish?"

"I don't know, I just like fish—and water."

Hmmm... Click!

Several years ago I went on a press trip. The plane landed first in Ketchikan, Alaska, one of the state's largest cities, with a population of a little over seven thousand. The locals grumble. They say it's getting too crowded.

If you wanted to complain, you could mention the weather. It was so freezing when we got there that not only could we see our breath, we could play cymbals with the icicles. I don't think I've ever been so cold.

We stood on a thick sheet of ice waiting for the tiny seaplane that would fly us far north, to a remote fishing lodge where it was even colder. This lodge was the only building on the island. It was once a whorehouse, so privacy was its redeeming feature. It was a place where you'd need to cuddle up to keep warm.

It's still very remote there—so private and far away that if you swallowed a fish bone, you'd probably choke to death before medical help arrived. Three guides lived at the lodge. Their job was to take guests like us out on small boats and to let them believe that they were catching the wild salmon and halibut so plentiful in those frigid waters, though in truth, it was the guides who did all the real work.

Our guide warned us that, if we fell overboard, the water was so frigid that we'd last for only a few seconds, not even a whole minute. Neither I nor my fellow food-writer companion fell in. We got back to the lodge safely and stretched out beside the roaring fire while the guides rustled up hot toddies and grilled the fish that "we" had caught. I'll remember that amazing meal forever.

So as I looked at David looking so concerned, my train of thought went like this: *Outdoors ... fish ... chef ... fabulous food. Alaska!* David didn't exactly warm to the idea.

So I suggested, "Chef in a seafood restaurant in Manhattan?"

"I'm a country boy," he said.

The day after my meeting with David, I received an e-mail from an old friend: "I'm looking for a young culinary-school graduate to be my sous-chef at the fishing lodge I'm opening in Florida. It's a new part of a six-restaurant complex and involves taking our guests bonefishing, teaching cooking classes, and cooking the daily catch."

David is off to paradise and a warm climate. He's off the hook. Gone fishing—and cooking!

Note: It also pays to have a network of really terrific friends.

Matter of Indisputable Fact

A flourishing network is more valuable than having money in the bank.

FOOD JOB: *Hospital Chef*

—Lynne Eddy, MS, RD, LDN, FADA, CHE

What industry has strong job growth, great job security, and generous benefits packages? How can I best use my credentials and culinary skills while balancing my professional and personal lives?

Why, you could apply to become manager or director of food services at a luxury independent-care or senior-living center.

It's no surprise that the healthcare industry is expanding to accommodate the growing number of aging baby boomers. Healthcare will generate 3.2 million new hourly and salaried jobs between now and 2018—more than any other industry—largely in response to the rapid growth of the elderly population.

Properties specializing in continuing-care retirement communities (CCRC) will need executive chefs trained in providing upscale dining experiences for these residents.

Healthy senior citizens who have downsized their homes are now living very active lives in exclusive adult communities with optional healthcare amenities. These aging baby boomers want white tablecloth restaurants serving genuine international cuisines. In assisted-care living, residents expect interesting flavor profiles and exquisite presentation of their meals. Who better to manage these operations than a culinary-school graduate armed with a bachelor of professional studies (BPS) degree?

Foodservice Management in Healthcare is a new elective class at the Culinary Institute of America. This uniquc course introduces students to food-service operations and management in various types of healthcare facilities. These include senior-living complexes, medical centers, nursing homes, rehabilitation facilities, assisted-care living centers, community hospitals, and on-demand room service.

In addition to business-management studies, entry-level chef/managers also learn about healthcare reform in what is now among the most highly regulated sectors of the food-service industry. Chefs also gain knowledge about equipment purchasing, clinical nutrition, and budgeting. If you are looking for a steady job that provides a good salary and benefits or a career that enables you to be good while doing good, this may be your ideal destination.

FOOD JOB: *Kiosk Chef*

Kiosks are achieving galloping success. At a supermarket in Texas, a cook demonstrates a suggested evening meal. She looks like a mom and works from a kiosk strategically placed next to the chicken, fish, and other meat displays. Customers are offered fully prepped ingredients and all the fixings required to serve two or a family of four. The system works wonderfully well.

A study conducted by the research company Knowledge Networks showed that in-store sampling not only has dramatic sales impact on the day of the sampling event but also increases sales of established products.

To apply for such a job, present yourself and your proposal to the public relations headquarters of a supermarket chain. Bring statistics proving you will increase the store's sales. Show a video of yourself in action, with customers if possible. This, you can also upload to YouTube and feature on your Facebook page. Wear an apron and a big smile.

Kiosks are popular in airports, shopping malls, and parks, too. Check kiosk designs online, and offer your services wherever your product fits a space—at the entrance to a movie theater, a skating rink or bowling alley or . . . you decide. Where do your cupcakes or other specialty foods fit best?

FOOD JOB: *Military Chef*

A cadet who has experienced the rigors of West Point may opt to work in a military-school kitchen, where one chef observed the following:

- Five thousand cadets were served a meal in fifteen to twenty-five minutes.
- Eight shining steel griddles were used to make ten thousand pancakes each morning.
- A German-built meat slicer was used to cut and portion a ten-pound ham or prime rib into deli-thin slices in two minutes.
- Every worker was spotless. Every countertop was spotless. Nothing fell on the floor.
- Not a crumb was left on any plate.

Food service is the second largest employer after the federal government. If government or military service provides the opportunity to "see the world," so might employment in the military food service industry. Officers eat well in executive dining rooms. Throughout the world, those who enlist must be fed; they provide work for chefs and line cooks everywhere. Note that it is not necessary to have served in the military to obtain employment in government service.

A DAY IN THE LIFE OF A 92G

by Daniel Jose Medina, student, the Culinary Institute of America

I chose to join the army as a 92G food-service specialist, in other words, as a cook. Yet I soon learned that army cooking doesn't start in the kitchen. It begins with basic training, a twelve-week introduction to military life and its chain of command. Only after successfully completing the course was I sent to the Army Culinary School in Fort Lee, Virginia, where I received culinary basic training for eight weeks—in cutting vegetables, making soups, grilling, and some baking.

I was then shipped to Airborne School, where I had to learn how to parachute from a plane. To this day, I still wonder whether this training was the military's version of takeout. I met my first platoon sergeant at Fort Bragg, North Carolina. As soon as I arrived at the base, I was told that my unit was already in the field. I was ordered to join them the next day, that is, after I'd marched in formation and enrolled in physical training ("PT" in military lingo) at the ungodly hour of 6:30 a.m. Soon after, I was issued my official weapon, not a whisk or a mixing spoon, not a sharp paring knife, but an assault rifle known as the M4.

Within an hour of becoming armed and having my clothing duffle unceremoniously dumped and inspected, I was ordered to get into the back of a truck to reach what, in military speak, is called a "field site." I was now part of a team and was responsible for feeding 450–800 hungry infantry soldiers.

My new schedule was as follows: wake at 2:00 a.m. every day for the next two weeks and get a few hours of sleep between breakfast and dinner. We usually started dinner at 12:30 p.m. and finished around 9:00 p.m. This was a very tough schedule to maintain. When all the cleaning was done, I went to work in the dining facility, also known as the D-Fac. There, morning shifts started at 4:00 a.m. and ended around 2:00 p.m., after which, we were given the rest of the day off.

That is, unless the company "needed" you. This "need" happened a lot, because "normal soldiers"—as army cooks call them—do not show up for duty until 6:15 a.m. They salute the flag at 6:30 a.m. and then perform PT, after which, at about 7:45 a.m., they head off for breakfast to be fed by we, the cooks.

The D-Fac opened at 7:30 a.m. and closed at 9:00 a.m. We served around 450 troops a day. As soon as breakfast ended, the scramble for lunch began. If you, the army cook, wanted time to eat lunch, you had to do it before 11:30 a.m., when the D-Fac opened its doors again. Eating lunch rarely happened. I was forced to eat after cleaning the kitchen.

After lunch was over, we sat down for what the army calls an "after-action review." The shift leader would discuss what had happened during the shift and would assign our next report times to us.

Army cooks serve at the mercy of the staff sergeant, who posts the schedule for each shift. The moment you arrive in the kitchen, you have to be ready to cook and ready for inspection in your cook's whites, which are always to be kept clean and pressed. Your rank- and name-tag serves as your total identity.

After my tours of duty were finished, I realized I wanted to learn more. I am currently enrolled in the Culinary Institute of America. I hope to graduate with an associate's degree in twenty-one months.

FOOD JOB: *Monastery Chef*

Monks and nuns raise money to help support their monasteries and convents by making and selling a variety of foods. These may include breads, cheeses, cookies, candies, fruitcakes, and preserves. Mary Jacobs, a reporter for the *Dallas Morning News* wrote, "Not all monastic communities with businesses have managed to balance the distractions of financial and commercial success with spiritual life." According to a *National Catholic Reporter* article, the brewery at Andech Monastery in Germany has "expanded to a multimillion-dollar business, staffed by 23 monks and 200 lay employees." Giuseppe Bellapadrona, the Vatican's farm and garden manager, reveals that annual production is valued at $330,000 and that it makes a healthy contribution to the cost of operating the pope's residence.

▶▶ FOOD FOR THOUGHT ◀◀

Pretzels are thought to have been invented by an Italian monk–baker in 610 AD. The original snack-food, they were made from dough scraps formed into a shape emulating arms folded over the chest in prayer. The monk gave the baked goods to students as rewards for good works. He called them *pretiolas,* which means "little rewards" in Latin.

FOOD JOB: *Museum Chef*

The restaurateur Danny Meyer has set the standard for museum dining. Meyer sets high standards for everything he undertakes. He is among the most highly regarded of restaurant owners in the United States. He expresses his philosophy in his book, *Setting the Table: The Transforming Power of Hospitality in Business.*

Any art-loving chef could write a business proposal for bringing a restaurant, a café, a kiosk, or a food truck to a museum. The wealth of hungry visitors—and therefore the potential for impressive profits—will convince management to offer you a job and, with any luck, free tickets to all the exhibits.

FOOD JOB: *Prison Chef*

The prison population in the United States has nearly quadrupled in the last twenty-five years. Two million people are currently incarcerated. Millions of dollars are spent to keep them there. It costs twenty-three times as much to keep a person in a prison as it does to house him or her in a community. It costs $50,000 a year to lodge a prison inmate, compared with $8,000 per pupil in a public school.

Becoming a prison chef is certainly challenging, but recently, a new opportunity has arisen. Prisons are also using chefs as teachers of the culinary arts for inmates, who may then use their skills to transition to the workplace when they are released. Care2 is one of several organizations that have initiated food-related prison programs. Check the availability of salaried and volunteer employment opportunities.

▶▶ FOOD FOR THOUGHT ◀◀

Prisoners on death row do not always know that what they request for their last supper is not necessarily what they will get (unless they ask for a burger and fries). This is not a meal to die for.

FOOD JOB: *Pizza Chef*

Pizza Hut, Domino's, and Papa John's were the top three searched restaurants, respectively, on Google in 2011.

FOOD JOB: *Personal Chef*

Cirque du Soleil employs teams of chefs who prepare food to keep the acrobats slim and trim while flying on the trapeze with the greatest of ease. The television program *Dancing with the Stars* employs a personal chef for the contestants.

A personal or private chef may find employment cooking for an athlete or working in the executive dining room at the World Series, the Super Bowl, or the US Open Tennis Championships.

FOOD JOB: *Research Chef*

The Research Chefs Association (RCA) is the premier source of culinary and technical information for the food industry. Its membership includes chefs and food scientists working in food manufacturing, chain restaurants, hotels, ingredient-supply companies, consulting, and academia. The organization works with educational institutions to offer fully integrated degree programs in culinology. Continuing education programs have also been created to cater to more seasoned chefs and food scientists. Degree courses are offered at the University of Nebraska and the Metropolitan Community College, both in Omaha. For more information contact the RCA at its management office via Culinology.com.

FOOD JOB: *Spa Chef*

"PILOT LIGHT: SPARRING WITH CALORIES"

By Ariane Batterberry, October 2011

It has always been a burning question, or at least a calorie-burning question: Is it possible to dine on food that is genuinely both delicious and sufficient, and still lose weight? Is it possible to create food that is far better than edible while working with a calorie count?

The growth in the number of spas in the United States has, in recent years, ballooned (excuse the pun). From 1999 to 2009 it went from 5,700 to 20,600. Only seven percent of these spas have restaurant facilities, thirteen percent if they are in hotels or resorts. But with wellness and the fight against obesity having become a national obsession, there are light choices scattered on menus from McDonald's on up, and the health police are watching.

To find out the answer to this burning question, I checked into Canyon Ranch in Lenox, Massachusetts, where corporate chef Scott Uehlein works as our own native Michel Guérard, creator of Cuisine Minceur. Scott, a CIA-trained chef and student of Madeleine Kamman, began his career as a chef at Los Abrigados Resort & Spa in Sedona, Arizona, and since then has become a leading go-to expert on healthful, low-calorie cuisine.

My first dinner readjusted my expectations. Scott says that he likes to build layers of flavor in food, and they are in evidence. A crunchy gazpacho with a deep taste of the essence of tomato and cubes of zucchini and sharpened with a blend of vinegars and a touch of cilantro, came to just forty-five calories, every single one packed with flavor. This was followed by two lamb chops (not three), carefully trimmed and perfectly grilled and accompanied by crisp polenta (390 calories total). Completing the meal was a sliver of "Berkshire plum Tatin," exquisitely caramelized (120 calories).

Ariane Batterberry is founding editor and co-publisher of Food Arts *magazine.*

FOOD JOB: *Calorie Counter*

You don't have to work in a fancy spa to become a spa chef. You will be welcome anywhere and everywhere if you can produce beautiful, flavorful food at an affordable price.

FOOD JOB: *Vineyard Chef*

Wine sales are becoming increasingly competitive. Customer loyalty may be increased when vineyard visitors dine in a restaurant located in the winery. A vineyard chef is in the happy position of combining wine and culinary knowledge.

FOOD JOB: *Vegetarian Chef*

There is a pesky problem with teetotaling and dessert- and coffee-refusing vegans and vegetarians. There are, though, "modified" vegetarians who refuse red meat but willingly accept fish and chicken. The more dedicated among them tend to challenge the server to reveal the previous living conditions of the chicken. (There are some folk who understand that having a free-range chicken is as dangerous as having a free-range boyfriend, because you never know where he has been!) Furthermore, they may insist that the food contain no salt, no butter, and, obviously, no ingredient to which they are allergic.

Preparing several vegetables and arranging them beautifully on the plate takes far more time on the part of the kitchen staff than tossing a steak on the grill and retrieving a baked potato from the oven. And despite a considerable amount of fetching and carrying, at the end of what may be a relatively small meal, the server can expect a tip, albeit calculated with excruciating accuracy.

FOOD JOB: *Zoo Chef*

A culinary student reveals that she loves animals and had previously considered becoming a veterinarian. "I just like to be around animals," she explains. She even considered writing a cookbook for her favorite Labrador. Her whole body lit up when I suggested that she might enjoy working at a zoo. Here's a little information about getting started.

Under the general classification of zoos, let's group chefs for aquariums as well. And would it be too great a stretch to add chefs for botanical gardens to this group as well? All these places attract thousands of visitors, all of whom must be fed.

There are two categories of chefs working at zoos. There are those who feed the animals and those who feed the staff, the board of trustees, thousands of schoolchildren, the visitors, volunteers, and the guests at formal fund-raisers.

The latter category may include provisioning the various food carts dotted about the grounds. Though hot dogs and lemonade remain popular, there are plenty of opportunities for other specialties too. For innovative ideas to use as a springboard, check into the entrepreneurs who are selling everything from tacos to little pies and apple turnovers from food trucks.

Zoo chefs earn an average of $43,000 a year, thanks to overtime, shift differentials, holiday pay, and other factors. The salary will of course vary widely depending on the part of the country where the facility is located and the prestige of the zoo itself.

In getting started, be aware that those responsible for feeding the animals must, at a minimum, have a high school diploma, but that most have bachelor's degrees in animal sciences or biology. Many have postgraduate degrees as well. Those who are feeding folks may need fewer formal credentials.

• •

My Word: Who Is in a Zoo?

The Smithsonian National Zoo was established on March 2, 1889, by an act of Congress, for "the advancement of science and the instruction and recreation of the people."

Today, the National Zoo exhibits living animal and plant collections and conducts research in conservation biology and reproductive science. Its mission is to provide leadership in animal care, science, education, and sustainability. Each year, more than two million people visit the National Zoo's 163-acre park, located in the heart of Washington, DC, to learn about the two thousand animals and nearly four hundred species represented there. The National Zoo maintains a staff of two hundred fifty between the Rock Creek and Front Royal facilities, including animal caretakers, veterinarians, and scientists. Likewise, more than one hundred facilities-maintenance staff, including chefs for humans, as well as thirty police officers are assigned to the zoo.

• •

Holy cow

By Jay Neal, Assistant Professor at the University of Houston

One Monday morning, I received a phone call from my boss. He told me he had arranged a large, yet simple party for Friday evening. All I had to do was bring the grill and burgers for two hundred people. It sounded simple enough. I recognized the address of the venue to be the Houston Zoo, because I had catered several events there in the past.

My boss had made all the arrangements and said the menu was burgers only. (He is a lawyer who wants to be a restaurateur. He knows everything; just ask him.) I placed all the orders and built in plenty of time for delivery and preparation.

The staff arrived on time and loaded the catering van. We arrived at the zoo early, unloaded the van, lit our grills and set up the buffet. The hostess greeted us and was thankful for the restaurant and my boss for making all the arrangements. She informed us that the National Association of Zoo Docent Conventioneers would be arriving soon.

I thought, "Wonderful, we are ready to go." We had our mesquite-wood-burning grills hot; the buffet line was set up with all the condiments. You could create Jimmy Buffet's Cheeseburger in Paradise franchise if you wanted to. The sensational aroma filled the air. It WAS paradise! Then *they* showed up; the docents.

In case you don't know, docents are loving, warm, and caring people who volunteer their precious time at the zoo to help care for our animal brothers and sisters. So it would make sense (it would seem), not to feed them our cousin, the cow.

Most docents are docile creatures, but they can become hostile when threatened by barbeques. I'm still waiting to see the home video commercial for "Vegetarians Gone Mad." Needless to say, things got ugly fast. Men shouted at us, while the women began a candlelight vigil for the creatures that had sacrificed so much for so little.

While this was going on, I called all of our seven properties around the city and borrowed every veggie burger they had. If only I had called the hostess and asked who the customer was, all this needless pain and suffering could have been avoided.

FRANCHISES

As Winston Churchill memorably said, "We are not at the end. We are not at the beginning of the end. But we are at the end of the beginning." He most certainly didn't mean that this is all there is for chefs to do: there are so many other food jobs to consider.

FOOD JOB: *Franchiser*

The Licensing Letter's "Royalty Trends Report" provides an extensive look at trends for royalty rates, guarantees, and advances for every property type and product category, including analysis of the key business factors that affect them. For more information about franchising, visit FranchiseHandBook.com, FranchiseSolutions.com, or FranNet.com.

Edible's Magazine-Publishing Franchises

The holding group Edible Communities features at least sixty-two local magazine franchises specializing in local food. These range from *Edible San Francisco* to *Edible Shasta Butte*. Licensees pay more than $90,000 to buy in—with one third due up front and the rest financed over five years—and they agree to publish the magazine in accordance with the company's specifications and to do so at least four times per year. Franchisees must also remit a royalty fee of 5 percent of total advertising revenue to corporate headquarters.

More Franchises

Some restaurants set their sights on international shores. FreshBerry, Saladworks, Orange Leaf, Wingstop, and Panda Express have signed franchise agreements in the Middle East, Singapore, Australia, and Mexico. Expansion announcements are made almost weekly as chain restaurants develop their dining footprints in countries around the globe.

The purchasing price of a fast-food franchise may range anywhere from $450,000 to $750,000 or even more, not including an initiation fee of approximately $50,000 depending on the franchise. Remodeling of an existing restaurant can cost more than a million dollars, particularly if the franchisee installs solar energy, LED lighting, or other green improvements.

A franchise agreement buys you the legal use of a brand name and proven business approaches, and bulk purchasing power, as well as marketing and training support.

Few franchisees make money the first year, and the parent company exercises almost total control of every aspect of the business. It can even allow another franchise to open across the street.

FOOD LOVERS FIND THEIR FORTUNES IN MANY DIVERSE FIELDS

FOOD JOB: *Butler*

Don't laugh; believe it. The rich are getting richer, and along with extreme wealth comes the irresistible desire to flaunt it. What could be grander than owning a small castle or large mansion, complete with a professional butler and a household staff?

At the French Culinary Institute in New York City, there are three classes, twenty-five to thirty hours each, which encompass the Estate Management Studies program. These classes are: Culinary Essentials, Essentials of Household Cleaning and Organization, and Laundry Essentials.

The class fee for Culinary Essentials and Laundry Essentials is $1,995 each. For the cleaning class, the fee is $1,750, in addition to which it is recommended that the student butler buy a $100 ironing board with a Teflon top rather than one with the traditional cloth cover.

If you aspire to the pinnacle of butlering, Brian Hoey, author of *Not in Front of the Corgis*, tells us that, "In Buckingham Palace alone, there are 339 full-time staff, eating up to 600 meals a day in the kitchens, but only about a dozen come into regular contact with the queen."

He further reports:

> The footmen and housemaids start with a basic salary of £13,634 a year [$21,542], which can rise after five years by £2,000 [$3,160] a year. With a promotion to senior footman, the salary increases to £15,634 [$24,702].
>
> A butler starts at an annual salary of £15,000 [$23,700] plus accommodations. For a liveried helper in the Royal Mews, who is required to have had some experience with horses and who will be seen riding behind the queen during one of the state carriages at official ceremonial occasions, the starting salary is £17,169 [$27,127], with livery provided. [Casual workers apparently receive less but no description is provided for what a casual worker is or does.]
>
> The queen's royal chef is the highest-paid member of the domestic household, with an annual salary of £45,000 [$71,100].

The rate of exchange varies from minute to minute but (roughly) £1 = $1.58.

►► FOOD FOR THOUGHT ◄◄

Walter Monkton was butler for the Duke of Windsor. He worked in this capacity, unsalaried, for twenty years. Upon his retirement, he was rewarded with a cigarette case. On it was engraved his name, spelled incorrectly. Whether or not he smoked, we may suppose that he fumed!

Recommended Book

The Butler's Guide to Clothes Care, Managing the Table, Running the Home, and Other Graces by Stanley Ager and Fiona St. Aubyn.

FOOD JOB: *Caterer*

Renny Reynolds, author of *The Art of the Party*, wrote, "Color can emphasize the theme of a party and help create the mood. What would a Mexican party be without bright colors like hot pink, turquoise, orange, and purple? The same colors would be totally inappropriate for most weddings. We think of weddings as white or pale, pastel-colored events—soft and romantic."

CATERING: IS IT FOR YOU?

By Bruce Mattel

FROM Catering: A Guide to Managing a Successful Business Operation

A successful caterer must be able to marry the culinary talents of a chef with the business savvy of a CEO. For anyone who wants to be a caterer, a passion for cooking and entertaining is a prerequisite. However, that alone is not a recipe for success.

Know Your Strengths

If you think that catering might be a career option for you, check your skills against the qualities that a successful caterer ought to have. Some of these qualifications may already be a natural part of your personality or education—other skills you might have to learn. Alternately, you could partner with another person or company to handle the part of the business that is not your strong suit. Here are several examples:

- If your culinary creativity soars, but your spelling and grammar are not the best, arrange for a professional food writer or freelance editor to proofread your letters, contracts, marketing copy, and menus on a case-by-case basis.

- If you are a talented chef with a sense of style but you don't have a clue about accounting practices, take a noncredit adult-education class at your local community college. Otherwise, hire an accountant or shadow a restaurant or catering manager to see how the books are done.

- If your food and business skills are terrific, but your style sense suffers, either concentrate on an area of catering that doesn't emphasize design as much or hire an assistant or catering manager with a sense of style.

- If your food sense, style, and business skills are all great, but you aren't mechanically inclined, offer a retainer to keep a handyman or refrigerator and appliance repair person on call. For major functions, include the cost of this person's services in the total bill as an insurance policy against culinary disaster.

Find Your Niche

Catering is a popular and competitive field. Caterers who seek out a specific niche market are often preferred when that specific style of catering is needed. And caterers who know how to customize their services to appeal to a clearly defined group or serve a specific type of event usually continue to grow their businesses.

In order to build up a clientele and maintain an established identity, clients must associate your business with the types of events that you cater, so choose your events carefully. If you are marketing yourself as upscale, it is okay to cater a simple barbecue, but just be aware that establishing and maintaining a consistent identity is important to your success.

Some caterers believe that they need to accommodate a client's every request, regardless of how this may affect their identity or reputation. Agreeing to serve pigs in a blanket, for example, may not fit with your identity, but by turning that familiar food into, for example, merguez sausage wrapped in filo dough and served with harissa sauce, you may keep your identity intact.

Qualifications of a Successful Caterer

1. Excellent organizational skills
2. Good time management skills
3. The ability to multitask
4. Quick thinking and good problem-solving skills
5. A friendly, hospitable personality
6. The ability to manage stress
7. An extensive knowledge of ingredients
8. High-level written and verbal communication skills
9. Natural leadership and motivational skills
10. Excellent networking skills
11. Proficiency in accounting principles
12. Good negotiation skills
13. A broad knowledge of cultural and religious customs
14. Basic mechanical skills

On-Premise Catering

Examples of on-premise catering operations include those found at restaurants, the banquet departments of hotels, cruise ships, country clubs, catering halls, and even some religious venues. On-premise operations should be located in desirable, safe locations and have ample parking.

The downside to starting an on-premise site is that the larger the facility and the closer it is to a densely populated area, the more expensive it will be to launch. However, to gain valuable experience or a steady income as a salaried employee, on-premise catering businesses are a great place to start.

Off-Premise Catering

The biggest benefit of an off-premise catering business is that it usually requires significantly less capital to establish than does an on-premise one. The production facility does not need to be in a highly visible location. Minimal parking is needed, and most consultations are held at the chosen event site in order to assess the venue and to plan ahead.

Many restaurant operators do off-premise catering as well. They already have a production facility and can fairly easily modify their operations for off-site events. One thing to remember is that off-premise caterers must rent equipment for the majority of their events. It is therefore important for a caterer to establish good relationships with reputable party-rental companies in order to ensure the quality of rented items.

Mobile Catering

Mobile catering is the most flexible off-premise type of catering and has gained enormous popularity of late. From the traditional trucks that bring breakfast and lunch to patrons at railroad stations, construction sites, and office parks to the RVs and trailers that focus on specific high-end cuisines, mobile catering is an excellent place to start for someone interested in the business. Many modern food trucks offer specific types of popular international street food, and they may collaborate with one another at events such as tailgate parties or concerts. In this way, the event coordinator can provide a variety of interesting, casual fare for the guests or attendees.

Transporting Food

The greatest challenge of off-premise catering is successfully transporting all food, equipment, and personnel to the event site. In all cases, proper care and forethought are needed when packing food for transport. Physical strength, coordination, and organization are necessary qualities for any off-premise catering crew. Endurance is paramount, as transportation adds many work hours to any given day.

The Catering Vehicle

Consider purchasing a station wagon, sport utility vehicle, or, optimally, a refrigerated truck. Any catering vehicle should have an automatic transmission so that anyone on your team can drive it. Whatever you purchase, register it as a commercial vehicle so that you can legally display signs and access reserved parking areas. For safe transportation, you will need bracing devices to hold containers, coolers, crates, and boxes, in order to prevent the food from shifting in transit. And always keep the vehicle well maintained and clean, because unsanitary conditions can lead to health department violations.

Marketing Plan

Your initial marketing plan should target the market outlined in your business plan. It must include funding for digital photos, business cards, brochures, stationery, vehicle signage, ads with local media, a website, and tastings for corporate marketing and event-planning executives, all during your first months of business.

Employees

The quality of a catering company's staff can determine whether the business will survive and grow or fail. Excellent food prepared by competent cooks but served by poorly trained or inexperienced waitstaff can easily spoil an event. Similarly, even the most competent servers cannot overcome poorly prepared food. Finding and managing staff can be the greatest challenge of running a catering business.

The professional caterer requires courage and persistence. And while presenting great food to your customers is key, being an excellent chef isn't enough. A caterer is a keen and savvy businessperson who understands and values every facet and function of the company. Before venturing into this arena, it is important to either take formal training or to apprentice with an excellent catering operation. It is worth all of the effort, though, because catering is a fulfilling and joyful area of the foodservice industry. You are most often working with people who are celebrating significant life events or business accomplishments, and this can add up to a satisfying career.

Bruce Mattel, CIA '80 Graduate and Associate Dean for Culinary Production, the Culinary Institute of America. This piece is excerpted from Catering: A Guide to Managing a Successful Business Operation *Wiley; 1st edition (February 26, 2008). It is a definitive work on this subject and essential reading for anyone considering catering as a career.*

FOOD JOB: *Wedding Food Planner*

An expert in the fields tells us, "Food is an important part of the work of a wedding planner. It must be appropriate to the space, served simultaneously to a hundred or more guests, accommodate all tastes and dietary demands, and remain on budget. Uncommon ingredients may need to be purchased from other countries and coaxed through customs agents."

Another expert warns, "The planner must be a good diplomat and be energetic, personable, tactful, able to work well under pressure and with all kinds of people who may (and often do) behave badly, while remaining confident, optimistic, flexible, and creative. A flair for the dramatic is helpful, but a sense of humor is essential. It is necessary to keep track of the many details while keeping everyone on speaking terms."

Many banquet departments of restaurants establish their fees as a percentage of the total food production costs.

FOOD JOB: *Food Truck Owner*

The phrases "keep on trucking" and "truck stop" have acquired entirely new meanings. Rice pudding, exotic ice cream, cupcakes, flavored popcorn, french fries, and Korean tacos are just a few among the dozens of street foods on the menus of flourishing food trucks now offering meals on wheels. A proprietor of a small operation in a busy location can make a fortune providing healthy, hearty, homemade sandwiches, lobster rolls, hot soup, or bowls of noodles with which to entice the lunch crowds.

An enterprising trucker named his vehicle K9. He caters to dogs. He crushes dog biscuits into what is essentially a canine ice cream cone and tops it with a chili burger. There's no telling who loved the idea more, the dogs or their owners.

The Not-So-Hidden Costs of Truck Ownership

The Globe and Mail reported that food trucks typically earn a profit equivalent to about 40 percent of total sales. This is after obtaining licenses and permits that are far from cheap. A new mobile catering permit from the San Francisco Police Department costs about $9,300.

A used hot-dog-style cart runs about $2,000, while refurbished trucks for driving and vending can sell for considerably more than $40,000, with some costing as much as $100,000.

Occasionally, an investor or partner may be willing to foot the bill for a start-up's food truck, but it is quite difficult to get a bank loan.

Insurance is an additional expense. An owner must protect the business, not only against collision and road hazards, but also against the possibility of being identified as the source of foodborne illness. Insurance companies may frown if they learn that a truck is storing and transporting one or more propane tanks, or, horror of horrors, that the chef is cooking over an open flame grill or using a hotter-'n-hell pizza oven inside a gasoline-fueled truck.

When the Wind Blows

Bad weather is a variable that is impossible to factor into a profit projection. Sales are also likely to plummet on national holidays, except for those few loyal customers who may prefer a turkey taco from a truck for Thanksgiving rather than attending a family gathering.

Permits

A permit may allow the purchaser to park in a public place at up to five different locations. Each must be at least two blocks or 300 feet away from another mobile catering vendor. If a truck is parked too close to a regular brick-and-mortar restaurant, it can (and often does) raise an objection as an unfair business practice. Parking on private property is strictly forbidden, and laws are vigorously enforced. Permits are nontransferable, and the wait to get one can extend for months if not years if the city council has restricted the number of mobile vendors allowed to operate within a specified geographical area. Some municipalities allow the food to be prepared in a different (licensed) facility, while others demand that all food be prepared in the truck itself and that it be properly refrigerated, not left to slosh about in a Styrofoam cooler.

Safety First

In many cities, the health inspector energetically enforces rigorous sanitation standards specific to food trucks.

Squirrels Kill

The National Highway Traffic Safety Administration recorded 173 fatal crashes and 12,000 injuries crashes involving animals. Drive carefully.

Spreading the Word

Social media continues to play a large role in food-truck success. For instance, more than 50 percent of Gorilla Cheese's customers track its location through social media. They tag street locations just like you might tag a friend on Facebook. Apps are proliferating. They announce specials and deals that can change by the hour.

Even big business is getting into the game. *Advertising Age* reported, "If McDonald's sees that a user has tagged it in a post ("I'm heading to McDonald's for lunch"), it can offer coupons before the user gets there. This is where Facebook's potential dominance becomes obvious—the ability to mine real-time conversations of more than 750 million users is not available on any other platform."

▶▶ FOOD FOR THOUGHT ◀◀

Today there are approximately three million food trucks operating in the United States, more than five million food carts, and an unknown number of food kiosks.

Fancy hot dogs, empanadas, dumplings, and Italian panini sandwiches are sold from kiosks at locations where there is high foot traffic—for example, Times Square. Tim Tompkins, president of the Times Square Alliance, a nonprofit business-improvement group for the area, revealed that such vendors pay either 10 percent of their sales or a flat fee, depending on which is greater. The flat fee for all four businesses, if open year round, would come to between $350,000 to $400,000 per year, an astronomical sum.

In New York City, pushcarts are not permitted to be pushed when they are selling food. The vending license requires them to stay in one designated spot.

FOOD JOB: *Picnic Preparer*

Consider starting a picnic service that caters to boaters, passengers of private planes, desk-bound workers, conference attendees, and anyone else hungry for lunch or dinner. Choose a memorable name for your company (and don't make it a cutesy one). Make a list of your specialties. Print some advertising fliers. Now find a licensed commercial kitchen, and you're in business. Don't forget the paper napkins.

> *They fried the fish with bacon, and were astonished; for no fish had ever seemed so delicious before. They did not know that the quicker a fresh-water fish is on the fire after he is caught, the better he is; and they reflected little upon what a sauce open-air sleeping, open-air exercise, bathing, and a large ingredient of hunger make, too.*
>
> —Mark Twain

• •

My Word

Untold millions toy with edible tidbits during the intermissions of charming concerts held in parks and museum courtyards. They love the idea of having a picnic in the park. Families backpack along country trails. They light campfires for burning hot dogs and s'mores. They bring food aboard small and large boats. Others spend their summer days and nights eating outdoors, seated around swimming pools or perched on patios. And there are the fortunate multitudes that feast alfresco at rock concerts and music festivals.

Eating outdoors is not everyone's idea of a picnic, but there are plenty of folks who think that nothing is finer than to bake clams on the beach, barbecue in the backyard, or carry a boxed lunch to the bleachers. Even places of worship hold a lot of outdoor suppers.

Dining out is the in thing to do.

In the United States, we have overcome a lot of the unpleasantness that folks in other countries have to deal with—ants and mosquitoes for instance, which, though invisible, were almost certainly there in the enchanting picnics that Édouard Manet painted so exquisitely.

We spray the hell out of the area where we plan to eat—and a generous radius around the picnic site as well. Then, just to be sure, we hang up those blue electric devices that zap any flying object that gets too close.

In Europe, picnickers go in for fancy picnic hampers with leather loops for holding a service of silverware for eight, but they never give a thought to bringing napkins. No one outside the United States bothers with napkins. We Americans insist on being provided with a napkin when handed a glass of iced tea or a gin and tonic. Even if the picnic is just a buttered roll and some coffee, there are always far more napkins than we could possible use. Paper plates and plastic forks are also the American way when we commune with nature.

• •

FOOD JOB: *Sandwich Maker*

From a tiny shack off the beaten track, an entrepreneur is operating a wildly profitable lunch-only sandwich business. His shop is located near to, but not in, a shopping mall, and it is close to several office buildings as well. He owns his little building. He arrives at 6:30 a.m. and makes super sandwiches, each to order. He uses great breads and the best ingredients. There are six choices and a daily special. His customers send their requests by e-mail. The sandwich bags are marked with the names of the customers and arranged alphabetically. The sandwich maker passes his sandwiches to his customers as they drive past his window. Each sandwich is $10, so there is no need to make change. This price includes a soft drink or bottled water, a little bag of chips, and a surprise—a few baby carrots with their fronds, a handful of cherries, or three marshmallows. He wishes to remain anonymous but acknowledges that he takes in upward of $250,000 a year. (In cash.)

►► FOOD FOR THOUGHT ◄◄

Grilled cheese sandwiches, in various configurations, have recently soared in popularity. Intrepid reporter Bret Thorn of *Nation's Restaurant News* gathered this information in April, which is, as you probably already knew, National Grilled Cheese Month:

- Cheeseboy in Boston serves goat cheese and grilled asparagus with apple-onion compote.

- The Union Kitchen restaurant in Houston is serving a $6.95 sandwich of Brie, avocado, sun-dried tomatoes, and roasted red bell peppers.
- Square Peg, a new restaurant in Philadelphia, has a $12 Mac & Cheese Grilled Cheese sandwich, served with a side of "drunken tomato soup," spiked with pepper-infused vodka.
- The Cadillac Grilled Cheese at Firefly restaurant in Washington, DC, is made with Gruyère, Cheddar, béchamel sauce, and garlic-herb butter. It's $11, served with mixed greens or fries.
- Lobster ME restaurant in Las Vegas offers a $10.50 Lobster Grilled Cheese, made of lobster, Gruyère, Brie, and cream cheese.

ANOTHER ANONYMOUS SANDWICH ENTREPRENEUR REVEALS HIS SECRETS

I don't have a culinary degree, but I can cook. I've started a small business making lunch for about thirty doctors in a medical practice. Mostly, I make sandwiches, but I vary the breads, rolls, and wraps and sometimes use panini as the base. I use the best ingredients I can lay my hands on, and always add a small "gift," even if it is just a handful of grapes, a peach, an apple, or any other fruit that is in season. When I'm feeling really generous, I bake a batch of cookies.

I keep the three most popular sandwiches on my list all the time, but I always have a couple of extra choices. As you can imagine, the packaging is nearly as important as the food, and I've found a distinctive box that not only looks great but also keeps the sandwiches in good shape.

The zoning law won't let me make the food at home, so I rent the kitchen at my church. (The cost is minimal.) I'm making enough profit to think about taking on a helper and expanding the business into an office building.

▶▶ FOOD FOR THOUGHT ◀◀

In 1597, William Shakespeare's *The Merry Wives of Windsor* referred to a drink as a "toast," based on the odd custom of tossing cubes of buttered toast into warm drinks at celebratory events.

FOOD JOB: *Table-Manners Trainer*

This is a great job for anyone who has witnessed barbarians at their plates. If, at a midweek breakfast meeting, a prospective employee orders a Bloody Mary, two eggs sunny-side up, bacon, sausage, *and* hash browns, where his prospective boss has asked only for a slice of dry toast and a pot of mint tea, the applicant probably won't get the nod.

The job seeker is judged not only by what he orders, but on how he speaks to the server, how much sugar he pours into his coffee, where he puts his elbows, how he holds his knife and fork, whether he tucks in his napkin, how he touches it to his lips, and whether he surreptitiously checks under the table for text messages. A hundred other clues reveal his worthiness for employment. Poor table manners may lose an applicant a job for which he is otherwise well qualified.

Table-manners trainers are employed by culinary schools, colleges, and corporations with clients in other countries.

▶▶ FOOD FOR THOUGHT ◀◀

An American was an honored guest at a banquet in Moscow. He was asked if he would like to have a second helping of the beef. He replied, in English, "Oh, no. No thank you—the spirit is willing but the flesh is weak." The translator reported that the guest had said, "The vodka was terrific but the meat was horrible!"

Recommended Book

Much Depends on Dinner: The Extraordinary History and Mythology, Allure and Obsessions, Perils and Taboos of an Ordinary Meal by Margaret Visser

CHAPTER 2

retail jobs

As for the notion of a "sucker is born every minute," you may know, in the early 1900s, George Smith made a confection on a stick for a Connecticut candy manufacturer. The candy was named for George Smith's other interest—the track—where Lolly Pop was one of the finest racehorses of the time.

- Butcher
- Cheese and Charcuterie
- Chocolatier
- Gourmet-Shop Owner
- Hummus Purveyor
- Ice Cream Sommelier
- Importer
- Fudge-Shop Entrepreneurs
- Professional Gift-Food Wrapper
- Professional Taster
- Salt-Shop Owner
- Supermarkets
- Tour Guide

IT HAS BEEN said that global food companies have "teeth." Indeed, their teeth can be compared to those of a giant squid wearing steel dentures and wielding tentacles that reach around the planet. Their embrace may be either menacing or benign, depending on how you view the state of affairs and the affairs of state. The only thing that can be said for certain is that, unless small enterprises are very nimble, they themselves are likely to be consumed.

Writing in *Entrepreneur*, Jennifer Wang reminds us of the following: "There was a time when a company's 'About Us' page didn't matter quite so much: a short bio, a mission statement and boom, done. These days, corporate-weary consumers care more and more about buying locally, supporting independent businesses and owning products that are made sustainably and responsibly. They want to know the story of what they're buying, who is selling it and what causes it may support. In a business landscape where success hinges on establishing a personal connection with customers and investors, the 'About Us' page has become prime real estate."

GETTING STARTED AS AN ENTREPRENEUR

No amount of book learning can compare with practical experience when it comes to developing the entrepreneurial instinct. Even so, it is essential for anyone planning to launch a new enterprise to know about zoning laws, food-safety regulations, and general business principles. Courses for entrepreneurs are offered at four-year and community colleges. There, students can learn business principles that may prevent many avoidable catastrophes.

The Road to Riches

The essence of entrepreneurship involves creativity, risk taking, and courage. It may help to define and study these foundational concepts:

1. What is an entrepreneur?
2. What qualities are needed to become a successful entrepreneur?
3. Compile a list of different categories of retail operation.
4. What are the characteristics of a cottage industry?
5. Examine the reasons that some retail stores succeed and others fail.
6. What are the characteristics of a successful retail business?

The best business plans are often the shortest, not fifty-page tomes, but bulleted lists of essentials:

- What am I selling?
- Who will buy it?
- Where will I find my customers?
- How do I price my product?
- How can I get financing?
- Whom will I hire?

▶▶ FOOD FOR THOUGHT ◀◀

Even those who no longer believe in the Tooth Fairy or the Easter Bunny still put their faith in Santa Claus—he may stimulate Christmas sales to climb through the roof.

Martha the Magnificent

—*David Kamp, author of* The United States of Arugula

The nineties were when the entrepreneurial spirit took hold of the food world. They were the years when an interloper named Martha Stewart swooped in and showed the veterans a thing or two about building a brand. A Connecticut-based caterer and former stockbroker of middle-class Polish American origins (née Martha Kostyra), Stewart made her first foray into public life in 1987, with her debut book, *Entertaining*, a gracious-living primer that combined James Beard's and Larry Forgione's love of culinary Americana with Ralph Lauren's jodhpur-fantasy approach to dress, table arrangement, and home décor. In the nineties, the unrelenting Stewart broadened her portfolio to include a magazine, many more books, TV programs, and various product lines, all incorporated in the aptly omnivorous-sounding title Martha Stewart Living Omnimedia.

Strawberry Jam as Retail Parable

Noodling around on Google, I discovered a strawberry-jam theory that goes like this: a customer wants a pot of strawberry jam, so she Googles those words. Up pop 1,500,000 strawberry jam references in less than a second—where to buy it, how to make it, etc.—all based on Google's unique algorithms.

One site offers twelve different kinds of strawberry jam. The customer is immediately overwhelmed. Twelve choices is six too many, so she goes to another site. There, only three kinds of strawberry jam are offered. Hmm. The customer decides that this company is way too small. (If I give them my credit card number, they'll probably steal my identity, and I'll never receive the jam.)

Click. And eureka! Here are six varieties of strawberry jam. She immediately chooses one variety and places her order with this company. Done and done. Strawberry jam arrives. Tastes good. Bank account and online identity are safe.

On the surface, this would seem to be totally irrelevant stuff, but it is actually invaluable information. If a fast-food restaurant offers more than six choices, the line slows and everyone complains. If a bakery offers six kinds of cupcakes, the buyers will buy at least one, maybe one of each. Offer six bagels, and even if we had planned to buy only one or two, we're more likely to buy 'em all, especially if the seventh is free.

Tip to store owners: put the free bagel or cupcake in a separate bag, just to make sure that your generosity is well appreciated.

►► FOOD FOR THOUGHT ◄◄

When a guest ordered a dozen oysters, one smart restaurateur always added a complimentary additional oyster—always on a small, separate plate so that it would be noticed. Guests often ordered twelve rather than six oysters, just to get the free one.

Smart Choices

Many chefs are wise, honest, and smart. They've figured out that it is shrewd to offer six choices, particularly on holiday menus. For Easter, there must be lamb, ham, a fish dish, a vegetarian dish, and two other selections. For Thanksgiving, the menu also needs to contain six options: turkey, turkey, turkey, turkey, or turkey. And one other choice.

Keeping the number of items down to six means that there will be less time devoted to interrogating the server: "Was the turkey raised humanely? Are there nuts in the dressing? Can I have the turkey with extra cranberries?"

When such conversations are kept to a minimum, the tables keep turning and reservations for the next seating are honored on time. And the satisfied guests will return the next year.

JOB OPPORTUNITIES IN THE RETAIL SECTOR

Small and large retail businesses and restaurant chains—such as Panera, Starbucks, Yum! Brands, and Darden—all employ real estate specialists; financial analysts; and advertising, marketing, and public relations experts in addition to recipe testers, recipe writers, and photographers. Is there a possible food job for you here?

A FEW INFLUENTIAL RETAILERS, PAST AND PRESENT:

- Balducci's
- Baskin Robbins
- Ben & Jerry's
- d'Artagnan
- Dean & DeLuca
- Rob Kaufelt
- Murray's Cheese
- Peet's Coffee & Tea
- Silver Palate
- Starbucks
- Steve Jenkins
- Trader Joe's
- Wegmans
- Whole Foods Market
- Williams-Sonoma
- Zabar's
- Zingerman's

FOOD JOB: *Butcher*

Birmingham News business reporter Michael Tomberlin wrote that Birmingham's Smart Butcher has installed the first-known butcher machine at the Lil Mart in Odenville, Alabama. With the push of a button, shoppers can buy fresh cuts of steak or sausages. They simply feed one or five bills into the machine or swipe a credit or debit card to purchase pork chops, steak, or ground beef.

FOOD JOB: *Chocolatier*

Carolus Linnaeus, that long-ago Swedish botanist who spent his life giving Latin names to plants (and to himself as well—he was born Carl von Linné), chose an especially apt one for the cacao tree. *Theobroma*, he called it, "food of the gods." The name was at once a tribute to the chocolate it produced and to the history it carried with it, for the Aztecs reserved the drinking of chocolate for their godlike royalty. The emperor Montezuma was served his fifty-cups-a-day rations in golden goblets. Each goblet was thrown away after a single use, thereby sustaining the emperor in style and presaging the disposable drinking cup by about four hundred years. During the intervening years, chocolate became an affordable luxury for almost everyone and a favored Valentine's Day gift.

Recipes for Success: David Bacco and Marcel Desaulniers

How original! David Bacco, a southern Californian chocolatier, pairs his handmade, artisanal chocolates with beer. Among his recommended pairings is Bell's Pale Ale with gingered macadamia nuts and a dark, bittersweet chocolate prepared with chardonnay, bacon, maple syrup, and sea salt. These combinations are fantastically good. Check them out at DavidBacco.com.

Marcel Desaulniers, author of *Death by Chocolate*, is an award-winning chef and the proud owner of Mad about Chocolate! a café in Williamsburg, Virginia. Upon selling his acclaimed restaurant the Trellis, Marcel recharged his batteries and opened his new venture, where he features his signature, over-the-top cookies, cakes, and brownies, as well as savory items like his hugely popular savory cheesecake. Somehow, he still manages to be home by dinnertime. Check out the restaurant at MadAboutChocolate.us.

▶▶ FOOD FOR THOUGHT ◀◀

A woman's longing for chocolate may not be entirely in her head. There are physiological reasons why women crave pickles during pregnancy and candy bars to ward off premenstrual blues. Menstruation leads to an increase in the metabolic rate. Women often consume an extra 150 calories a day during this period. They experience a hunger for ice cream and other dairy products and for sweets, including chocolate and fruit. These foods satisfy the body's requirement for calcium and additional calories during pregnancy.

Craving Immediate Satisfaction

Some cravings have nutritional bases, while others may result from powerful emotional needs. Professor Adam Drewnowski, director of the Nutritional Sciences Program at the University of Washington in Seattle, theorizes that foods high in fat and sugar stimulate the brain to produce endorphins, the same chemicals responsible for the feelings of calm and well-being described by distance runners.

A candy bar or a pint of ice cream may soothe the pain of a lost job or love. Sometimes, nothing else will work (except, possibly, chicken soup). But when facing such a deprivation, it may be wise to heed the advice of the experts and choose from lower-calorie alternatives: broccoli might do the trick as a mood elevator, although there is not a shred of scientific evidence to support this theory.

Note: We should always listen to nutritionists, but we do not always need to give them our undivided attention. Some dieticians have a theory that red wine is good for you. So is exercise. This could lead a person to embark on a regime of jogging from bar to bar.

No Laughing Matter

Laughing gas makes chocolate taste even more chocolatey. Attendees of the Institute of Food Technologists' Annual Meeting and Food Expo were startled to receive the information from U.K. scientists that nitrous oxide, pumped under pressure into liquid chocolate, produces a more intense cocoa flavor. The testers also found that the gas caused chocolate to melt more rapidly in the mouth. "Bubbles are undervalued as a food ingredient," reported lead researcher, Keshavan Niranjan. Clearly this kind of research will be no laughing matter to the candy men. For them, going to work can sometimes be a barrel of fun.

Sweet Teeth

A sweet tooth: is it innate or acquired? We are descended from a long line of fruit-eating primates. Our cousins, chimpanzees, dip their food in salty water and have developed the ability to poke sticks into honeycombs. They can open hard-shelled nuts and gather termites and other insects that are part of their daily diet. Female chimps are better at this than male chimpanzees. Boys excel at bashing other animals in the head and killing them. A girl sits quietly beside her mother and learns how to copy her. Boys sit still for thirty seconds and then take off to join their pals. Evolution continues to evolve.

►► FOOD FOR THOUGHT ◄◄

- Many advances in food technology stem from research originally conducted by the military and NASA. For example, during one of our recent wars, American scientists developed a new kind of chocolate dessert that won't melt in the hand, even when marching through a desert.

- Biochemists are unraveling the DNA of chocolate, hoping to prevent the fungus that is devastating cacao trees in Brazil and other countries.
- Eating chocolate can contribute to the occurrence of seizures because it increases electrical activity in the brain.
- A business card is a self-branding tool that creates a lasting impression of you, your style and your business. Make sure yours conveys the message you want to send. Having a chocolate business card may be cute but will be disastrous if it melts in the recipient's pocket.
- The French Pastry School at City Colleges of Chicago offers a course in the art of *pastillage*, a sugar that is pulled, blown, and cast to make ornate showpieces. See FrenchPastrySchool.com.
- New advertising messages suggest that chocolate is heart-healthy (especially on Valentine's Day).
- When people declare that they'd kill for a chocolate bar, they don't actually mean what they say. Strictly speaking, an addict may kill for a fix but chocoholics experience a craving, not an addiction.
- The world's most expensive chocolate Easter egg sold for $10,000 in 2012, cracking a Guinness world record.
- Chocolate is the third-largest traded commodity after sugar and coffee.
- Fifty million workers are involved in cacao farming throughout the world.
- The major chocolate companies are Cargill, Nestle, Hershey, Cadbury, and Mars. Together, they generate $80 billion in annual revenues.

FOOD JOB: *Cheese and Charcuterie*

One of the more interesting ideas is to have a restaurant that serves only cheeses, charcuterie (cooked meats, served cold), and wine.

FOOD JOB: *Gourmet-Shop Owner*

How Wine Turned Me Into a Citizen

It was Carl Sagan, the famous astronomer, astrophysicist, and cosmologist, who suggested, "It pays to keep an open mind, but not so open your brains fall out." I mention this proposition to emphasize how vital it is to do serious but skeptical research before embarking on any business endeavor—or any endeavor at all, for that matter.

The only way to learn the retail business is to spend a few years working in a store.

I learned this the hard way…

After spending a shockingly short time at the London Cordon Bleu School of Cookery (known today as Le Cordon Bleu, London), I decided to open my very own cooking school in Greensboro, North Carolina. I named it La Bonne Femme. Of course, nobody in Greensboro had the least idea what this meant. As a dish, it is a seductively tasty combination of garlic, onions, bacon, and mushrooms in a red-wine sauce to accompany a thick veal chop or chicken leg. As a namesake, it evokes "the Good Wife." I preferred to think of myself, and of the shop, as the Good Woman.

I set up my cooking school in a beautiful, isolated little house in the woods where nobody could find it. Nevertheless, word of mouth was generous. The school thrived. It thrived so mightily—on a small scale mind you—that I decided to expand into a shop where I could sell the same soufflé dishes, rolling pins, and other gadgets and utensils I was using in my classes. That worked, too.

Next, I considered how neat it would be to sell what were then quaintly called "gourmet" foods. A glass-door refrigerator displayed great cheeses. There were exotic coffee beans, teas, chocolates, and all manner of good things to eat. I arranged to have baguettes, croissants, and brioches flown in from New York.

There were only two things missing in my little corner of paradise: one was wine ... so I decided to import it. The law required wine sellers to become US citizens. I became a US citizen.

The place was simply charming.

There now remained only one missing thing: customers.

Lesson one: Don't choose a fancy name for a business or for your identity as a personal chef or for a service or for a blog or for a book title.

Lesson two: Each town has a doomed location. There, every enterprise is destined to fail. Before investing in a cash register, make sure that you know that you have chosen the best possible location. Know who your customers and suppliers are likely to be. Make sure there is enough parking for the crowds that will flock to your store. Check the zoning. Get insurance. Explore all the hidden costs including taxes and garbage and snow removal. Register your name. Make friends with the bank manager. Have a marketing and publicity plan. Be realistic about drawing up a profit-and-loss statement. Think carefully about your ability to withstand extreme stress.

And as a rousing chorus of Les Bonne Femmes would say: *Bonne chance!* (Good luck!)

★ RARE FOOD JOB: *Ice Cream Sommelier*

Recently, in the *Los Angeles Times*, I came across an article about Katherine Montero, a self-described "ice cream sommelier." She graduated with a business degree from Harvard University and an interest in molecular gastronomy and biology. She's created a job for herself working with a chef in an ice cream laboratory in Miami. She produces flavors so intense that they will change the color of contact lenses (no, not literally!). She and her partner have dreamed up some truly weird flavors, including pizza ice cream, a combination of tomato marmalade and basil served with a curl of Parmesan cheese. There's also maple syrup ice cream served with a strip of crisp bacon and chocolate molé ice cream. Those who yearn for plain old vanilla ice cream may be out of luck, because there is a never-ending parade of people who are willing to try anything at least once.

I mention these rare food jobs in order to make a point: When you can identify the thing you truly love, you can scoop up a career wrapped around the object of your affection.

★ RARE FOOD JOB: *Professional Taster*

If you believe that you have a vibrant palate and can accurately identify each flavor when the menu offers lasagna with four cheeses, then you may be able to earn a living as a professional taster. Here are some professionals who do just that:

- Chef (of course)
- Tea taster
- Coffee taster
- Cheese taster
- Sommelier
- Flavor creator
- Food purchasing agent

RARE FOOD JOB: *Hummus Purveyor*

New York magazine reports that Ori Apple, a French Culinary Institute graduate and former line cook for the high-end New York restaurant Lespinasse, owns Hummus Place, which is devoted exclusively to the sale of—you guessed it—hummus. Factoring in all the hummus aficionados from all the Mediterranean nations that pride themselves on the stuff—not to mention the area's legions of vegetarians and connoisseurs of Middle Eastern food in general—Apple and his partners figured that they had a built-in constituency. Indeed, no place has taken the chickpea spread as seriously—or devoted itself to it as single-mindedly—as has this twenty-eight-seat shrine to the dense, creamy, tahini-enriched dip. We probably shouldn't be surprised to know that Hummus Place is located in New York's Greenwich Village.

There also is a nearby store doing a brisk business selling only French fries, though not the kind traditionally made in Belgium, served in a paper cone with mayonnaise.

FOOD JOB: *Fudge-Shop Entrepreneur*

Why is it that, when on vacation, there is always a little shop selling homemade fudge? If you can get to the bottom of vacationers' affection for fudge, you may have a sweet career ahead of you, even if it only thrives during the tourist season.

FOOD JOB: *Professional Gift-Food Wrapper*

Here are some tips and ideas for gift-wrapping batches of cookies, your own homegrown tomatoes, hunks of cheese, or pounds of coffee. All of these inspirations sprang from the fertile mind of Elaine

Yannuzzi, former owner/president of Expression Unltd., one of the country's leading gift and gourmet stores and originator of the concept of the gusseted bag for packaging food gifts. Master these presentation ideas, and offer your services as an in-store gift-wrapping specialist. You will become an invaluable employee. Take a few samples of your work when you go for an interview, and leave your goodies behind you at the store to reiterate your skills and good taste!

1) A Basket of Breads

Make a visual plan. Decide whether you will fill the bottom of the basket with excelsior or a folded napkin or kitchen towel. The bread must fill the basket completely and must build the center up so that the basket has a bountiful look.

Basically, all you need is an attractive basket, at least ten inches in diameter, an assortment of breads of different shapes, colors, and types, and about three yards of wide ribbon for the bow. Work from the back to the front of the basket. A round flattish bread, such as Boboli, makes a particularly effective rear centerpiece.

Fill in the empty spaces with breadsticks, and tuck in some shiny green leaves or fresh foliage. Decorate with a big ribbon bow tied to the basket handle or wired to the side of the basket.

2) Bread in a Flower Pot

If you are a baker, give the gift of bread in a flowerpot. Use a regular red-clay garden flowerpot, wash it in hot soapy water, and let it dry. Butter the interior generously, covering the hole with a small piece of buttered foil. Coat the sides of the pot with toasted breadcrumbs.

Make a basic yeast bread dough, and fill the pot three-quarters full. Oil the top of the dough and set in a warm place to double in size. (One rising will be enough.) Bake in a preheated 350-degree oven for thirty minutes if you are using a large pot, fifteen if a small one. The bread cooks quickly as a result of the additional heat from the clay pot. It is done when it sounds hollow when tapped and when the top is golden brown. Leave the bread to partially cool in the pot for fifteen minutes before removing it from the pot to cool completely. To decorate the pot, glue a pretty fabric ribbon around the lip and attach a bow to the front. Set the baked bread back in the pot and wrap with cellophane.

3) Fruits and Vegetables

Fill a white or colored colander with arrangements of vegetables placed around a bottle of fine olive oil in the center. Fill in the spaces with little radishes and fresh herbs.

Similarly, fill a colander with a variety of colorful larger fruits, interspersing these with several kinds of berries. In the center, place a jar of Melba or other fruit sauce, and at the last minute, tuck in a carton of super-premium ice cream.

4) Stack Packs

To form a gift stack of foods, select a collection of goods, making sure that at least one is flat and large. This will form the base. Take the tallest, most cylindrical item, such as a bottle, tall jar, or a box of crackers, and attach it to base's center with rolled, double-sided, heavy-duty tape.

Separate the other elements into groups of similar shapes and sizes. Arrange the foods in a circle around your centerpiece on top of the original base. Alternate shapes, interspersing long items with round ones and so on. Don't be afraid to stack one thing on top of another. A jar of preserves may be topped with a round mini-wheel of cheese stacked on top of it; pasta can be topped with a jar of a sauce; a jar of specialty mustard may be topped with a chunk of pâté; a package of risotto rice with a small container of saffron.

When you are satisfied with the shape, secure it in place with tape. You might decorate the pack with colorful paper before you wrap it or intersperse the stack with wrapped candies or fresh flowers.

Cut a piece of cellophane large enough for the ends to meet five to six inches above the tallest point of the pack. Depending on its width, you may have to crisscross pieces and tape the sides closed. Gather the cellophane up over the package, crimp it at the top of the tallest item, and tie with a ribbon. Make sure the cellophane is pulled up tightly around the package so as to hold the construction securely in place.

A professional food-gift wrapper can transform even a simple box of crackers into an attractive gift.

• •

My Word: Gift Basket Giver

I went food shopping in Adams Fairacre Farms, a locally owned Hudson Valley, New York, food market, which carries picture-perfect fruits and vegetables, many organically grown by nearby farmers. They offer smoked salmon and bacon supplied from a local smokehouse. There is free-range poultry—including duck, goose, young turkey, and poussins—and pastured, grass-fed beef and lamb. There is an impressive array of cheeses, as well as crème fraîche, yogurt, and hand-churned sweet and salted butter. There is honey personally delivered by a neighborhood beekeeper, as well as farmhouse pickles and preserves. There are ice creams and sorbets from an ultra-premium creamery.

There are handmade chocolates and cookies and vast selections of breads, biscotti, and cookies from brick-oven bakeries short distances away. There is a marvelous range of local beers, ciders, and juice drinks.

"Aha," thought I, "here's a business—a food job!"

There are more than a million visitors to the Hudson Valley every year. Many travelers are looking for a gift to take home to the kind person who looked after the children, or the dogs and cats, or who watered the plants.

How about a gift basket overflowing with artisanal foods and local wines?

No matter where you live, there are regional specialties to arrange in attractive containers, to be hand-delivered or mailed.

Offer your creative services to food shops, florists, hotels, bed and breakfasts, historical homes, wineries, and wherever tourists tour. Suggest different price points and several options, and be willing to do the mailing for your clients. Give a commission to sites that display your actual or photographed gift basket ideas, or make a contribution to a worthy local cause for every basket purchased. Use social networks for your marketing.

With perseverance and a little capital, you can quickly establish your own business.

• •

FOOD JOB: *Salt-Shop Owner*

It may be a trend, or merely a fad, but those with a few extra pennies in their pockets have become inordinately interested in single-ingredient retailing. There are stores selling only olive oil, only spices, only tea, and perhaps most surprisingly, just salt.

Of course, salt is—well—the salt of the earth, but here are a few other facts to enrich your life:

▸▸ FOOD FOR THOUGHT ◂◂

- Sprinkling table-quality salt on food as a seasoning was once a privilege affordable only by the wealthy. Hence, those seated "beneath the salt" were designated lesser mortals.
- Animals followed paths to salt licks. Their paths turned into well-traveled roads that connected cities.
- Salt was the first internationally used commodity of trade and the first commodity to be monopolized.

Recommended Book

Salt: A World History by Mark Kurlansky

FOOD JOB: *Supermarkets*

You may have noticed that when you shop at the grocery store at the beach, there are only three kinds of cereal, along with three kinds of lettuce: wilted, more wilted, and not worth buying. Yet the local population appears to be quite adequately nourished.

There is an army of employees behind the scenes. In addition to all the obvious front-of-the-house jobs—the managers, cashiers, stockers, and baggers—there are chefs, cooks, butchers, bakers, and fish folk. There are sweepers and cleaners, and in some stores, wine experts.

Supermarkets are like villages, with a place for everybody and every kind of expert. If you just enjoy being around food, you can find employment in a supermarket.

U.S. SUPERMARKET FACTS AND FIGURES

Number of employees	3.4 million
Total supermarket sales, 2011	$584.369 billion
Number of supermarkets with $2 million or more in annual sales, 2011	36,569
Net profit after taxes, 2011	1.09%
Median total store size, in square feet, 2010	46,000
Median weekly sales per supermarket, 2010	$466,011
Percentage of disposable income spent on food, 2010 On food at home On food away from home	9.4% 5.5% 3.9%
Weekly sales per square foot of selling area, 2010	$11.78
Sales per customer transaction, 2010	$26.78
Sales per labor hour, 2010	$166.55
Average number of trips per week consumers make to the supermarket, 2012	2.2
Average number of items carried in a supermarket, 2010	38,718

Sources: US Department of Labor, US Department of Agriculture, Progressive Grocer *magazine, US Census Bureau, and Food Marketing Institute.*

▶▶ FOOD FOR THOUGHT ◀◀

According to the USDA's Economic Research Service report *The Relationship Between National Brand and Private Label Food*, the average price of supermarkets' private-label foods is about 23 percent lower than those of national brands.

FOOD JOB: *Tour Guide*

Culinary tourism is among the fastest growing niches in the US travel industry. This is a great career if you relish the challenge of creating your own business and enjoy meeting new people.

Brooke Dojny, food writer, writes about stops on the culinary tourism trail:

> There are places of interest to food lovers everywhere in the United States these days: an olive ranch in Sonoma, California; a barbecue pit in Charleston, South Carolina; a clam shack in Penobscot, Maine; a bagel factory in Brooklyn, New York; a tortilla maker in Santa Fe, New Mexico; a cheese maker in Ashland, Wisconsin; and an Indian grocery in Dallas, Texas. Wineries, brew pubs, farms, and farmers' markets east, west, north, and south are all of interest to food lovers.

For instance, Deborah Orrill, a Dallas resident, fashioned a five-day trip that includes a lobster boat excursion, visits to a cheese maker, a seafood smoking plant, a couple of organic farms, oyster and mussel farms, a crab lunch with a cookbook author, and a final stop on the last day at the farmers' market, "where everything kind of comes together." The group of five to eight people is housed in a small inn. They eat a few restaurant meals, but they also cook some dinners using ingredients they've gathered during the day.

Some tours combine food and cooking with other creative endeavors. Gigia Kolouch runs weeklong trips in California's Sonoma and Marin Counties that she calls "Journeys of the Senses." In addition to touring a creamery, an olive ranch, an herb farm, a winery, and the huge and fabulous Frank Lloyd Wright Marin Civic Center Farmers' Market, the tour group visits artists and artisans' studios.

Susan Rosenbaum organizes three separate New York City "melting pot" tours.

In Charleston, South Carolina, Amanda Dew Manning, a tenth-generation Charlestonian, runs three regular culinary walking tours of her city every week plus daylong trips outside the city. A typical walking tour of downtown Charleston emphasizes South Carolina's rich food history and its local cuisine and includes stops at the city's famous covered market, artisan bakeries, a chocolatier, and shops selling Low Country products.

How to Get Started as a Food Tour Guide

Recognize your own culinary knowledge, and set yourself up as an expert. If need be, seek help from other experts in your area, whether local historians, gardeners, farmers, etc. Librarians and newspaper food editors can help you with your research.

Never surprise vendors. Schedule visits with them well ahead of time, and make every effort to avoid their busiest times. A homemade food gift is also a nice touch.

Have frank conversations with vendors about whether they expect payment or whether their compensation will be in the form of goods sold to tour participants. Settle all details regarding transportation, accommodations, meals, and the total number of clients you can handle.

Decide how to market the tour. Give your company an appealing name. Build your own website, but investigate other online marketing venues (e.g. ShawGuides.com), as well as state tourism departments. Consider hiring a professional marketing consultant.

FOOD JOB: *Importer*

For special occasions, special ingredients may need to be purchased from other countries and coaxed past the watchful eyes of customs agents. All major food-processing companies employ specialists familiar with the intricacies of international trade and with rules pertaining to food safety. To get started in this ever-expanding field, explore the National Association of Specialty Food Trade (NASFT) at SpecialtyFood.com/nasft.

CHAPTER 3

art, design, and creativity

Computers are to design as microwaves are to cooking.

—MILTON GLASER, DESIGNER OF
THE I ♥ NEW YORK LOGO

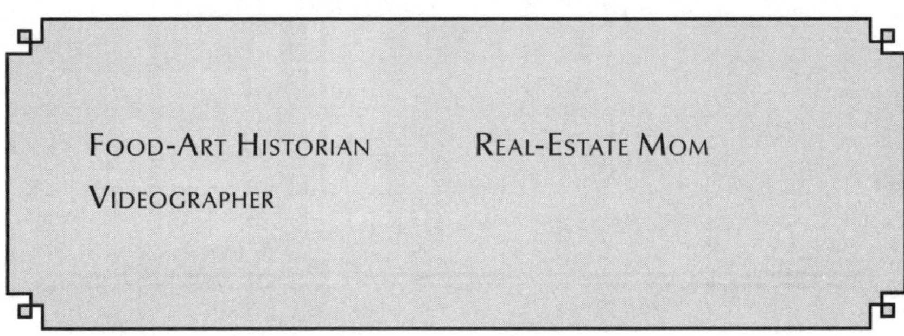
Food-Art Historian
Real-Estate Mom
Videographer

CREATIVITY: WHAT IS it and why is it important in the culinary world? Jewelers, potters, glass blowers, and craftspeople use every medium, from clay to precious metals and gemstones. Commercial designers and manufacturers produce a dazzling array of kitchen equipment and elegant, useful tools for cooks. In kind, food too is a medium used to render images and to be made into objects for everyday use.

Food enters art in everything from shopping bags to Christmas-tree ornaments and greetings cards. Still-life paintings depict the last supper; hunting expeditions; picnics beside the sea; silver bowls of ripe fruit; tables laden with simple loaves of crusty bread, cheese, and goblets of wine; or entire meals of ham, pheasant, figs, cheese, and cherries.

These are treasures to last, for gastronomic eternity, in the form of fine art.

• •

My Word: Food Becomes Art

We tend to think of creative people as great artists or musicians like Picasso or Mozart, not as the kind of people who might build things like the Gotham Bar and Grill in New York City. But restaurateur Alfred Portale has made that very place famous with his stunning, architectural food pyramids. When we come to praise famous men and women, we may forget their names but not their creations. (Though, could it be said that for all his accomplishments, Caesar is now remembered mainly for his salad?)

A creative genius is one who doesn't stop with salt and pepper but who marches on to discover the delights of combining the salt and caramel. Inventive chefs have reimagined food itself. Ferran Adria, Grant Achatz, and Heston Blumenthal are leaders among those who have gone where others feared to tread. We can confidently anticipate that legions of synchronously swimming chefs will continue to splash in their sparkling waters.

• •

CREATIVE SOLUTIONS TO STIMULATE BUSINESS

Hard times bring about interesting solutions. It was during the 1997 economic slump that a group of restaurateurs got together and came up with the concept of the $19.97 prix fixe lunch. The idea caught fire and continues to attract new business. It made sense, because it introduced a new clientele to restaurants and enabled restaurants to maintain their purchases from vendors. Increased business made it possible for kitchen workers and servers to hold on to their jobs.

Creativity comes in many guises.

Here's an example of a simple yet creative gift for a friend: Fill a plastic (medical) glove with Hershey's kisses. Attach a note with the words: "I'd like to give you a hand."

Three Creative Eggs

The first was a brown egg in an eggcup. The top had been removed. Inside was a miniature soufflé. The second egg was not an egg at all but was nestled into an eggcup. The cook had molded the white likeness of an egg from vanilla ice cream. Inside, the "yolk" was a passion-fruit sorbet. The third egg was also a fantasy, this time in the likeness of a fried egg. The "white" was formed from white chocolate, and the "yolk" was apricot mousse.

Recommended Book

Imagine: How Creativity Works by Jonah Lehrer

• •

My Word

There are those who invent clocks and others who tell the time. There are architects who design buildings and artisans who paint them. There are craftsmen who make violins and musicians who compose and perform concertos. Plumbers, electricians, and vacuum-cleaner engineers also invent novel solutions to problems. So do chefs. They are creative geniuses too.

We all know chefs who acquire or are endowed with exceptional ability. Some are intellectual giants. Some are blessed with intuitive talent. If we tried to make a list of influential chefs, it would reach back to Lucullus, who drew his last breath in 56 BC. We could trace a glorious gastronomic path through the prism of Apicius, who sighed away his final moment on earth in 25 BC. We'd mention Taillevent (1310–1395) and François Rabelais (ca. 1494–1553), who tirelessly described sixty ways to cook an egg. (In his five-novel cycle *The Life of Gargantua and of Pantagruel*, Rabelais wrote, "Drink always and you shall never die." Unfortunately, he did.) We'd add to our list of creative cooks Catherine de' Medici, who arrived from Italy as a tiny, betrothed fourteen-year-old and became the queen of France. She changed the culinary landscape by introducing the French court to truffles, Parmesan cheese, artichokes, quenelles, roast duckling with orange sauce, and pasta—lots and lots of pasta.

Each stage in the evolution of our culinary journey takes us to new heights. From the seventeenth-century influence of François Pierre de la Varenne, we stride through the history of gastronomy to honor Jean Anthelme Brillat-Savarin, Marcel Boulestin, Marie-Antonin Carême, Alexandre-Etienne Choron, Adolphe Dugléré, and Nicolas Appert (inventor of canning). From Auguste Escoffier, Alain Chapel, Alain Ducasse, and Alain Senderens, we move onward to Ferdinand Point, Guy Savoy, and Gordon Ramsay, and still further on to Chef Boyardee and his discovery of 365 ways to use leftover hot dogs.

It has been observed that there wouldn't have been a Renaissance without the creation of pasta. Hungry men growl, and with rumbling tummies foment revolutions, whereas the well-fed sing happy songs and create everlasting beauty. With a bellyful of spaghetti, a person can contemplate creation itself.

It was the ancient Greek philosopher Epicurus—alive from 341 BC to 269 BC—who wisely declared, "The beginning and root of all good is to make the stomach happy; wisdom and learning are founded on that." If only those ancient Greeks still ruled the world! We would all be living in paradise instead of dwelling in perpetual poverty.

Do you remember the dictum of King Henri IV, alleged patron of that venerable inn, La Tour d'Argent? He pronounced his monarchal philosophy thusly: "If God allows me to live, and I will see that there is not a single laborer in my kingdom who does not have a chicken in his pot every Sunday." This declaration was made in the mid-1500s, before the Colonel had even fried his first chicken. Thus we stride through the first stirrings of culinary creationism and evolve from sauce béarnaise to green goddess dressing, from poulet *demi deuil* with a fine Bordeaux to chicken nuggets with Diet Coke. We have indeed traveled far and wide, though sometimes we cross bridges that do not always lead anywhere.

• •

▶▶ FOOD FOR THOUGHT ◀◀

- Antoine-Augustin Parmentier was the French pharmacist who persuaded Parisians to set aside their suspicion of potatoes.
- Chef Maurice Edmond Curnonsky described French fries as being among "the most spiritual creations of Parisian genius."
- The original French fries are thought to have been invented during the French Revolution. It is said that they were eaten beneath a bridge in Paris and were known by that name, as pommes Pont-Neuf.

DEFINING CREATIVITY

Creativity is a capacity that can be developed. It is based on the fundamentals of technical knowledge and soaring imagination. Leonardo da Vinci had to understand the elements of anatomy in order to paint the *Mona Lisa* and *The Last Supper*. Picasso had to understand the fundamentals of art before creating his own Cubist art. Every great chef begins to climb the ladder to stardom only after fully understanding the pure ecstasy of a well-constructed consommé. It is this grasp of complex simplicity that separates the sous from the celebs. To invent a new dish is to pay homage to all who cooked before, as well as to all the consumers who declared chefs to be artists.

FOOD IN FINE ART

Stroll through a museum and you will be astonished to see how frequently artists use food as their inspiration. An art historian could make an entire career just writing and lecturing on the topic of apples in art.

Carl Warner describes his work as a food-landscape photographer: "Making landscapes out of food seems a rather unusual thing to do for a living, and people often ask, 'What made you start doing this?' It seems that the burning heart of this question is really the curiosity about what it is that motivates any human being to do something out of the ordinary, and my short answer to this is usually, a simple, because I had the idea and I chose to do something with it."

Recommended Book

Carl Warner's *Food Landscapes* is a fantastic book that belongs on every food lover's shelf. It will become a treasured possession of anyone who receives it as a gift, too.

FOOD JOB: *Food-Art Historian*

A historian interested in food-as-art can create a unique career as a researcher, writer, teacher, museum lecturer, or exhibit curator. I met a young man who had yearned to be a painter. Sadly, he'd listened to his parents' forecasts on the inevitable fate of the starving artist. Instead of following his heart, he'd become a chef. Eventually, though, he landed a job at the Philadelphia Museum of Art. He was appointed chef of the private dining room, where he created the exquisite hand-painted menus that many guests treasure as souvenirs. He said that he would occasionally model the food on his plates after paintings on the museum walls. His was a dream deferred and reimagined.

Recipe for Success

British culinary historian Gillian Riley is one of the world's foremost authorities on the subject of food in art. She may devote an entire evening to an erudite discourse, say, on the still-life paintings of the Spanish artist Luis Egidio Meléndez (1715–1780).

During a lecture at the National Arts Club in New York City, Ms. Riley may point to what at first seems to be a random selection of objects tipped out on a kitchen table. Under her eye, it becomes a rigorous, perfectionist's arrangement illustrating a precise theme: a meal, a recipe, a gastronomic event. The artist may in fact have painted the gathered ingredients for a gazpacho, a salad, a dessert of fresh and preserved fruit. In another painting, he may have hinted at a whole meal—fresh crusty bread, jamòn, and figs—or made a composition of cheese, fruit, and wine.

Recommended Book

A Feast for the Eyes: Evocative Recipes and Surprising Tales Inspired by Paintings in the National Gallery by Gillian Riley. (Admire her other glorious art books, too.)

MAKING A DATE WITH HISTORY

After spending eleven years as the White House's executive chef, Walter Scheib teamed up with acclaimed caterer Abigail Kirsch, as well as Design Cuisine, a Washington, DC, catering company, to reproduce celebrated state dinners, Christmas feasts, small lunches, and other special-occasion meals from US history.

To reproduce a historic meal, for example, a Shakespearean supper, a good cook and inspired storyteller can add to the joy of the occasion by recounting gossip from the period. If you lived near a maritime museum, you might scour its archives for material relating to fishing or to the diets of long-ago sailor-explorers. If you are knowledgeable on the subject of herbs, you might research period gardens and offer your services creating kitchen gardens for historic homes. If you are adept at hearth cooking, you might suggest giving cooking demonstrations, using authentic techniques. Or, with a little help from your friends, you might even re-create the last supper on the *Titanic*.

THE LAST FIRST-CLASS MENU SERVED ON THE *RMS TITANIC*, ON APRIL 14, 1912

FIRST COURSE

Hors d'Oeuvres

Oysters

SECOND COURSE

Consommé Olga

Cream of Barley

THIRD COURSE

Poached Salmon with Mousseline Sauce, Cucumbers

FOURTH COURSE

Filet Mignons Lili

Sauté of Chicken, Lyonnaise

Vegetable Marrow Farci

FIFTH COURSE

Lamb, Mint Sauce

Roast Duckling, Apple Sauce

Sirloin of Beef, Château Potatoes

Green Peas

Creamed Carrots

Boiled Rice

Parmentier Boiled New Potatoes

SIXTH COURSE

Punch Romaine

SEVENTH COURSE

Roast Squab & Cress

EIGHTH COURSE

Cold Asparagus Vinaigrette

NINTH COURSE

Pâté de Foie Gras

Celery

TENTH COURSE

Waldorf Pudding

Peaches in Chartreuse Jelly

Chocolate & Vanilla Éclairs

French Ice Cream

Each of these ten courses was paired with an appropriate wine. After dessert, there was a service of fresh fruits and cheeses, then coffee and cigars, port wine, brandies, *alcools blancs*, and liqueurs. This was truly a meal to die for.

FOOD IN FOLK ART

Women and girls, men and boys—all delight in decorating the everyday objects they use in the spaces in which they live and work. The work of the early American settlers is a reflection of the spirit of the times. Utility came first, beauty followed. Samplers were not only for decoration; they were used to teach children reading, writing, and arithmetic. Sewing was not a hobby; it was a necessity. All the family clothes had to be made at home. Mothers and grandmothers made quilts and rugs to keep themselves and their children warm, with little inkling that they were also creating art.

Men and women have always been artisans, using whatever materials they had at hand—metal and wood, tin and pewter, rags and whale bones and scraps of cloth. The early settlers, too, fabricated weather vanes, sculptures, teapots, and kitchen utensils. Neither fancy nor frivolous, their work is nonetheless filled with the exuberance of experimentation. It may be described as naïve, but its very innocence is the essence of its charm. It is no small wonder that many such objects have endured and become part of our treasured heritage.

A new handmade gift is cherished every bit as much as an heirloom. Like the work of those who lived before us, we need little or no formal training. The important thing is to continue to create with our own unique signatures.

A EUREKA MOMENT

An idea for specialization can spring from anywhere. At the James Beard House, I saw a poster announcing an event entitled "Dumplings and Dynasties." Wow! An entire career could be predicated on this concept. It could even become a kind of Alex Haley *Roots*, Joseph Campbell *Power of the Myth*, or Ken Burns's *The Civil War*—with music and dance! How fabulous this could be. Dumplings and Dynasties:

The Origins of Everything Edible! Imagine a series of wedding-ceremony traditions around the world. Edible Dumplings and Dynasties animated in living color!

FOOD JOB: *Videographer*

A videographer provides vital visuals for cooking instruction, for animating the interiors of restaurants, for memorializing food festivals, and for recording conferences. Video can also be used to enliven websites, sales pitches, and proposals. Even job applications will get added depth and interest in the subject. Videographers have become valued members of many culinary teams.

If you can secure the funding, you can travel the universe as a food videographer. Pick your topic. It could be anything, from a documentary about fair-trade coffee to recording a family gathering to filming instructional videos on table manners and other rules of etiquette. Indeed, every aspect of teaching and learning about food preparation and service can be enriched when a speaker is seen as well as heard. Online courses and cooking demonstrations are more interesting when accompanied by a lively video. A profitable business may await a professional who specializes in creating short-form video content for websites—whether of conferences, lectures, or interviews; to augment food-blog content; or for marketing materials, say, to promote a food truck or introduce a new line of barbecue sauces. To get started, create some sample material and write a proposal detailing your fees.

RARE FOOD JOB: *Real-Estate Mom*

The oddest "job" I have ever had was at the invitation of a very large home builder. I was asked to stand in the kitchen of a model home, look like a mom, and cook little snacks for the house hunters. It was a hugely successful promotion. Not surprisingly, everyone gathered in the kitchen. Neighbors met neighbors and shared notes about schools and other areas of mutual interest. Sales soared.

CHAPTER 4

all things media

publishing, tv, the internet, and radio

Anyone can become a writer: the trick is to keep a roof over your head at the same time.

—BEN STEIN

Anthologist

App Developer

Blogger

Cartoonist

Catalog Compiler

Chef Biographer

Cookbook Author

Cookbook Reviewer

Cookbook Translator

Director of Digital Publishing

Food-App Develope

Food-Etiquette Columnist

Food-Politics Writer

Food-Related Game-Show Producer

Ghostwriter

Literary Agent

Magazine Columnist

Menu Writer

Newspaper Food Writer

Playwright

Radio Host

Restaurant Apology Writer

Restaurant Reviewer

Science Writer

Travel Writer

Wikipedia Writer

SMALL CHANGES LOOM LARGE

PRINT PUBLISHING HAS rapidly progressed from paper to screen. This change is revolutionary. It is even more momentous and consequential than the invention of the Gutenberg printing press circa 1440.

Today, an event can be broadcast simultaneously, wirelessly, and globally, and viewed by millions. Paradoxically, though, marketers are narrowcasting; they are desperately seeking ever-thinner slices of the pie. They must identify micro-niches for their products in order to remain competitive.

We can see this fracturing of large entities into smaller, more clearly defined units in every aspect of commerce—huge supermarkets spin off smaller shops that sell only fresh foods. Large department stores splinter into smaller specialty stores. Restaurants specialize in only one cuisine, or even a single food—whether noodles, sushi, pizza, sandwiches, bagels, tacos, doughnuts, ice cream, cupcakes, fried chicken, or burgers with fizzing brown drinks. One restaurant in Manhattan sells only rice pudding. Another offers only French fries. All are thriving.

TV networks have divided, and subdivided, into special-interest cable channels—nature and weather, home and garden, food and fashion, history and mystery, old movies and new religions, sports, crime and politics. Each segment has its leaders and followers.

Doctors and dentists have morphed into micro-specialists, as have artists, musicians, theologians, chefs, athletes, financiers, and food writers.

Books, magazines, and newspapers take aim at clearly defined demographics. Magazine articles are getting shorter. Sound bites are merely nibbles. Texting is instantaneous. It has become challenging for writers to hold the attention of people who read articles while watching television, while eating ice cream on a stick, while holding a smart phone, while seated on a loved one's knee.

WHO WANTS TO BE A FOOD WRITER?

Your first task as a writer may be to narrow your options. If you say that you would like to be a generalist, you are looking at the vast blue sky through a telescope. It is crucial to narrow your focus by carefully studying your options. Instead of a telescope, change your focus; peer through a microscope at one specific sector of the huge publishing universe.

Make up your mind about whether you want to be a newspaper columnist, to write for a consumer magazine like *Edible Hudson Valley*, *Fine Cooking*, or *Saveur*, or to write for a trade journal such as *Nation's Restaurant News* or *Pizza Today*. Or, you might have luck proposing a regular column for a publication that didn't have a food section until you came along and suggested it. Be aware that Wegmans and other supermarket chains publish food magazines. Medical-insurance companies issue magazines for those on special diets. Restaurants and food companies distribute newsletters, as do specialty food retailers, so your options are in fact much broader than may at first have seemed obvious.

A Word of Advice for Food Writers

Buy as many magazines as you can afford. Examine every inch of every page, and pay particular attention to the advertisements. These provide clues about the readership. If a given magazine's ads are for expensive cars, costly jewels, and luxurious perfumes, this may be your desired destination. If not, you may feel more comfortable trying to attract the attention of a college community or a posse of bearded bikers.

PUBLISHING: COOKBOOKS

A Guide to a Slippery Slope

The wise are forever issuing dire warnings about slippery slopes. Here is one that has become a very steep slide indeed. Traditional publishers are taking fewer risks on unknown authors and are producing fewer cookbooks. This means that there is less need to maintain high-priced publishing offices in high-rent districts. Costs are cut as publishers' profits decline. The agonized staff is laid off or offered freelance or part-time employment without traditional benefits.

When the demand for physical, hard-, or soft-cover books is reduced, there are fewer orders placed with printers. Fewer printed books result in empty warehouses, and this, in turn, means that there is a less inventory to insure. Fewer trucks are needed to carry books to and from bookstores. We are all painfully aware of the demise of small, independent, neighborhood bookstores, and even of the disappearance of large bookstore chains. Even so, don't abandon hope.

►► FOOD FOR THOUGHT ◄◄

The following fact was provided by R. R. Bowker at the Roger Smith Cookbook Conference in New York City in 2012: Cookbooks account for 4 percent of all book purchases.

The speaker went on to ask the following questions:

- Who buys cookbooks, professionals or home cooks? Answer: both.
- Where do they buy cookbooks, from bookstores or online? Answer: both.
- How does a prospective buyer hear about a cookbook at a time when there are fewer newspaper and magazine reviews and virtually no extensive author or media tours? Answer: Radio interviews and bloggers spread the word. Amazon is the key to sales.
- Why does a buyer purchase a specific book? Answer: Most books are bought as gifts. There is a spike in cookbook sales during the Christmas season. (Diet books, however, are not given as gifts but are purchased by the intended user.)
- What is the average price paid for a cookbook: Who buys a fifty-dollar cookbook? Answer: some people—a few.

Purchasing decisions are based on

- how many children there are in the recipient's household;
- whether the buyer or recipient is married or single;
- whether he or she is high school or college-educated;
- and whether or not the buyer has some income to spare.

Profile of a Cookbook Buyer

Women buy 69 percent of all cookbooks. The largest purchasing group is between the ages of thirty and forty-four, though there has been growth in the eighteen- to twenty-nine-year-old group. This change is attributed to cable-TV cooking programs.

Conclusions: Fewer cookbooks are published every year. Thousands upon thousands of recipes are available online, *for free*, so a prospective author must ask: who truly needs, or wants, or will buy my book? This is a harsh reality, but it is vitally important to nail this information down.

▶▶ FOOD FOR THOUGHT ◀◀

We are rapidly becoming a cooking-illiterate nation. It is therefore essential to have a clear profile of the prospective buyers of your book. Ask yourself, "To whom am I speaking?" Answer—honestly. It is essential to develop a marketing plan the moment a contract is signed.

Time Elapses

The rapid increase in e-book sales means that it is no longer necessary to have two publishing seasons. In theory at least, a book can be available as soon as it is deemed ready for electronic publication.

Money Matters

If a book doesn't physically exist, what is it worth and how much can an author or a publisher earn from it? Everyone in publishing is currently wrestling with this conundrum, and lawsuits are twisting and turning before stern-faced judges who struggle to render Solomonic decisions. "Collusion" and "price fixing" are words that have reentered the lexicon of late.

Winners and Losers

Author advances and royalties are no longer contractual certainties. They now often exist only in the wishful eye of the author, and may hop, skip, and jump according to the idiosyncrasies of each publisher. Certainly the old 7.5 percent royalty rate for a soft-cover book is no longer the norm in all circumstances, and some publishers no longer provide any advance payment at all. Indeed, the publisher may now require an investment from the writer to cover editing, fact-checking, indexing, design, and other preproduction costs. The publisher will often pay for the printing of a book, or its conversion into an e-book, in exchange for 50 percent of the profits. A few publishers are offering authors 70 percent royalty rates, or even higher, but these come with plenty of fine-print caveats. Book publishing is changing so rapidly that there is no single model to point to.

Every writer is responsible for his or her own research into how to get the best possible contract, but a knowledgeable, well-connected literary agent is as essential to this process as a good lawyer is to a defendant pleading a case. The ability to strike a great deal in the new high-tech publishing world has become vastly more complicated, but it also offers great new opportunities for writers and publishers alike.

How the System Works

In the *New Yorker*, on April 26, 2010, Ken Auletta broke down the costs and profits involved in a typical book in the following manner:

> A simplified version of a [traditional] publisher's costs might run as follows: On a new, $26 hardcover book, the publisher typically receives $13 dollars. Authors are paid royalties of about fifteen percent of the cover price; this accounts for $3.90. Perhaps $1.80 goes to the costs of paper, printing, and binding, $1 to marketing, and $1.70 to distribution. The remaining $4.60 must pay for rent, editors, a sales force, and any write-offs of unearned author advances. Bookstores return about thirty-five per cent of the hardcovers they buy, and publishers write off the cost of producing those books. Profit margins are slim.

On the Topic of Despair

> "When finally I delivered my typescript to my publishers, they looked at it coldly. I had been a long time about it—it was twice as long as they had been led to expect ... they hoped the expenditure would be justified. I hoped so, too. And went home to a house empty, divested of the evidence of two years' work. The whole ... project was relegated to the back of my mind."

This is Elizabeth David, writing about her book *Italian Food*, the same Elizabeth David whom the *London Sunday Times* described as "among the greatest writer-cooks of our times." David's book has remained in print since it was first published in 1954.

M.F.K. Fisher, the Other Culinary Goddess

I was proud to serve as president of Les Dames d'Escoffier. Every year, we honored a star from our dining and drinking galaxy. During this time, I stumbled across the writings of M.F.K. Fisher, and I applauded her designation as America's so-called "epicure laureate." I unhesitatingly chose M.F.K. when it was my turn to choose the honoree for our annual dinner.

The New York Public Library's private dining room was the destination for the event. A committee formed to plan the evening. Tables were set with beautiful floral cloths, upon which her books were placed as the centerpieces.

I stepped into the library elevator and pressed the button for the third floor. At that instant, a seemingly homeless woman shuffled through the closing doors. "Crumbs!" I thought. What could I say? "Grrrumph! Madam! This is a private dinner. Buzz off"? No, I couldn't possibly say that.

But what? How could I explain the situation politely? It took only a moment to arrive at our destination. The host of the hospitality committee stepped forward to greet us. "Welcome, welcome, Ms. Fisher!" she gushed.

The French Chef Cooks and Writes

French Recipes for American Cooks was the first title. In 1953, Julia Child received an advance of $200 from her publisher, Houghton Mifflin. The manuscript was ultimately rejected in 1959. *Mastering the Art of French Cooking* was published in 1961. After several years of publishing success and generating considerable profit for its publisher, Julia was asked to pay the cost of adding photographs. She refused.

Mastering the Art of French Cooking sold more than one hundred thousand copies within one year of publication, and by 1969, sales had surpassed six hundred thousand copies. A decade later, it was in its fiftieth printing. It is a classic that will continue to delight generations of home and professional cooks (without photographs).

Julia Child was neither French, nor, strictly speaking, a chef. This title was chosen for her TV show because the words the *French Chef* fit nicely in *TV Guide*.

Single-Subject Cookbooks

Gin, rum, vodka, and whiskey are among the more than thirty single-subject cookbooks that explore the history and culture of drinks and foods. These illustrated books are published as part of Reaktion Books' Edible Series and are written by learned authors. They cover the gamut of our most popular foods and include such titles as *Ice Cream: A Global History* by Laura Weiss and *Cake: A Global History* by Nicola Humble. Also on the list are cheese, chocolate, bread, cake, and pie. To access the complete list, go to Edible-Series.Blogspot.com. Submit a proposal if you glimpse an opportunity for yourself.

My Word: Evolution of the Single-Subject Cookbook

I started writing small, single-subject cookbooks in 1969, so the idea has been around for simply ages. The concept was and still is immensely popular. My small company, Irena Chalmers Cookbooks, published The Great American Cooking School Cookbooks series and the Books by Cooks series way back in 1983. They are all out of print now. Most books have a shelf life somewhere between milk and yogurt, but you can buy them online now for just a penny or a nickel.

Maybe one or more of them could be an inspiration to you. Help yourself! Following is a partial list of books we published:

American Food and California Wine

Bountiful Bread: Basics to Brioches

Christmas Feasts from History

Cooking from a Country Kitchen

Cooking of the South

Dim Sum & Chinese One-Dish Meals

Dinner in Half an Hour

Fair Game: A Hunter's Cookbook

Fine, Fresh Food—Fast

Fresh Garden Vegetables

Ice Cream and Ices

Microwave Cooking: Meals in Minutes

Old Fashioned Desserts

Omelettes and Soufflés

Pasta! Cooking It, Loving It

Quiche and Pâté

Romantic and Classic Cakes

Soups and Salads

Successful Parties: Simple and Elegant

All of these were paperback cookbooks. Our small book, *Napkin Folding*, sold more than a million copies. Who folds napkins? Apparently many still do.

The Demise of the Hardcover Book

If we no longer yearn to own hardcover cookbooks, do we need literary agents to sell our proposals to publishers? The answer to this vexing question is still yes—unless you can figure out the complexities of learning how to do your own formatting and coding for an e-book. But be sure to check Amazon's Self-Publish with Us page, as well as their Kindle-direct publishing page at KDP.Amazon.com.

▸▸ FOOD FOR THOUGHT ◂◂

The number of independent bookstores has declined rapidly in recent years. According to *USA Today*, they account for only an estimated 6 percent of the total retail book market, whereas Amazon accounts for an estimated 22.6 percent, and chains like Barnes and Noble are struggling to hold on to 17.3 percent. Big box stores like Target and Wal-Mart carry primarily best-selling titles, along with a few cookbooks from authors with TV platforms.

FOOD JOB: *Cookbook Author*

It is easy to understand why sales of *365 Ways to Cook Chicken* would have a better shot at commercial success than *365 Ways to Use Leftover Okra* or why *Simply Sensational Salads* would be a bigger hit than

Winter Root Vegetables from Uncle Dmitri's Ukrainian Garden. The subject matter matters.

But how can you account for the million-copy sales of *The Sweet Potato Queens' Big-Ass Cookbook (and Financial Planner)* by Jill Conner Browne? The book is jam packed with dozens of heart-stopping, butt-enlarging recipes from the Queens' basic food groups: sweet, salty, fried, and au gratin.

How can you explain why folks rushed out to buy *The Mafia Cookbook*? Did they become misty-eyed when they heard the most famous line in the movie, *The Godfather*: "Leave the gun; take the cannoli."?

Things to Consider When Making a Cookbook Proposal

- What are your credentials?
- Do you have a platform? Are you a television food star or cooking-school teacher? Or do you have access to some other constituency that might buy a few thousand copies of your book? (For example, the Potato Council might give away a book entitled *Potato Salads: Fifty Favorite Recipes* to its best customers or to any food writer who writes a column on the topic of potatoes.)
- Do you have new, interesting, and reliable information to share?
- Do you have plenty of time to write your proposal?
- Who will buy your book? In other words, who cares? For example, millions of people have high cholesterol. Ought you to write a breakfast cookbook that includes eggs, butter, and other such forbidden ingredients?

▶▶ FOOD FOR THOUGHT ◀◀

- Numerous studies have revealed that eating two eggs a day has an almost undetectable effect on serum cholesterol for two-thirds of the population. The slightly worrisome aspect of this research is that you may not know if you belong to the other third.
- Writing and publishing a cookbook is just the beginning; the hard part is selling it.

THE COOKBOOK PROPOSAL

- State your idea clearly and concisely. You are doomed if you take too long to express your idea. If you can't describe it in one sentence, forget about it.
- Provide sales information about books on similar topics.
- Describe the specific market (this means likely readers) for your proposed book.
- Describe your qualifications, including only those that are relevant to this specific project.
- Write the introduction and a sample chapter.
- Compile the table of contents now. This is an essential step. It will provide you with a road map for your journey later.
- Include eight sample recipes with head notes. Ask a cooking-illiterate friend to test the recipes. This will insure that you have not forgotten any ingredients and that your directions are totally clear to a novice.
- Propose a working title. Among the best ever are: *The Joy of Cooking*, *Mastering the Art of French Cooking*, *How to Cook Everything*, and *The Cake Bible*.

BIBLICAL BOOK TITLES

I published Rose Levy Beranbaum's first cookbook, *Romantic and Classic Cakes*. Her manuscript subsequently evolved into *The Cake Bible*. At the time, she asked me what I thought of the title. I was horrified. I told her I'd definitely steer clear of bibles—any religious person would be shocked—shocked!—at the idea of linking the Bible with devil's food or frosted chocolate cakes. I pointed out that rich desserts are frequently called sinful and that religious people are (mostly) opposed to sin. Besides, no nonreligious person would even think of buying a book with the word *bible* in the title.

I was wrong (again)!

COOKBOOK "BIBLES" LISTED ON AMAZON

Meatball Cookbook Bible

Barbeque Bible

Best Ribs Ever: A Barbecue Bible Cookbook

New Bible Cookbook

Paula Deen's Southern Cooking Bible

Appetizer Bible

Sexy Forever Recipe Bible

Yogurt Bible

Louisiana Seafood Bible

Berry Bible

Pasta Bible

Gluten-Free, Wheat-Free and Dairy-Free

Recipes: More Than 100 Mouth-Watering

Recipes for the Whole Family (A Cook's Bible)

There are still more bibles, past and present, and undoubtedly there will be more published in the future.

BOOK IT!

by Judy Gelman, Book Club Cookbook *author and website creator*

In 2002, my friend Vicki Levy Krupp and I were having coffee and discussing our respective book clubs. Both groups had been pairing food with the reading selections and had been looking for ways to spice up the discussions with recipes connecting to the books we were reading. If *we* are interested in exploring thematic foods at our meetings, we reasoned, there must be plenty of other book clubs interested in doing the same. We noted the lack of any cookbook or guide for book clubs interested in integrating food into their book club discussions. Thus, the idea for our first book, *The Book Club Cookbook,* was born.

I've always been interested in how food is used to tell a story or to help set the mood, the time period, or the place. I still recall foods mentioned in my favorite children's books, and as an adult, I've savored foods mentioned in writing, from Jo's failed dinner in Louisa May Alcott's *Little Women* to Jhumpa Lahiri's tantalizing descriptions of Indian foods in her stories.

My professional background had been in public relations. Vicki and I, while both "foodies," had no formal training in cooking or recipe writing, and neither of us had ever written a book, let alone a cookbook. We labored over the book proposal and sample material and sent it out to several dozen literary agents, most of whom turned us down. But we landed with a good agent, who sold our book to a publisher. We got down to work in earnest.

Early in the process, we took a recipe-writing course and purchased what would become our bible, *The Recipe Writer's Handbook* by Barbara Gibbs Ostmann and Jane L. Baker.

Our early concept for the book was to survey book clubs across the country to find out what titles were "hot," and then feature our own ideas for book and food pairings after deciding which titles to feature. But when we began interviewing book club members across the country, we learned that many of these groups were already integrating food into their meetings in amazingly creative ways. We decided to include these ideas in the book, along with recipes from as many of the living authors whose work was to be featured in our book as possible. *The Book Club Cookbook,* which is now in its second edition, is a compilation of ideas from authors, book clubs, restaurants, and a few of our own. I fell in love with the research for this book, especially exploring the history and culture behind many of the recipes, such as negus (a mulled, spiced wine) in Charlotte Bronte's *Jane Eyre*, to the fruit dessert prepared by Lewis and Clark for the Corps of Discovery paired with Stephen Ambrose's *Undaunted Courage*, to the Southern Ambrosia and Lane Cake mentioned in Harper Lee's *To Kill a Mockingbird*.

Pairing food and literature for our next book on youth book clubs, *The Kids' Book Club Book*, allowed me to explore food in those childhood favorites such as *Half Magic* (Toledo hot fudge dope) and *The Phantom Tollbooth* ("Subtraction Stew" from the author!).

We also created a Web site for our book, BookClubCookBook.com, and it evolved over time. A few authors asked us if would be possible to connect with book clubs through our website, and the site has now become a very useful resource for book clubs—they can find recipes from their favorite authors tied to their books, food and book pairing ideas, and reading recommendations. We had a growing audience of readers and book club members who visit our site with some regularity, and it became a natural place for authors and publishers to promote books to a highly coveted audience. Given the popularity of author recipes in our first two books, our third book, *Table of Contents*, featured recipes from fifty popular contemporary authors—from Gregory Maguire's whimsically named Oh Sweet Ozcrust Glinda Tart paired with *Wicked* to Laura Lippman's Cheese Straws.

My interest in food as a story-telling device naturally extended to television, and after being addicted to *Mad Men* from day one, I found myself fascinated by the food and drink—and the real-life restaurants and bars—depicted in the show. Together with my husband, Peter Zheutlin, we wrote *The Unofficial Mad Men Cookbook: Inside the Kitchens, Bars, and Restaurants of Mad Men* in 2011. We both grew up in the 1960s close to Manhattan, so we enjoyed peeking back into the adult world we glimpsed as kids.

The research, especially for historic recipes, was one of my favorite aspects of writing *The Unofficial Mad Men Cookbook*. We knew from the beginning we wanted authentic 1960s recipes for the food and drinks featured in *Mad Men*. I pored over hundreds of cookbooks from the 1960s—from Betty Crocker to Julia Child to *The Stork Club Bar Book* (many at the Schlesinger library in Cambridge, Massachusetts, as well as my own collection). We also searched through period magazines and advertising and requested recipes from those restaurants, bars, and hotels depicted in the show that still exist. Another highlight of writing the book was working with these legendary establishments, such as Sardi's and Keens' Steakhouse, on recipes from the era. One reviewer said our book bordered on "culinary anthropology," which we took as a high compliment because our goal was to get the historical detail exactly right, just as *Mad Men* does. Historical context was critical. It was fascinating, for example, to learn why dishes such as Sole Amandine in particular and French cooking in general were suddenly so fashionable in the early 1960s. (Short answer: the combined influence of Julia Child and the Kennedys' passion for French food.) Or to discover that the sudden popularity of faux Polynesian cuisine, like that served as Trader Vic's and other so-called tiki restaurants, was related to the influence of Hawaii statehood on 1960s culture; Americans were suddenly eating rumaki and drinking mai tais, using Hula-Hoops, and watching movies such as *Blue Hawaii* starring Elvis Presley.

Being able to combine my passions for food, literature, and popular culture have become my life's work.

FOOD JOB: *Cookbook Translator*

You might think it would be easy to translate a cookbook from one language to another. It isn't. The flour in France is not the same as the flour in the United States or Canada. The fat content in the butter isn't the same. Translating metric units of measure into pounds, ounces, and standard box sizes is challenging. Every recipe has to be retested.

The cost of food photographs is enormous, whereas the cost of translating recipes is relatively small and might considerably extend the sales of an existing cookbook. If this challenge appeals to you, you might offer your services to a publisher.

Julia Child is perched on the uppermost rung of the best-seller lists. But neither she nor James Beard wrote original recipes. What they both did, superbly, was to write recipes in their own inimitable voices. James's are divine invitations to dine. Julia's two volumes of *Mastering the Art of French Cooking* survive and thrive because the recipes are masterpieces of accuracy and clarity. They have been published in a digital version but have not been translated into French. Maybe you would like to offer to translate them?

Opportunity Seized

Elizabeth Andoh is the director and instructor of her own cooking schools in Tokyo and Osaka. She grew up in the United States and attended the University of Michigan, where an adviser suggested that she apply for a postgraduate fellowship in Japan. If she didn't, nobody would, and the funding would dry up. This was the beginning of an extraordinarily successful career that came to encompass both teaching and writing. Andoh is now the author of several highly regarded books on Japanese cooking. She has written for many prestigious magazines and is admired as the foremost expert on the food and culture of Japan writing in English. She speaks the language fluently and flawlessly.

Recommended Books

Washoku: Recipes from the Japanese Home Kitchen by Elizabeth Andoh

Kibō (Brimming with Hope): Recipes and Stories from Japan's Tohoku by Elizabeth Andoh

• •

My Word: Opportunity Lost

I asked my students to write a restaurant review. Paul's was outstanding. Not only had he described the food at Café des Artistes with professional skill, he had also evoked the charming atmosphere of this lovely, romantic restaurant. He had included colorful reproductions of Howard Chandler Christy's murals of frolicking, semi-naked nymphs found at the establishment, along with a copy of the restaurant's menu and the wine list. I was dazzled and delighted.

Purely by chance that evening, I ran into George and Jenifer Lang, the Café's owners. I told them about the superb review I had just received from my clever student. George asked to see the material, and I told him that I would ask Paul's permission. Then, generous as always, he invited Paul to have lunch with him at the Café. Paul was thrilled—dancing 'round the classroom, showing off.

I brought Paul a copy of George's memoir, *Nobody Knows the Truffles I've Seen*, and I instructed him, firmly, to read every page. Paul peeked inside the cover and discovered that George was Hungarian. "My family is Hungarian," he remarked.

"Do you speak the language," I inquired.

"Yes, I speak five languages."

At the next class I was eager to learn about the lunch.

"Oh, I didn't go," said Paul.

"What!" I exclaimed, "Did you let George know you weren't coming?"

"No."

Instead, Paul had accepted his fiancée's father's offer of a job in the insurance business in Iowa. It came with a car and medical benefits. He hadn't known that medical care is free in Europe.

It turns out that George Lang had been looking for a smart culinary-school graduate to assist him while he restored Gundel, a famed, historic restaurant in Budapest.

Had Paul shown up for the lunch speaking Hungarian and with considerable culinary knowledge, George would likely have offered him a job as his personal assistant. Paul would have been able to rub shoulders with every one of the bright, shining stars of the restaurant world, all of whom were George's associates. Paul could have gotten along without a car. He could have taken the fast train to Paris, to London, to Madrid, to all of Europe, and beyond.

A few months later, Paul called to tell me that he had broken up with his fiancée. He wanted to know if the job with George was still available.

The answer was a resounding no. He had been afraid to take a risk and had missed the opportunity of a lifetime.

• •

FOOD JOB: *Chef Biographer*

Writing a memoir or an autobiography is like preparing yourself to go to confession. You have to examine your conscience, and that entails honesty. You can't write an effective memoir if you're worried about family and friends looking over your shoulder. Even if the truth hurts, if it is truthful then there's no other way to present it. At the very least, readers will recognize the courage in that and respect you for it.

—Frank McCourt

►► FOOD FOR THOUGHT ◄◄

Classes in memoir writing are offered at many community colleges and universities.

Victoria Riccardi Writes Her Own Story

Victoria Riccardi is the author of *Untangling my Chopsticks: A Culinary Sojourn in Kyoto.* It is a culinary and personal journey to discover and understand the heart of modern Kyoto and the beauty, culture, customs, and flavors of Japan today. In it, she looks back on the year she spent living in Kyoto, Japan, studying tea *kaiseki*. Here, especially for this book, she explains the essentials of writing a memoir:

> If you are thinking about writing a memoir ask yourself what do you want to share and what do you *need* to share with the world? What haunts you? What are you passionate about?
>
> *Untangling My Chopsticks* is the story I wanted to share about tea *kaiseki*—no one had written about it and I studied it—and knew what it was like to be a young American woman making her way in one of the most impenetrable cultures on earth.
>
> Why did I care? What haunted me?
>
> Tea *kaiseki* is dying out. I hoped to share the beauty and mystery of Japan with others, particularly with those who had lived through the Second World War.
>
> I needed a theme to create boundaries and maintain focus. Like any good nonfiction, I wanted my book to read something like a novel, with strong characters, good dialogue, a clear narrative arc, and a strong ending. The pacing had to keep the reader turning pages.
>
> My challenge was I couldn't change real life or alter truth but the writing had to be compelling. These are the questions I asked myself:
>
> FORM: Should I tell my story from the perspective of the reader discovering Japan just as I did or begin just landing in Kyoto and pull them deeper into the story over time—reveal the humanity of my experience—enable readers to see themselves

on the pages and identify with my experience by including vignettes and essays that jump around in time, but bring the reader to a deeper understanding of the topic?

TONE: indicates the writer's attitude toward what she is writing about. My approach was that Japan was mysterious, exotic, fascinating, and ultimately a gift. I wrote with a sense of wonderment.

TENSE: the inevitable past versus present dilemma! The present tense gives the sense of immediacy but can feel forced. Also it is difficult because it can create two different "NOWs"; the now of the story itself and the now from the perspective of the story being told.

I chose to write in the past tense. I recreated the dialogue through letters, diaries, pictures, slides, and my memory, which vividly recalled conversations, emotions, and moments because everything about Japan was so wildly different from my previous life.

The narrative arc reaches its climax when I try to decide whether to stay in Japan and gorge myself on the perfect situation that I have struggled so hard to attain or to leave the country still wanting more.

In the end, I leave, but I return thirteen years later to close the circle, to see how Kyoto has changed, and to put the entire experience into a living context.

My agent wanted more personal musings, thoughts, and comments. The editor wanted to cut that out and focus on cooking. I decided to offer a bit of both, in order to help the reader experience Japan in all its elements. I wasn't enthusiastic about including recipes. I thought that they would detract from the chapter endings, but the editor insisted, and ultimately, I think they added an additional flavor.

Recommended Books

Writing the Memoir: From Truth to Art by Judith Barrington

Inventing the Truth: The Art and Craft of Memoir edited by William Zinsser

The Sharper Your Knife, the Less You Cry by Kathleen Flinn

M. F. K. Fisher and Me: A Memoir of Food and Friendship by Jeannette Ferrary

Julia Child: A Life by Laura Shapiro

The Solace of Food: A Life of James Beard by Robert Clark

Masters of American Cookery: M. F. K. Fisher, James Beard, Craig Claiborne, Julia Child (At Table) by Betty Fussell

There are many more exemplary books in this category, all of which greatly contribute to the understanding of those who achieved top-tier success. Librarians are willing guides.

FOOD JOB: *Anthologist*

There is an interesting food job for researchers who are devoted detectives: the ferreting out of writings in defined areas. For example, anthologists locate, organize, and edit the material collected in books and series such as the Best Food Writing, Success Stories of Food Entrepreneurs, or the Greatest Lines from Food Advertisers. An anthologist might compile a collection on the origins of food phrases and idioms such as "the peanut gallery," "bring home the bacon," "egg on her face," "cream of the crop," or "cut the mustard."

FOOD JOB: *Travel Writer*

My Word

The typical Frenchman thinks that the world is made up of the French—and of those less fortunate. Indeed, it is impossible to think of food without putting France into a separate, exalted place. Watch a group of French carpenters or plumbers sharing lunch on the job—a meal made up of bread, cheese, perhaps a little sausage, and a measure of wine. Eavesdrop on a group of housewives waiting their turn in the butcher's shop, or three or four businessmen assembled in a fine restaurant. They will be sharing memories of their Breton grandmother's matelote of eel with wine, cream, eggs, and shallots, even prunes. "Did you ever eat a matelote with prunes?" one will ask, and another will launch into a tale of cassoulet from Toulouse—full of beans and sausage, duck, pork, and lamb—which took six hours to cook and three more to eat. Another will recall, his tongue passing over his lips, a certain earthenware pot always filled with a Burgundian beef stew—a stew perfected by time and hallowed by generations, a noble stew, with lardons of salt pork, dark woodland mushrooms, tiny white onions, a crust of bread to soak up the gravy, and a liter or two of wine, all served on Sundays that seemed never to end....

ADVICE FROM A TRAVEL WRITER

By Sharon Hudgins, Award-winning food and travel writer

Everyone, from novice journalists to experienced cookbook authors, still confronts the same set of challenges when writing about the cuisine of another country, region, or ethnic group. During more than twenty years of working in this field, I've developed a set of guidelines for planning projects, doing background and on-site research (the fun part—eating!), and for writing accurate accounts of the foods of people living in other parts of the world.

One rule is fundamental: You *must* go to the country that you're writing about. That might seem an obvious statement, but I've known cookbook authors and magazine journalists in the United States who intended to write about another country's cuisine without ever actually traveling there themselves. They claimed they could do all the necessary research in the United States, eat at selected foreign restaurants in America, and then write authoritatively about the foods of the foreign countries they were assigned to cover—even though they'd never set foot in even one of the countries.

I strongly disagree with that approach. There is no substitute for eating another country's food on its home soil. Turn the tables and think about it. If you've ever eaten Tex-Mex food in India, Russian food in Turkey, or Thai food in Finland, you'll understand my argument. It's just not the same. Yes, of course, there are many fine restaurants that reproduce the dishes of one country in another, but the cuisine of any country is rooted in the geography, climate, agriculture, animal husbandry, cooking methods, and customs of that particular place. You just can't experience it in the same way anywhere else.

So buy a plane or boat ticket, get a rail or bus pass, rent a car or bicycle—and go there. You might find pleasures such as those Rosemary Barron writes about in the introduction to her book *Flavors of Greece*:

> Greek food is inspired by the heady perfumed fragrances that float on the Greek air; those aromatic scents are echoed in many of their dishes ... On shopping trips to the market, shapes, textures, and colors assault the senses, excite and entice—glossy multicolored vegetables and lush juicy fruits; plump nuts and seeds; boxes of dried fruits; strange-shaped sausages and meats from every part of an animal; sea-fresh fish you have never seen before; barrels of salted fish and taramá; hard and soft cheeses, crumbly white or creamy golden, some wrapped in animal skins; and more kinds of olives and beans than you ever imagined. Even the water in Greece seems special; Greeks say that some dishes, particularly those based on vegetables, cannot be made properly outside Greece because the water is not the same.
>
> *Reproduced by kind permission from* Flavours of Greece *by Rosemary Barron, published by Grub Street, London, England*

• •

My Word: Dining Abroad

Malaysia, it's a land of steamed dumplings and tropical fruits, of chili, curry, Chinese congee, and croissants, of street vendors and open markets selling locally grown greens and produce from around the world. The supermarket in Kuala Lumpur is as well stocked as its counterpart in Washington, DC; New York; or San Francisco, but drop into a restaurant in the crowded Indian section of town, and you'll find that there are no plates on the table. The food is served on banana leaves, and we all eat with our hands. The noise skipping and crashing against the tin ceiling makes conversation impossible. Smiles, gestures, and hearty appetites are the order of the day. Ask for tea, and you'll get a performance. A contortionist waiter holds a steaming pot in his right hand and raises it high above his head. He twists his body ever so slightly as he pours the tea over his shoulder and behind his back into a cup held in his left hand. He puts it in front of you with the happy expression of—

Little Jack Horner
Who Sat in a corner,
Eating his Christmas pie.
He put in his thumb,
And he pulled out a plum
And said, "What a good boy am I!"

(16th Century nursery rhyme attributed to the Bishop of Glastonbury)

• •

►► FOOD FOR THOUGHT ◄◄

In a letter to a playmate in Ohio, an expatriate child mourned the food inadequacies of a faraway country: "There's no chocolate syrup, peanut butter, SpaghettiOs, Hawaiian punch, Good Humor bars, hot dogs, potato chips, grape juice, bubble gum, Fluffernutter, Pop-Tarts, fish fingers, tuna melts, bologna sandwiches, popcorn, Slurpees, M&M's—there's nothing to eat in France."

All Wrapped Up

Almost every culture does the same thing, but each does it differently. They all enclose portions of food in edible wrappings in order to make the contents go further, but the choice of wrap makes each variation distinctive. Some people eat burgers between the two halves of a bun or pastrami between two slices of rye. Others wrap their food in lettuce leaves, cabbage leaves, grape leaves, banana leaves, palm fronds, or corn husks. Morsels of food are enclosed in plain pastry, puff pastry, wet noodles, or various papers—rice paper, parchment paper, even newspaper.

A bewildering variety of meats, fish, cheese, vegetables, nuts, and fruits turn up inside blintzes and buns, burritos, cannelloni, chimichangas, crêpes, dumplings, egg rolls, empanadas, fajitas, knishes, kreplach, quesadillas, ravioli, spring rolls, strudels, tortellini, turnovers, and won tons. And an entire fortune can be contained inside a single cookie.

FOOD JOB: *Food-Politics Writer*

The International Association of Culinary Professionals (IACP) has created a new food-book award category concerned with the impact of food choices on personal and planetary health. It encompasses issues related to farming and fishing, buying and selling, abundance and scarcity, the joy of plenty and the fear of hunger and deprivation. It includes books related to science and technology, food processing, marketing and publicity, packaging and distribution, ethical and cultural issues related to food, and the influence of law and politics on our daily diets. For more information, contact the IACP at IACP.com/contact.

FOOD JOB: *Ghostwriter*

Being a ghostwriter is an honorable profession. Some chefs can't spell. They may tend to produce recipes for the home cook that require more detailed information than they are willing or able to communicate. They may need help from skilled writers and knowledgeable cooking professionals willing to toil in anonymity. If you like this idea, send a cover letter and your résumé to the literary agents and publishers revealed in the acknowledgement sections and title pages of cookbooks. Stress your credentials as a super-accurate recipe tester able to speak in the voice of your employer. Include samples of three or four different writing styles.

Your material must show an understanding of the home cook, who may or may not understand that separating five eggs doesn't mean putting two on the counter and three on the table; that "bake blind" isn't meant literally; or that "stand under cold running water" refers to the ingredient, not the cook.

FOOD JOB: *Science Writer*

A 1930 study at the University of Missouri proved that meat cooked at a constant temperature loses less moisture than meat given an initial searing to "seal" in the juices. Seared steak is less juicy, not more so. Harold McGee, author of *On Food and Cooking*, confirms this finding. But he also maintains that seared steak tastes better.

Searching for the Truth

Journalists, reporters, and television stars generally influence public opinion on food and eating behavior more effectively than do professionals in the field. Surveys reveal that most Americans rely on news stories to decide which foods to eat. We receive more information about nutrition from the media than we do from doctors or dietitians. In general, science writers may tackle such subjects as the value of teaching chimpanzees how to play tic-tac-toe or brain research that has led to the development of a computer system enabling a quadriplegic person to provide himself with a cup of coffee. Science writers specializing in food may consider other topics for exploration, such as

- food irradiation;
- the use of hormones in beef;
- the effects of additives and preservatives in processed foods;
- surveys of agricultural and marine biotechnology;
- fish farming or transgenic salmon;
- food labeling;
- the comparative nutritional value of organically versus conventionally grown produce;
- historical food facts and myths, whether related to potatoes, pasta, tomatoes, or the Salem witches (who, it is believed, may have evidenced a sort of madness as a result of eating contaminated rye flour);
- mad-cow disease;
- salt, and reasons not to restrict it in a normal diet;
- and omega-3 fatty acids and their effectiveness.

Definition of Junk Science

The JunkScience website explains: "A pseudoscience is an established body of knowledge which masquerades as science in an attempt to claim a legitimacy which it would not otherwise be able to achieve on its own terms; it is often known as fringe or alternative science. The most important of its defects is usually the lack of carefully controlled and thoughtfully interpreted experiments which provide the foundation of the natural sciences and which contribute to their advancement. In legitimate science misinterpretations are self-correcting if not by the original researchers themselves, then through the critical scrutiny of the greater scientific community."

FOOD JOB: *Director of Digital Publishing*

Publishers now employ specialists in digital publishing and e-book development. This high-tech work requires the ability to convert book content into a diversity of platforms, including Kindle, Nook, and other e-readers, as well as different manufacturers' tablets and smartphones. To get started, compile a list of cookbook publishers (as gleaned from a bookstore) and apply for an existing or proposed job as director of digital publishing. E-books are going even more high-tech. Hidden eyes know whether the reader of an e-book has finished the book, or whether or not he stopped reading at a long or complicated description. These are just two among several commonly tracked reading behaviors. This kind of information is already influencing the kinds of books that publishers will accept.

FOOD JOB: *Catalog Compiler*

Writing catalog copy requires the ability to strip a product to its sexy, bare bones. Think of the available space for the copy as though it were luxury real estate. You will succeed if you can use a skeletal listing to create a selling description, as in the following examples from *Newsweek*. The name of the company offering each product precedes its description; its website follows:

> MAMA LIL'S, SEATTLE. Howard Lev's Hungarian goathorn peppers, preserved in perfectly spiced olive oil, come "kick-butt" hot and sweet. mamalils.com
>
> FRA' MANI HANDCRAFTED SALUMI, OAKLAND, CALIF. Star chef Paul Bertolli has spent a decade perfecting his sublime cured meat. Smoked and sweet sausage, fennel salami, bresola, mortadella, and more. framani.com

> Kasia's Deli Chicago. These dumplings fit our romantic imagination, turned out by a Polish grandmother in her deli kitchen. Kasia Bober's pierogi are award-winning and available by mail. kasiasdeli.com

Winning writers keep it short. The Gettysburg Address contains 272 words. *The Cat in the Hat* contains sixteen unique words. A bag of potato chips contains some chips and 401 words.

FOOD JOB: *Literary Food Expert*

Life as a literary food expert is enriching in many ways. Following is an extract from Linda Wolfe's memorable book *The Literary Gourmet: Menus from Masterpieces*:

> Food, with its kaleidoscope of odors and textures, colors and flavors, gives writers the prime equipment for creating the semblance of reality that is the first requirement of their job.
>
> The great literary food writers have concocted many a pioneer pudding and peasant soup and aristocratic herb sauce in order to make their heroes' lives sound actual and real. But some of their depictions of meals and table talk and manners have been so fine that much of what we know best of ancient life, or even of the more recent life of the French nobility, of English gentry, or American homesteaders, we know through the carefully detailed dinner of fiction writers and poets.
>
> Food has provided them with turning points in their plots: lovely ladies have been headed down the primrose path to sin with a sirloin steak, as Theodore Dreiser does it in *Sister Carrie,* or with a platter of quail in plumage, as Gustave Flaubert does it in *Madame Bovary*; shrewish heroines have been subdued with the offer of teacakes or mustard sauce on beef; sated lovers have

renewed their passion over deviled chicken; and fictional families in trouble have been held together with a pan of freshly-baked biscuits or a well-roasted goose.

From Cervantes' character, Sancho Panza, who pragmatically is willing to forsake the promise of nobility for a plate of simple stew, to Tolstoy's Levin, who ascetically longs for Russian cabbage soup though he is served with the finest French luxuries, food is the vehicle that transports and reveals the innermost workings of their characters. Even the ancient biblical story of Jacob and Esau first shows Esau's fatal flaw of rashness through the very nature of food that tempts that hasty man to betray himself: not a milk-fed kid or some fine honey cakes, but pottage, mere lentil pottage.

The Literary Gourmet: Menus from Masterpieces *is available in E-Book and Print-on-Demand from Argo Navis Author Services.*

FOOD JOB: *Literary Agent*

The following words are shared by Lisa Ekus. The Lisa Ekus Group's website is LisaEkus.com:

> Since 2000, we have been offering personalized, detail-oriented services to veteran authors and newcomers alike. The agency represents more than 120 authors—many of whom have published multiple books—and numerous publishers, both national and international.
>
> We specialize in cookbooks and food-related titles, but have represented a number of health and women's nonfiction topics as well. . . .
>
> Here are a few of the key responsibilities we assume as an agent:

- Analyze industry trends, in order to approach the most appropriate publishers
- Consult on the "readiness" of each proposal, providing suggestions for revision based on feedback from editors
- Create a plan and timeline for proposal submission
- Negotiate publishing contracts to reflect the best possible terms and conditions, with respect to rights, royalties, options, copyrights, style, format, promotion, publicity and advertising
- Sell subsidiary rights as applicable
- Provide constructive advice when analyzing prospective works, proposals, and manuscripts
- Match clients with editors who are looking for specific projects
- Respond promptly and reliably through the entire publishing process
- Believe in each and every client!

If this job appeals to you, compile a list of literary agents specializing in food books. These are often thanked in book's acknowledgments section. Join professional organizations, including the International Association of Culinary Professionals, and attend food-writing conferences where agents and authors gather.

LITERARY AGENTS CONNECT THE DOTS: FROM BOOK IDEA TO BOOK STORE, AND BEYOND

Lisa Ekus answers the questions: What is a literary agent? Do I need one if I want to write a cookbook?

"I love reading cookbooks. How can I make a food job out of that?"

"I've lost count of how many times I've been asked these questions. Like a memorable dish made of the best ingredients, a great agent is one part editor and coach, one part advocate, one part broker, and one part marketer and trend spotter. She is a visionary savant, spiced with wit and sage advice. The best agent buys the champagne when the book idea is sold to a publisher.

The Responsibilities of the Literary Agent

A literary agent represents an author's book or book idea to publishers and ensures that any agreement made with a publisher is fair and reasonable. It is as important to find the right literary agent—one who will represent your work passionately—as it is to find the right publisher.

It is only a small group of literary agents that devotes its energies primarily to cookbooks and culinary subjects. Most of them work on the East or West Coasts, where the large publishing houses are located. They can be hard to find outside of culinary organizations like the International Association of Culinary Professionals (IACP). Many authors thank their agents in the acknowledgment sections of their books, so with just a little detective work, you can easily track them down.

Having [literary] representation tells an editor that your book project has been vetted by a professional who thinks highly enough of you or your topic to take it on."

WHERE THE LITERARY AGENTS ARE

It is almost as difficult to find an agent as it is to find a publisher these days. An agent won't waste her or his time trying to sell a proposal unless she or he thinks it will find a home. So before you write a proposal, it is important to know what you're getting yourself into. Writing a cookbook, no matter how great the idea, is not easy. As Susan R. Friedland, a veteran executive editor and the director of cooking publishing at HarperCollins, recently pointed out in a remarkably insightful *Food Arts* article, "Nowadays, even famous chefs find it as challenging to get a book published as to score a multi-star review in a major metropolitan daily." Friedland adds, "A wise chef, who is lucky enough to have stirred the interest of a publisher or has the urge to write a cookbook, should hire an agent, preferably one who represents other cookbook authors and knows the terrain. It's advisable to ask around to get recommendations from colleagues and then interview several potential agents. It's important to find a compatible agent, as you will be spending a fair amount of time together (if not in person, by e-mail and telephone) and will want to partner with someone with whom you can work well."

Other than access to publishers—which is critically important—the agent negotiates the author's contract. The focus is on: (1) the amount of money given to the author as an advance, (2) manuscript delivery dates, and (3) royalty scales. If these terms sound unfamiliar, you need an agent.

Usually, an agent asks the author to sign a contract stipulating that the agency will receive a commission for her services, in the form of a percentage of the funds advanced to the author and of all future book royalties. This is generally in the 15 percent range.

The author receives payment in stages. The first payment is received when the contract is signed, and following payments are distributed throughout, at different points in the process. Each installment is contingent on the author meeting the terms of the contract. Usually, there are no more than three payments. This typical schedule is a kind of insurance for the publisher, who wants to make sure that the author won't complain too loudly or actually refuse to make any of the editor's suggested changes.

The agent also negotiates the answers to vexing questions, such as who pays for things such as photography. Sometimes, a publisher will advance the cost of photography, to be deducted from the author's future earnings. Agents often find and negotiate with the author's collaborators, or—as is often the case with cookbook authors who are also restaurant chefs and are stuck in their kitchens—with the occasional ghostwriter. Occasionally, the agent is able to persuade the publisher to pay for the book's index, though frequently this cost is billed to the author.

Becoming a Literary Agent

Sadly, one is not born a literary agent. Rather, one becomes a literary agent over time and with experience. Just ask legendary literary agent Jane Dystel, founder and president of Dystel & Goderich Literary Management. To get started in this field, apply for a position with an agency that is representing the kind of books that appeal to you. While you are sure to learn all the steps involved in selling a book to the right publisher, it is most critical that you love to read. All literary agents start by reading through the "slush" pile of book proposals that come in to agencies, seeking that rare gem that will lead to a great book.

FOOD JOB: *Playwright*

Any culinarian who yearns to become a playwright or movie maker will be inspired by the success of such hit movies as *Ratatouille*, *Babette's Feast*, *Julie and Julia*, and of plays including *Fully Committed*, *Sideways*, and *My Kitchen Wars*. We likewise seem to be eternally hungry for new food- or restaurant-themed television series.

Acting the Part

The setting of the off- and then on-Broadway play *Fully Committed* is a Manhattan-based "global fusion" restaurant. In one scene, the reservations clerk juggles many calls while reading menu items over the phone to a Midwesterner thinking about making a reservation for dinner. The clerk recites from the menu, "Jicama-smoked Scottish wood squab poached in ginger broth and wrapped in wilted spinach ... and herb-crusted grouper speckled with fresh hyssop oil on a bed of wild ramps ... and Argentinean cedar-roasted milk-fed organic chicken ..." Clearly, the unheard response from the caller is "Huh?"

My Kitchen Wars is reviewed as "A one-woman play written by Betty Fussell. She describes her world as a war story. The warrior is a woman, the battleground is the kitchen, and the weapons are the *batterie de cuisine* with which the author evokes her era's domestic battles. As much about hunger—emotional, sexual, intellectual—as it is about food, this fierce and funny memoir takes no prisoners. The action takes place in a kitchen as the protagonist prepares a three-course dinner."

Nora Ephron wrote about food too. She wrote about the Pillsbury Bake-Off and was nominated for an Academy Award for writing the script for *When Harry Met Sally*, with its memorable scene in Katz's Delicatessen: "I'll have what she's having." She also wrote the script for and directed *Julie and Julia*. She loved food, hated egg-white omelets, and had memorable feelings about mashed potatoes.

• •

My Word: The New "Moo-Vee"

I've been thinking about the movie *Ratatouille* and how kind it was for Pixar to make a film just for us—the food fanatics. And the more I think about it, the more I long to make a sequel for the less fortunate, the fast-food folk who may be unfamiliar with the fact that *Ratatouille* was about more than rats—it was about food.

Rats! What's so great about rats other than *King Rat* (the movie about a prison camp in Japan) and the Rat Pack—Frank Sinatra, "Dino" Martin, and Sammy Davis Jr.? After all, as the comedian and actress Lily Tomlin famously observed, "The trouble with the rat race is that even if you win, you're still a rat." No one I know likes rats. (We don't eat rats—or mice, owls, or pussy cats either, for that matter.) So there'll be no rats in my new movie; nor mice, not even one named Mickey or Stuart (as in Stuart Little). For that matter, nor will there be any Chicken Little, Doolittle, or any animal from the Orwellian animal farm, nor any from Edward Albee's *Zoo Story*, nor any likeness to the little foxes or to Red Riding Hood's wolf in sheep's clothing, nor to any other of the badly behaved animals fabled by Aesop, Grimm, and Rowling.

But as I cast about, looking for a lovable animal to feature in my movie, I fell into a deep despond. Alfred Hitchcock has filmed all the birds and bees. Dinosaurs have been done to Jurassic death. We already know about lovable pigs like Miss Piggy, the Three Little Pigs, and Babe. We know about the wolves who raised Romulus and Remus, the apes who raised Tarzan, and the monkeys who kidnapped Mowgli. Penguins? Overdone. Talking goldfish? Cats in hats? Oh dear! What's left? Shaggy dogs? One hundred and one dalmatians? Done. Lassie has come home already, as has the adorable Toto. How about horses: Trigger? Flicka? Black Beauty? The Black Stallion? Racehorses like Seabiscuit, who come from behind to end up in front? All done. We've also read about all the biblical animals led by Noah onto the begetting love boat known as the Arc. Donkeys? There was an animated donkey in *Shrek*. Pinocchio was turned into a donkey and sold to a circus, where many animals were taught how to behave unnaturally.

Democrats are represented as donkeys. Republicans are portrayed as elephants (but not like Dumbo or Babar).

I considered a frog for a leading role in my movie. A frog like Kermit, perhaps, or the kind of frog that turns into a handsome prince?—though never into a pretty princess. And that led me to think about Charles, Prince of Wales, and Moby Dick, another sort of whale and you'll surely remember Willy, Free Willy (the Whale?). And Flipper? And toads? Kenneth Graham wrote of Badger Mole and Toad of Toad Hall in the *Wind in the Willows*. And then I considered the idea of rabbits like those created memorably in pastels by Beatrix Potter, and Pooh the Bear, who loved honey, and then I gave up because I realized at last I couldn't do any better than Edward Lear, who wrote about Owls and Pussycats:

The Owl and the Pussycat went to sea
In a beautiful pea-green boat,
They took some honey, and plenty of money
Wrapped in a five pound note.
... and were married next day
By the Turkey who lives on the hill.
They dined on mince and slices of quince,
Which they ate with a runcible spoon;
And hand in hand, on the edge of the sand,
They danced by the light of the moon.

Edward Lear wrote this charming verse in 1871, and it immediately made me think about the cow that jumped over the moon possibly wearing a milk mustache.

• •

►► FOOD FOR THOUGHT ◄◄

The closest I ever came to writing a movie was to name my publishing company the Runcible Spoon. I didn't know then and don't know now what a runcible spoon is. (Perhaps, that's why my company went bust.)

FOOD JOB: *Cookbook Reviewer*

Becoming a cookbook reviewer is a great occupation for a cookbook lover, particularly when you have gained experience by reading actively. By saying "actively," as opposed to "passively," I mean that you have read many books and have acquired enough knowledge to make informed comparisons with similar publications in specific areas. For example, you might be able to compare books on the cooking of Tuscany or Ireland or cookbooks for the blind and for other people with disabilities or books on quick meals, using only five ingredients, prepared in fifteen minutes, and costing five dollars.

Truth to Tell

If an author declares that a recipe can be prepared in fifteen minutes, the critic must determine whether this feat is possible for a mom juggling small children, a buzzing iPhone, and a guest sipping a glass of wine in the kitchen, or whether it is possible only for an experienced cook.

A food-book reviewer is the first cousin of the restaurant reviewer. Both professions require the critic to have good taste, an in-depth understanding of food, knowledge of the industry, and the ability to write well and quickly.

The Best-of-the-Best Book Reviewers

If you are looking for a model of brilliant cookbook and food-book reviewing, I urge you to check out the website for the Manhattan-based Kitchen Arts & Letters bookstore, at KitchenArtsAndLetters.com. Check the current newsletter. You won't find a better example of dazzling erudition.

Here's a customer review of Kitchen Arts & Letters written by one of its many admirers, "Kelly K.": "This place is cookbook heaven! The selection is outstanding, the staff so darn knowledgeable, and the service always courteous and friendly. Whether you are a first time cook or an industry legend, this place caters to all. Believe me, I was living in London the last four years, and while London has its own well respected cookbook shop, the range at Kitchen Arts & Letters is far more extensive. I love both shops, but if I had to choose, KA&L would win!"

A Matter of Judgment

Every book critic brings a personal perspective to the task. The celebrity of the author may sway one judge's opinion, while another reviewer may have a bias *against* a popular TV star or celebrity.

The Reviewing Process

A conscientious cookbook reviewer reads the author's introduction. It provides an insight into the author's objective. Further exploration will determine if a goal has been scored, as it were.

When writing a review, only the opening lines surpass the concluding paragraph in importance. Don't let your report stop abruptly, as though you had somewhere to go. Your final words let your reader know your opinion decisively.

It's not necessarily required that you damn a book with faint praise. If you want to damn it, damn it! You can't be sued. The First Amendment protects your right to speak your opinion freely. However, you can be at legal risk if you have knowingly slandered the author.

A cookbook writer may have spent years writing a book, so it is essential that it receive careful consideration—not a desultory flipping through of pages, a mere glance at the photographs, and the tossing off of a vapid opinion. A conscientious cookbook reviewer even scrutinizes the index to ensure that it is composed logically before rendering a final opinion.

Even when a book review is afforded a mere twenty words, it can still have a significant impact on a reader's attention. Here is a great example from *Newsweek* magazine: "In his book, *Simple Pleasures*, Alfred Portale pares his complex cuisine to the basics. Who knew making roast cod with escargot butter could be this easy?"

How to Get Started

The fastest way to get started as a cookbook reviewer is to blog extensively on the topic of cookbooks. You can request review copies from publishers or publicists. You can find publishers' addresses online. Read publishers' catalogs for forthcoming releases and study announcements in the trade publication *Publishers Weekly*, or, as a last resort, buy already published books. If you post intelligent reviews on Amazon, you may be placed on their mailing lists.

▸▸ FOOD FOR THOUGHT ◂◂

The sales potential of a book shouldn't have any part in the decision as to whether or not it should receive a glowing review.

Many otherwise sensible folk have the quaint idea that they could easily write a cookbook if only they had the time. Sadly, having a collection of recipes is not sufficient for the creation of a marketable cookbook; there is a craft to writing as well as an art. I suggest that if you really want a cookbook, it is far easier and faster to go out and buy one. Cheaper, too.

Chefs have become among the most prolific of cookbook writers. It seems that once they get started, they find it more or less impossible to purge the urge to write not one, but many cookbooks. "Why?" we may ask. After all, we the people go to restaurants to eat food we can't or don't want to cook at home. Some serious chefs know this to be true. They don't write cookbooks for consumers, they write for other chefs—and to burnish their brands.

The most elite of the elite chefs compose almost incomprehensible fantasies to delight fellow professionals. Among the demigods of molecular gastronomy are chefs Ferran Adria, Grant Achatz, and Heston Blumenthal, who is also the author of *In Search of Perfection*.

Note: the words *molecular* and *gastronomy* are despised by those who practice these alchemic arts. This is entirely understandable. These chefs are teaching we mere mortals to achieve a deeper understanding of the very meaning of food, as interpreted through all our senses, not only sight and smell, but touch and sound, too. They lead us to view Food as Art, Reason, Technology, and Science. (Experts in this field are not, however, known as FARTS.) Strictly regimented traditional cooking has transcended itself and become what is derisively known as molecular gastronomy. The preferable term is "modernist."

FOOD JOB: *Magazine Columnist*

Begin your journey as a food writer by buying an armload of magazines—as many as you can afford. Or go to a library where you can find many back issues of food magazines in the archives. Study the open letter from the editor; examine every page, every quadrant of every page, and every advertisement on every page. Take notes. Ask yourself important questions, such as: Who are the readers of this publication? What are their education and income levels? Why are advertisers paying to have a presence in this publication?

By the end of your research, you will have a pretty good idea about the DNA of each publication, and you'll be in a position to see whether your ideas will be a good fit with them. This is a kind of dating game in which you decide whether or not to make a proposal for an article or (better yet) make a pitch for a permanent spot on the writing staff.

Finding a Topic

Could you offer to write a brief paragraph about the food-related history of the city in which you live? For example, the tale is told of Mlle. Evelyne Claudine de Saint-Évremond, daughter of a distinguished French courtier. She was an immigrant who established a salon (vulgarly known as a bordello), in one of New York City's most exclusive residential districts. In no time at all, her name was abbreviated to "Eve." The ladies in her employ soon became known as "Eve's Apples." The establishment where they resided was cryptically referred to as the Big Apple. Visitations were therapeutic, for, as everyone knows, "An apple a day . . ."

Consumer Magazines: Who Is Reading What?

The Audit Bureau of Circulations reports on newsstand sales of consumer magazines. The latest figures are mostly depressing: single-copy purchases have tumbled by as much as 50 percent in the last three years. That's the bad news, but there is some good news: Subscriptions to periodicals are remaining fairly stable, and online publications are finding new readers. E-book readership is escalating rapidly. It is estimated that sales will reach $10 billion by 2016. Sales on Amazon now far exceed those in bookstores.

What Can I Earn If I Work in the Food Media?

- An editorial assistant working at a food magazine may earn $25,000–$30,000.
- An associate food editor earns about $50,000.
- A food editor whose name is listed on the masthead earns close to $70,000.
- The executive editor takes home between $90,000 and $125,000.
- Customarily, these positions are filled by graduates of professional culinary schools. A degree in journalism is a good credential too, as is experience working in the hospitality industry.

Pitching a Story

To pitch a story, you will need to write what is known as a query letter, not more than three or four paragraphs. In it, state your idea clearly, list your qualifications, and anticipate any questions. Keep the control in your own hands. If you have sent a query letter and have followed up with three telephone calls asking to speak to the food editor only to be told that the person you are trying to reach is unavailable, then you have your answer. It is “No thanks.”

Sample Query Letter

Dear Ms. Stalwart:

I have been reading your magazine for several years and have noticed that you are interested in politics. Last January, I was appointed to the position of White House sous-chef. Are you interested in an article about the food that will be served to the 1,000 guests of the forthcoming wedding? I have obtained written permission to publish this information from the State Department.

I am a freelance writer and have had my work published in several magazines. I am also the author of *White House Weddings*, published by Hope Springs Eternal Books last year. It currently has a five-star ranking on Amazon and has been reprinted three times.

I will call you on Wednesday afternoon at 3 p.m., or you can reach me at isee@mmmgood.net.

Yours Sincerely,

Max A. Million

Yes, No, Maybe ... Not

Some editors will accept a query by e-mail, while others prefer a hard copy. If you decide to go with a hard copy, use good stationery. Spell the name of the editor correctly, and if you are in doubt as to whether Pat is a man or a woman, just call the publication and ask. (I once received a letter addressed to Ilona Chompers. I saved it but didn't answer it.)

Note: If a publication requests that you do not send samples of your work—do not send samples of your work.

Legal Issues

As Margaret Happel Perry tells us, "You [the writer] are responsible for getting permission from the chef or any other person, to feature them in your article and to use their photograph. You are also responsible for obtaining *written* permission to use or adapt their recipes. You are responsible to let the magazine know if there are any limiting conditions attached to the article. For example: do the recipes have to be resubmitted to the chef (or other featured author), if they have been changed during the testing process?"

Organizing an Article

Write a working title. You can change it later when you experience a more brilliant flash of inspiration. Having even a temporary title will keep you on track.

For your article, gather information from every possible source. Going out and actually talking to experts in the field is the pathway to the best research.

Organize your work. Concentrate on the opening and closing sentences. Then write the body of the article as though tracing a cardiogram; develop a rhythmic progression of peaks and reflecting pools.

Rewrite the opening.

Rewrite the conclusion.

Rewrite the body.

Several times.

Review your work, and correct all egregious errors. Improve every poor choice of words and remove any redundant references. Make sure that all subjects agree with their verbs and vise versa. Don't muddle past, present, and future tenses. Read your manuscript aloud. Your ear will hear errors that your eye has missed.

And there you (almost) have it.

▸▸ FOOD FOR THOUGHT ◂◂

AARP: The Magazine's circulation is twenty-four million. The emphasis is on older people. *People* magazine's circulation is four million. It is devoted solely to people. *Every Day with Rachael Ray* magazine has a circulation of 1.7 million. Its content is related to people and food. There are 1.57 million readers of *Bon Appétit*, and *Food Network* magazine has a circulation of 1.37 million.

My conclusion is that, if you are looking for a wide circulation, write about people and food, but don't limit your search to food magazines. Explore corporate newsletters and real estate publications and local magazines of all kinds.

The editor of one consumer magazine compared the frenzied rush immediately prior to "closing" each issue to working in a whorehouse. She said, "There's a lot of hanging around, punctuated by short, sharp bursts of intense activity."

FOOD JOB: *Newspaper Food Writer*

Trade councils such as the Blueberry Council, the Cranberry Marketing Committee, and the Beef Council provide recipes for newspapers. They are free. Photographs are also given. Free. It can be very difficult for a freelance food writer to make a living when competing against free material.

The best hope for a food writer who yearns to write for a newspaper is as a journalist. Instead of writing recipes that include honey as an ingredient, report on the huge increase in the number of beekeepers. Focus on investigative journalism, politics, or celebrities. Food stories appear in every section of the paper.

Some food writers make a specialty of "the best"—the best takeout food, the best sandwiches, the best coffee, and the best of the best. Others become experts in health issues or food trends or write commentaries on the food scene.

Be sure to double-check any word-count requirements in your contract before submitting your article. If you are over or under, the editor may reject your work rather than try to shorten or lengthen your submission.

How to Get Started

One way to get started is to pitch ideas for a newspaper's blog, Twitter feed, or other online presence. Establishing a relationship with the permanent staff will put you in a good position for being awarded a byline of your own. Specialize in business stories, interpreting food-science news, people profiles, or in reporting on local entrepreneurs. Become a specialist rather than a generalist. Check grammar and spelling carefully, and make triply sure that your facts are checked, your quotes are accurate, and that all permissions are obtained (in writing) when necessary.

If you are asked for a previously published clip of your work, make sure that you have at least ten—twenty even—not just a single article. Having more work to show will prove that you are a serious writer willing to work hard at your craft. Having a blog with many dozens of postings is a very easy way for an editor to review your writings. It is a great advantage to be able to take your own terrific photographs too.

FOOD JOB: *Restaurant Apology Writer*

The letter writer who can strike just the right tone of voice (somewhere between saying "sorry" and servile groveling) is a valuable member of the restaurant staff. As Fred G. Sampson wrote in *Nation's Restaurant News*, "Complaining is synonymous with disapproving, denouncing, dissenting, reproaching, grumbling, whimpering, remonstrating, fretting, protesting, fussing, moaning, objecting to, entering a demurrer, defying, carping, imputing, attacking, refuting, grousing and bellyaching. But no matter what you call it, a customer complaint must be handled with dispatch."

Restaurateurs and apology writers must remember that, as Bill Marvin, the "Restaurant Doctor" wrote, "Fifteen percent of unresolved complaints will result in a loss of business. A typical business hears from only four percent of its dissatisfied guests; the other 96 percent quietly go away, and 91 percent will never come back."

FOOD JOB: *Restaurant Reviewer*

Alan Richman's *Fork It Over: The Intrepid Adventures of a Professional Eater* chronicles his brilliant career as a wonderfully witty restaurant critic. He says, "Everybody thinks that what I do for a living is the gastronomic counterpart of test-driving a Mercedes sports coupe or helping Las Vegas chorus girls get dressed. Actually, the job is part analysis ('Is it good?'), part self-analysis ('Am I the only one who'll like it?') and part gluttony ('Good or not, I ate it all')." Richman doesn't dwell on extraneous matters (i.e., S-E-X). He leaves such ruminations to John Lanchester, who, in his novel *The Debt to Pleasure*, reveals his philosophy about more or less everything, from the erotica of distaste to the psychology of the menu.

It has been said by a reviewer: "Restaurant critics learn to live in an atmosphere where their presence—if detected—is met with groveling and cringing fear, and, more than occasionally, hostile loathing. But being liked is not part of the job. Honesty is."

Sometimes, though, honesty can be quite brutal. Restaurant critic A. A. Gill, writing in *Vanity Fair* magazine, characterized one meal—from the menu of a restaurant that, for decency's sake, shall here remain nameless—in the following manner. He likened the fish and foie gras dumplings to "fishy liver-filled condoms," and called them "vile, with a savor that lingered like a lovelorn drunk and tasted as if your mouth had been used as the swab bin in an animal hospital." That's telling it like it is, by Jove, as is a Pete Wells *New York Times* review of Guy Fieri's restaurant, in which he asks the following question: "Hey, did you try that blue drink, the one that glows like nuclear waste? The watermelon margarita? Any idea why it tastes like some combination of radiator fluid and formaldehyde?"

Becoming a Restaurant Reviewer

Restaurant reviewing in America was not a real, bona fide job until it was invented by Craig Claiborne, who pioneered the art of observing, writing, and rating restaurants in his role as the first male food editor of the *New York Times*. In his biography of Claiborne, *The Man Who Changed the Way We Eat*, author Thomas McNamee wrote:

> [Claiborne] saw himself as a critic on a par with the paper's critics of books, art, music, and drama, and he was determined to bring to his work a rigor and gravity equal to theirs. He wrote with vigor, honesty and knowledge having previously studied in Lausanne, Switzerland at the École Hôtelière de Lausanne, where he absorbed the principles of classic cooking and the art of refined service and management. In the United States he instituted a star system for ranking not only the quality of the food and service, but also every minute aspect of the dining experience.

The triumvirate of Craig Claiborne, James Beard, and Julia Child was the initial catalyst that propelled the United States from the dark ages of dining into an ever-more-refined sophistication at the most exalted levels of fine dining. Interestingly, both Claiborne and Beard were gay men who were unconditionally accepted, indeed, embraced, by the leading food professionals and by legions of admirers. Each man also had a mother who was an outstanding American cook and who ran a boarding house. James Beard's mother lived in Portland, Oregon, while Craig Claiborne's lived in Sunflower, Mississippi.

These men (and their moms) were equally responsible for awakening a respect for food in America, and though they rather disliked each other, their undeniable influence on the way we eat continues to reverberate today. Their books have sold in the hundreds of thousands (though it must be said, both performed terribly on television!).

AN (UNSERIOUS) NEW RESTAURANT-RATING SYSTEM

FWC: Families with children

UTFLOTB: Under thirty-five, living on the brink

WOOF: Well off older folk

OFLOM: Over fifty, lots of money

GVLF: Great view, lousy food

RP: Romantic and pricy

Ultimately, there are as many different forms of criticism as there are critics, but if one were to make the broadest distinction, on one side of which lie those hypocritical critics who tend to eviscerate and disable efforts, often while advertising their own erudition and good taste.

—Kathryn Harrison

FOOD JOB: *Cartoonist*

Here is a marvelous job for a witty food-scene observer. All you need to do is to look, listen, laugh, and draw. There surely must be a fertile market for your talents, whether your cartoons come attached to a regular humor column, in single frames, on greeting cards, or as pithy observations on everything from calendars to note cards and mugs. The universe is wide open. Draw a dozen sample cartoons and send a proposal to a publication that you hope will run them.

How to Get Started

The wikiHow website offers this advice to aspiring cartoonists: "Search online, or in the Artists' Market catalog (in the reference section of the library), for companies with open submissions policies. Also consider entering greeting card contests. Carefully read each company's submission guidelines to learn how to send in your cartoon ideas. Every company will have slightly different requirements, so you will need to tailor your submissions to each one. Accompany your cartoon with a (witty) cover letter.

Accept rejection without becoming distraught or discouraged. Competition in these markets is keen. Consider contacting greeting-card producers. Follow up your first sale with more ideas. Keep the style of the artwork consistent. Among the most prolific cartoonists are those who create a single character that is featured in every panel—for example, you could feature a novice cook or a crazy chef. There are certainly plenty of role models to be found."

Recommended Book

How's the Squid?: A Book of Food Cartoons by Jack Ziegler

FOOD JOB: *Food-Etiquette Columnist*

What advice do you give to a date who thinks that you haven't noticed that he is texting while you are talking? How do you tell a dining companion to come off it when he suggests that the wine needs to breathe? If you know the answers to such questions, write them up and suggest them as a series to your local newspaper.

▶▶ FOOD FOR THOUGHT ◀◀

As Ben Stein, American opinionator, writer, wit, and actor said, "Being a freelance writer is the most insecure existence imaginable. It mandates saving, ingenuity, and nonstop work and creativity. Freelancers never have a day off. Never. They can go months without a check. They absolutely have to save. They have to have five different levels of fallback plans and financial escape hatches."

FOOD JOB: *Menu Writer*

There is no denying the fact that menu writing is a fine art. One must consider numerous elements when composing a menu, not all of which may be obvious. Menus must be written with a mind toward maintaining a balance among and between a kitchen's staff and equipment—for instance, so that neither the grill nor the ovens nor the stovetop are likely to be overloaded at any one time. Purchasing and accounting folk must calculate the costs of labor and ingredients in order to determine optimal prices for a menu, but there are plenty of other things to think about when it comes to parlaying it into a profitable poem. The ultimate goal is to fulfill the expectations of the guests. The language of the menu sets the style of the room and the service.

A menu's graphic design is extremely important too. The menu designs for the Four Seasons restaurant in Manhattan still carries its original logo: four trees, each depicted in one of the four seasons. The menu items are centered on the page, and each word on each line is composed with infinite care. There are no dollar signs:

SELECTED MAIN COURSES FROM THE MENU OF THE FOUR SEASONS, SPRING 1960

Broiled Maine Lobster 6.50

The Classic Truite au Bleu 5.50

Summer Sole, Four Seasons 4.95

Baby Flounder Stuffed with Crabmeat, Sauce Mornay 5.25

Crisped Duckling with Calamondin Oranges, Flambé 5.95

Coq au Vin Rouge 5.00

Baked Veal Chop, Grand-Mère 5.75

Baby Pheasant in Golden Sauce 6.25

Roast Rack of Lamb for Two 14.00

Two Thrushes en Brochette 7.50

Filet of Beef Poivre 8.00

Heart of the Prime Rib 5.75

SELECTED MAIN COURSES FROM THE MENU OF THE FOUR SEASONS, SPRING 2010

Maryland Crab Cakes, Mustard Sauce 46

Dover Sole, Lemon-Caper Sauce Market Price [xx]

Wild Striped Bass, Wilted Pea Shoots,
Watercress-Ginger Bouillon 38

Whole Grilled Turbot 45

Loin of Rabbit, Baby Carrots and Turnips, Lavender Sauce 44

Crisp Farmhouse Duck, Plums 49

Whole Roasted Free-Range Chicken,
Morel Mushrooms, Ramps 38

Filet of Bison, Foie Gras, Périgord Black Truffle 56

Aged Sirloin Steak, Béarnaise Sauce 55

▶▶ FOOD FOR THOUGHT ◀◀

- When the Four Seasons opened, the restaurant critic Silas Spitzer wrote in the December 1959 issue of *Holiday* magazine that the menu represented "the New American Cuisine." It was the first time that this phrase was used in print.
- Strictly speaking, seasonal menus have become something of an anachronism. We can get asparagus and strawberries—indeed almost any ingredient—at any time of the year, so with the exception of soft-shell crabs and shad, there are few delicacies that arrive and leave only in their season. Modern chefs have decided that there are now fifty-two seasons in a year; their menus change every week.
- Contemporary restaurants do not add cents to the dollar amount. Instead of listing "Roast Chicken, $20.95," such an item might appear as "Farmer Brown's Napa Valley, Free-Range Organic Roasted Chicken, $40."

CAN YOU SPELL THAT PLEASE?

Following is an extract from the menu of tThe Millennium at Chanterelle, New Year's Eve, 1999: "Reservations can be booked from 5:30 p.m. to 11:00 p.m. The six-course degustation highlighting the best wines of the century is $1,400. The ten-course *Tour de Force* menu with the greatest wines from each decade is $2,400." A pretty penny, indeed! Following was the first of the *amuse-gueules* (appetizers) from the menu:

Oscetra Caviar: Cool Foie Gras, Warm Pemaquid Oysters
with Cabbage and Black Caviar
Billecart-Salmon Cuvee Nicolas Francois 1990

(Note: Is Oscetra spelled correctly? Or is it Osetra? I'm just askin' dear Reader.)

MENU BLOOPERS, AS COMPILED BY HENRY ALFORD FOR *THE NEW YORK TIMES* MAGAZINE, 1993:

Cream Cheese and Ox

Tuna Nickwash

Grilled Fresh Tuna Served with Soap

Special Big Leg with Lice

Baked Zit

Sautéed Couch

Smoke with fish and cucumber

Reuban

Rubbin Special

Meatball's Plain

Live Worst

Chocolate Mouse Tort

No Poatato on the Weekend

MARRIAGES MADE IN THE KITCHEN

Upon matching a dish coupled of two ingredients, "rice and seafood," you might then put such a dish on the menu for $3.50. Or, you could name the same concoction Maine Lobster and Seafood Saffron Risotto, whereupon you might price it at thirty-five dollars or more.

One of celebrated chef Thomas Keller's signature dishes is Oysters and Pearls, a sabayon of pearl tapioca with Island Creek oysters and white sturgeon. The combination is a marriage of a high-priced ingredient with a low-priced one, but results in a very high-priced menu item indeed.

In 2009, on the $275 prix fixe menu at his restaurant Per Se, Keller offered the following choice: "Elysian Fields Farm's carré d'agneau rôti entier, ris d'agneau, herb-scented panisse, summer squash, violet artichokes, pickled garlic and za'atar—scented yogurt with lamb jus." (In other words, lamb and sweetbreads with gravy, and four veg.)

The Fine Art of Menu Writing

A menu must be appropriate to the room in which it is to be read. As with fashion, every detail must be in harmony with the desired result, whether this be a hushed temple of gastronomy or a boisterous neighborhood joint in a college town. This means, or should mean, being sensitive to the economy: wine and food prices should be humbler during hard times. After all, a menu should reflect what guests want to eat. This reality check may not always conform to what the cook wants to cook.

People want to eat different kinds of foods at different times of day and on different days in the week. So what is a menu to be: sophisticated, elegant, contemporary, or trendy? Casual chic or country?

▸▸ FOOD FOR THOUGHT ◂◂

A small group of influential American food writers were invited to visit the great French restaurants. They had lunch at La Maison Troisgros in Roanne, where they were served a salad of foie gras and haricots verts with a warm vinaigrette dressing. They swooned. They adored it. However when it was adapted into print for the delectation of their hometown readers, the dish underwent the cruel pencil of the editor. In translation, it became bologna, frozen string beans, and Thousand Island dressing!

Recommended Book

Menu Design in America: 1850–1985 by Steven Heller and John Mariani

THE INTERNET

When I launched my own blog, foodjobsbook.com, I was told to write a description of it in order to keep myself on track. This is what I wrote a few years ago, and it still holds true to my objective now: "The *Food Jobs* blog is a natural expansion of food jobs covered in my Food Jobs books, and is (I hope) a lively discussion of issues and topics related to the food industry. It is also a place to share thoughts, musings, and occasional dashes of humor that may amuse and possibly inspire others to join or celebrate the food world with its many colors, tastes, smells, and flavors."

It can really help you to maintain focus if you'll just take the time to figure out your purpose. When asked to describe myself in three words, I chose *writer*, *speaker*, and *mentor*. Which words would you choose? And do they describe the work you are doing?

How to Get Started on a Blog

Writing a blog is, or should be, different from writing a magazine article. Blog posts should be less about soaring flights of literary fancy and more about the direct relay of information.

The most important question to ask yourself is: "Why am I doing this?"

It is a lot of work.

Do you have something to say? Do you have something to say that anyone wants to read? It isn't enough to simply say that you want to start a blog. If no one reads your work, it doesn't mean that you don't exist, but it is pretty close to that cruel reality. Do you want to showcase your brilliant writing, hoping an editor will offer you a book contract? It happens, but only rarely. Don't hold your breath.

In the meantime, make sure everything that you write is organized in a permanent archive and sorted by topic. For example, my own blog posts reflect the headings in my books: "Restaurants and Foodservice," "Science and Technology," "Publishing," "Education," and so on. When I know where to put things, it makes it easier to find them again.

How to Make a Fortune

Do you want to make money as a blogger? Forget it. There isn't any unless you are attracting at least five thousand visitors a day. But not making any money at it is not a reason not to write a blog (note that a triple negative makes an absolute positive).

How to Sell Yourself

Figure out what you are selling. Are you providing content in order to promote a product or a service or to share your personal opinions? If the latter, decide whether you want to be a lonely monk who spends a lifetime illuminating a few manuscript pages or whether you want your Facebook fan page to have ten thousand likes.

Focus. Identify a topic and stick to it tightly. It could be anything, from describing your life as a recipe tester at a tiny urban or incubator kitchen to providing seasonal recipes for your infant or fellow gluten-free dieters to descriptions of your life as a pastry chef living in Paris or Beirut. Your field of interest must be endlessly interesting to *you* first of all, or you may simply get bored with it and stop writing.

Stopping writing is the absolute worst thing you can do. You must commit to writing something, anything, even if it is just a few sentences, at least three times a week. This last requirement is, however, subject to controversy. Deb Perelman, a.k.a. the Smitten Kitchen blogger, reveals that she doesn't post a recipe until she is absolutely sure she is ready to send it forth. Judging by the popularity of her site, it appears that her fans are willing to wait.

How to Get Organized

It is essential to understand how the blogosphere works. Don't think of yourself as a victim of technology. It isn't that difficult to understand. Here are some basics:

- Blog headlines must jump out in Google searches. For example, the title, "A New Study of Obesity Looks for Larger Test Group" might produce a chuckle, but a surfing reader may not stumble across such a post at all. For such a topic, it is better to use a simple headline such as "Obesity Research." Don't try to be too clever or too enigmatic. I love the title *Wry Martinis* by Christopher Buckley, but while this was a great title of a book, it might be less successful as a blog heading.
- Use bullets frequently. They get the reader to the point quickly.
- Keep postings short, 350–500 words. Anything longer will exceed the attention span of the vast majority of blog readers.
- Keep recipes even shorter than commentaries. Use as few ingredients as possible, and provide concise directions. Embed videos. Provide app shopping lists.
- Readers like visuals. Add photographs, particularly if you have access to good lighting.
- Typos diminish your credibility, as do factual errors.

- Add links to help expand the reader's knowledge.
- Blogger Denise Graveline suggests commenting on other bloggers' sites, telling them what you like about their blogs, providing your own contact information, or asking them to link with your site.
- Google ranks all websites on their search results based, in part, on the number of other sites which link to them (and on the reputations and popularity of these linking sites).
- Install Google analytics to obtain weekly records of your traffic and of the days and times when the most readers visit your site. You will be able to see which of your topics were the most popular, where your fans are coming from, and how much time they are spending with you.

Advantages of Blogging

You own all your own material. The copyrights belong to you, not to a publisher who may wish to reprint your recipes in an anthology without further payment to you.

You can be your own PR company, directing traffic to your site by providing (not too frequent) mentions on your Facebook page and Twitter feeds.

You can use your blog to make your business more successful.

You control your own destiny as a blogger. You don't have to wait for an editor to accept or reject your work. You don't have to agree to make all the ghastly and totally unreasonable changes that are inevitably required. You can write exactly what you wish to write. So there!

Owning your own blog is like getting a gift from your fairy godmother. It grants you the freedom to stride forward in any direction you please. You choose. Every decision about the way your work is presented is yours to make. You can create one-word sentences and invent your own rules of grammar with no one to carp or criticize. And you can publish your work immediately.

Locating the Best Blogs

Go to the *GreenBee* blog and check out their article "50 of the World's Best Food Blogs." Analyze the content of each. Critique the graphic design. See if you can figure out what it is that made these blogs the crème of the crop. Why are readers flocking to these few sites and ignoring hundreds of thousands of others? In other words, who is speaking to whom—and how and why are they speaking?

Decide on an easy-to-remember name for your blog, and register it at Blogger. It costs about ten dollars to do so. My own blog www.foodjobsbook.com had to be named this because the domain FoodJobs.com was not available.

▸▸ FOOD FOR THOUGHT ◂◂

Remember, everything you write may likely be retrievable forever, so learn how to be your own editor.

> *Don't compromise your principles. That can mean a lot of things, from the kind of language and advertising you use, to what you write about. Just don't try to be all things to all people—be yourself.*
>
> —CakeWrecks.com

FOOD JOB: *Food-App Developer*

A 2012 cookbook conference organized by Andrew F. Smith offered a panel discussion on the emergence of cooking apps. One panelist claimed that cooking apps took over the conversation about a year and a half ago, right after iPads were introduced. Everyone saw the app as the successful merger of cookbooks and TV. Did that really happen? Tech developers love apps, but what about the readers and writers of cookbooks? Here today, but what about tomorrow?

If not apps, then what? What are cooks looking for? Recipes? As features multiply, will there be major differences between an app and an enhanced e-book, or an interactive website and a vlog? Are apps, even the most sophisticated ones, becoming instantly obsolete as features change so rapidly? And what about what seems to be one of the newer food trends: the rise of the YouTube chef?

We can expect these amateur chefs (and pros, too) to multiply like rabbits in the years ahead, at least on the web. As a content creator, how do you compete? As a user, how do you choose and navigate? To learn more on this topic, and to listen to other sessions of this extraordinarily useful and popular conference, access the Roger Smith Cookbook Conference Archive.

FOOD JOB: *Wikipedia Writer*

I was giving a talk at New York University when a student raised her hand and asked why I wasn't listed on *Wikipedia*. I told her that the idea had never entered my mind. She asked if she could write the entry. I was delighted and readily agreed. The research took rather longer than she had anticipated, but she enjoyed the process so much that she contacted several other food authors and chefs proposing her *Wikipedia* services. She now makes a comfortable living working full-time writing *Wikipedia* culinary profiles. Her fee is based on the number of hours she estimates will be required. Establish an hourly rate for yourself; calculate the time you think you will spend. Double it. It will undoubtedly take much longer than you initially think.

My Word: Funny Foods

You've probably noticed that studio audiences tend to chortle every time a television chef uses an odd ingredient. Garlic, it seems, is a naughty word. Sure it has a connection with slaying vampires, and it makes your breath smell, well, "emphatic" is perhaps the word I'm looking for, but why people laugh when they hear the word "garlic" is a bit of a mystery.

We chuckle at maraschino cherries, pistachio ice cream, and Jell-O. We giggle at any mention of Wonder Bread or fruitcake or Brussels sprouts. We scoff at classic American foods like spaghetti and meatballs, tuna-noodle casserole, Hamburger Helper, and green goddess dressing.

But it is not only TV audiences who find foods funny. We elitists, too, will snicker—for instance, at the very idea of canned cream-of-mushroom soup used as a "sauce." It has been many years since we thought it a treat to open a can of fruit cocktail. The culinary masterpieces of yesteryear have passed into the realm of the passé. No longer do we salivate over chicken à la king, beef Wellington, lobster thermidor, angels on horseback, angel-food cake, Boston cream pie, or cherries jubilee. Even thinking about them is like seeing your entire life flash before your eyes. Food snobs sneer at cream-filled, jam-packed doughnuts, though heaven knows it's not only the men in blue who love 'em.

Some foods fail to achieve fashionability at all. Instead, they remain in the realm of the weird. It's that way with beets. Beets should be taken seriously. They are put up on pedestals at Harvard. It is not surprising that Harvard College, an institution with a pronounced affection for the color crimson, should have come up with the idea of Harvard beets.

Pickled beets are a puzzle. You see them at every salad bar, but you hardly ever catch anyone actually helping themselves to a spoonful of them. At some of the poshest European spas, however, extremely well nourished patrons are offered regular doses of fresh beet juice and are told it will be a big help with weight control. (They pay handsomely for advice like this.)

Out in the country, they grow a big orange-colored beet known as the mangelwurzel, which tastes just as horrible as it sounds. The natives eat it but only if there is no alternative.

• •

FOOD JOB: *Food-Related Game-Show Producer*

Isn't this a good idea? Start your own game show. Invite celebrity chefs as guests. The world seems to love winners and losers (and food fights) and people who make other people laugh.

FOOD JOB: *Television Professionals*

As a last resort, a food-job seeker might consider the possibility of becoming a celebrity chef. Barring that, a culinarian who is also an actor might offer an invaluable service as a media trainer. No one has discovered how to predict the magic that makes one person shine on television and another whither in the bright lights.

But on-air talent is only part of the story. Behind each celebrity chef, there are producers, directors, shoppers, dishwashers, food stylists, recipe writers, camera operators, and other crew.

As the range of food-oriented television programming grows, so do the possibilities for employment. Not everyone can be Guy Fieri or Alton Brown, Giada De Laurentiis or Tom Colicchio—and not everyone wants to be—but if you have an interest in the medium, there may be a job for you there in some capacity.

• •

My Word: Tuning in to TV Celebrities

The TV Food Network was launched on November 23, 1993, at a splashy press party at the Rainbow Room in Manhattan. When Reese Schonfeld, then the TVFN president, gave the word, the gathered food media hushed, and he began to roll out his vision for a bold new concept: a 24/7 food channel. What a fabulous idea.

Reese Schonfeld was a very big big-shot back then. He was managing editor of United Press Movietone and Vice President of United Press International. He founded the Independent Television News Association, the first satellite-delivered television news service. With his pal Ted Turner, he created CNN. Reese served as its first president.

Today, one hundred million households can tune into the Food Network. There are stations in New York, Atlanta, Los Angeles, San Francisco, Chicago, Detroit, and Knoxville. There are viewers in Canada, Australia, New Zealand, Korea, Thailand, Singapore, Philippines, Monaco, Polynesia, and Great Britain. More people watch the Food Network than CNN. It no longer aims to teach cooking techniques or kitchen skills. Instead, it has lurched into the production of cooking shows featuring the assembly of store-bought components, and of cooking-competition shows that choose winners and losers. It also has an unfathomable addiction to cupcakes.

What is turning this huge audience on to all of its culinary idols, as featured on the Food Network? There is big boy Mario Batali. There is Anthony Bourdain. And there was Paula Deen, the Southern belle who dared to serve grits with grape jelly and red-eye gravy. There is Sandra Lee, who—upon throwing together a store-bought package of lady fingers, a plastic container of vanilla pudding, a whisper of artificial rum flavoring, a jar of jam, and a squirt of whipped topping—declares her creation "mostly homemade." Vast swaths of people appear to have the time to watch others cook and eat, and exclaim how good it all smells—but to have no time to cook for themselves.

Everything smells fabulous on the television screen. This phenomenon is frequently noted by Ina Garten, the "Barefoot Contessa," who cooks for her well-heeled pals. It is as equally well-known to the perpetually smiling and cleavage-revealing Giada, to the lovely Lydia, to Nigella "La Bella" Lawson, and to sweet Sara Moulton. Tyler Florence knows this, as do Bobby Flay, Michael, George, and Dave, and the beloved Mr. Chris Kimball of America's Test Kitchen.

• •

Breaking into the Food Media

In the IACP's newsletter, *Frontburner*, David Joachim published an interview with the Emmy-nominated food-show producer and director Irene Wong. In it, she revealed the following:

> If you want to be in front of the camera, my advice is to watch a lot of food programs. Get an idea of why each show works. Why is *Diners, Drive-Ins and Dives* among the most popular shows on the Food Network? Why is Rachael Ray so appealing? They're giving the audience something they want. Figure out how you are going to deliver what you want to say about food, but also what the audience wants to hear. Find out what your food identity is, what your food voice is. Your brand. Make it stand out from everyone else. If you're the only person who can deliver your brand, that

will make you more attractive to television executives, because you will be irreplaceable.

David Joachim is an author, editor, and collaborator on more than forty cookbooks and is a frequent television guest.

Mario Speaks

"Everyone has to fall into a niche," says TV culinary personality and chef Mario Batali. "I'm the Italian guy. Emeril [Lagasse is] the exuberant New Orleans guy with the big eyebrows who yells a lot. Bobby [Flay is] the grilling guy. Rachael Ray is the cheerleader-type girl who makes things at home the way a regular person would. Giada [De Laurentiis is] the beautiful girl with the nice rack who does simple Italian food. As silly as the whole Food Network is, it gives us all a soapbox to talk about the things we care about." (And from which to sell branded foods, pots, pans, specialty foods, and whatever else they can dream up.)

Turning up the Heat

The Food Network is shamelessly derivative, but it isn't alone. Science channels are morphing into food channels, and travel, adventure, and survival channels are following the same path. Competition is hot and getting hotter. Wars are being fought; battles are being won—and lost.

Who can make the most divine ice cream while marooned on a blazing tropical island with no utensils and no ingredients? (Don't even think of using palm oil!) You have just thirty minutes before the scheduled arrival of 2,602 Carnival Cruise Lines passengers. The winner is ... wait for it ... the Instantly Iced Sandy Snapping Turtle Smoothie!

Who'll take the cake in a contest of transporting turrets of spun sugar from here to there without dropping them? Who will be the judge of the judged? Who will deliver the next incandescent banality?

The erudite National Public Radio talk-show host Leonard Lopate described our insatiable appetite for culinary voyeurism as follows: "We continue our obsession with diets, dietary delusions, and Star-Treky molecular gastronomists, who boldly go where no chefs have gone before."

Recommended Book

Watching What We Eat: The Evolution of Television Cooking Shows, by Kathleen Collins

That's Entertainment

Food is now both entertainment and theater. As chef Michael Lomonaco declared, "Cooking is performing." Mary Sue Milliken, one half of the TV cooking duo known as "Too Hot Tamales," has compared the choreography of cooking in a restaurant to dance: "I tell my staff that, all day, it's preparation for 6 p.m. When the curtain rises, you dance through service. If you've had a good performance, you feel it. You know it when the line cooks are synchronized; they're flowing like a dance."

Q & A

Renowned chef and restaurateur Thomas Keller was asked whether or not it was true that a dancer had trained the servers at Per Se, his Manhattan restaurant. He responded simply: "A famous dancer taught Per Se's waitstaff to move elegantly, offering interesting insights into spatial elements, gestures—how to move around when coming into others' space."

Culinary Media Stars

Aarón Sanchez
Aarti Sequeira
Alexandra Guarnaschelli
Alton Brown
Bobby Flay
Cat Cora
Claire Robinson
David Chang
Dione Lucas
Emeril Lagasse
Giada De Laurentiis
Guy Fieri
Jacques Pépin
James Beard
John Ash
Julia Child
Lidia Bastianich
Mario Batali
Martha Stewart
Martin Yan
Ming Tsai
Nigella Lawson
Anne Burrell
Paula Deen
Pierre Franey
Rachael Ray
Sandra Lee
Sarah Moulton
The Frugal Gourmet
The Galloping Gourmet
"Two Fat Ladies"
"Too Hot Tamales"
Tyler Florence
Wolfgang Puck

Add your own favorite stars to this list.

What's for Dinner?

It is interesting to observe that we are most content when eating what we have eaten before. Every religious and national holiday is celebrated with traditional foods. We are all turkey-eating Americans on Thanksgiving Day and corned-beef Irish on St. Patrick's Day. We believe it to be important to have baked (not roasted) ham on Easter Sunday and hot dogs and hamburgers on the Fourth of July (American Independence Day).

▸▸ FOOD FOR THOUGHT ◂◂

The crime rate in the United States is at its lowest on Thanksgiving Day between noon and six o'clock. Families are at home eating turkey, watching football, sleeping, or complaining about the in-laws.

Recommended Books

It seems that many professional chefs are returning to home cooking. Take a look at Tyler Florence's *Tyler Florence Family Meal*, at Thomas Keller's *Ad Hoc at Home Cookbook*, or at *Jean-Georges: Cooking at Home with a Four-Star Chef*, by Jean-Georges Vongerichten. They are all leading us back into the kitchen and proving that you *can* go home again.

▸▸ FOOD FOR THOUGHT ◂◂

In 1946, the NBC network produced a cooking program called *Elsie Presents*. The show was sponsored by Borden, Inc., and featured a puppet of the company's mascot, Elsie the Cow, who wore a string of pearls and a frilly apron. The host of the cooking segments was James Beard. It ran for two years, until the program was canceled and Elsie kicked the bucket.

RADIO

FOOD JOB: *Radio Host*

Being the host of a food-focused radio show must surely be among the most desirable of careers for anyone knowledgeable about food. If you would love to have your own radio program, this is how to get started.

Address a proposal to the radio-station manager in which you describe your idea in one short paragraph. For inspiration consider *Food and Drink* magazine, a lively weekly radio program that celebrates the joys of food and drink. Late-breaking culinary news is heard there first, along with interviews and fascinating reports on the American food chain—the voyage of food from farm, to store, to skillet, to the plate.

Bullet points are always good to use in proposals. Using *Food and Drink* magazine again as an example, if you were pitching that show, you might characterize it in the following manner:

- *Food and Drink* magazine is modeled on the ideal buffet reception. It is a fast-paced buffet party where the talk is fascinating, the food is fabulous, and the punch carries a terrific wallop.

- The best-known and least-known small-scale food artisans, wine and beer makers, and connoisseurs are invited to present their opinions through tightly focused interviews and personal commentary.

- Listeners will meet cookbook authors, food-business entrepreneurs, chefs, restaurateurs, food-truck owners, farmers, physicians, nutritionists, food-safety regulators, beekeepers, bread bakers, and critics.

- On the menu, too, are those responsible for feeding school children, hospital patients, the military, astronauts, and those working in the kitchens of federal prisons, museums, zoos, and as the caterers of grand parties.

- When our guests can't come to talk to us, we will go to them, even if the journey takes us to the galley of the *Queen Mary 2* or to the White House.

- The subject matter of *Food and Drink* magazine is the stuff of life. Food fads will be explored; food trends will be tracked.

There will be reports on the latest supermarket innovations, on new apps and restaurant openings.

- The show will serve an audience hungry for information about food and the food market: what is in season—what is available at which supermarket, specialty food store, or mail-order catalog?
- Listeners will learn about the latest scientific findings concerning nutrition and agriculture.

Suggested show format, with additional time to be allotted for commercial messages:

1. Message from the host/teasers/food news 4:00
2. Interview/produced story (major topic of the week) 3:30
3. Quiz question 0:20
4. Interview/commentary/produced story 2:00
5. New product review 2:00
6. Cookbook review 2:30
7. Person-of-the-week profile 2:00
8. Wine/beer segment 2:30
9. Supermarket news 2:00
10. The fresh report 2:30
11. Interview with person of the week 4:00
12. Listener mail with responses from an expert 2:00
13. Nutrition news 2:00
14. Closing commentary 1:30

You will be taken seriously if you provide this kind of detailed proposal. Remember as well, that some universities have their own radio stations. This may offer an opening for you too.

CHAPTER 5

science and technology

It was placed on the same magnitude of important discoveries as the printing press, cotton gin, steamboat, paper clips, Kleenex, contour sheets, and disposable diapers . . .

—DAVID KAMP ON THE CUISINART FOOD PROCESSOR, *THE UNITED STATES OF ARUGULA*

- Adverse-Food-and-Drug-Interaction Researcher
- Allergy Researcher
- Anthropologist
- Dietician
- Food Behaviorist
- Flavor Maker
- Food Behavior Researcher
- Label Designer
- Safety Inspector
- Robotics Engineer
- Vegetarian Dietician
- Vending Machine Engineer

CAREERS IN FOOD SCIENCE

SCIENCE REACHES EVER more extensively into the world of food. As nations address issues related to world hunger, there is an urgent need to learn how to grow food more efficiently, to grow it in inhospitable land, and to invent new methods of irrigation. There are unlimited possibilities for employment in many fields relating to food science. They loom large once you accept the premise that growing, preparing, and cooking food is a marriage of science and art. Whether you are more interested in the medicinal value of herbs or flavors developed in chemistry labs, science and technology offer numerous ways to turn your appreciation of food into a profession.

In *Discover* magazine, Jeffrey Klugar writes that, "In the United States alone, there are more than 75 science-based companies churning out artificial flavors. Each of these labs serves hundreds of brand-name food manufacturers, who include their inventions into nearly everything we eat, from frozen dinners and tacos to Tootsie Rolls."

A Few New Technologies

- Researchers at the University of Minnesota have reported the identification of "bisin," a naturally occurring compound produced by some types of bacteria that reduces the growth of harmful organisms including *E. coli*, *Listeria*, and *Salmonella*. The discovery could extend the shelf-life of many foods by several months. (Bisin is chemically related to risin, which is used to keep processed cheese sterile.)

- Cooking with light instead of heat.
- Containers have been engineered with tabs, like soda cans. Flip the tab and contents will be almost instantly reheated.
- An edible film made from natural ingredients was recently invented that may eventually replace plastic wrap.
- The University of Missouri–Columbia's campus dining halls are planning the implementation of a system for recycling food waste as fertilizer with which to grow more food. In addition, the dining halls use about three thousand gallons of cooking oil per year, which the school plans to turn into bio-diesel fuel for the trucks that will haul the fertilizer mash around campus.

FOOD JOB: *Adverse-Food-and-Drug-Interaction Researcher*

Among the newer food science fields is the study of adverse food and medicine interactions. *New York Times* columnist Maureen Dowd described the possible side effects of a drug extensively advertised on television, writing that the warnings of the side effects "may include dry mouth, deadened emotions, tremors, insomnia, constipation, incontinence, deflated libido, inflated libido, overeating, loss of appetite, increased blood pressure, hives, acne, shortness of breath, death, and memory loss." The urgent, though mixed message is, go to your doctor and ask for it. It will make you better—or much, much worse! Clearly there is plenty of useful work for culinary experts with extensive knowledge of pharmacology.

John Thor Arnason is a biologist at the University of Ottawa. He and his colleague Brian C. Foster have examined the effect on drugs on more than 450 foods. Food and drug interactions are significantly important: grapefruit and olive oil may inhibit the efficacy of some statins. Beers with high hop content may reduce the effect of cancer drugs such as Tamoxifen. It has also been reported, "the anti-oxidant, resveratrol, found in red wine, nuts, and dark chocolate could reduce the effectiveness of some drugs."

FOOD JOB: *Allergy Researcher*

Many people believe that they are allergic to specific foods, but in fact, genuine food allergies, which attack the body's immune system and may become life threatening, show up in only 1 to 2 percent of the adult population.

A far more common experience is food intolerance—a disagreeable reaction that bears many of the symptoms of an allergy, among them upset stomach, vomiting, diarrhea, and itching. Food intolerances are extremely unpleasant, but they won't kill you.

The season of the year plays a significant role in the intensity of intolerance and allergic reactions to some foods. For example, someone who is allergic to cantaloupe may be more susceptible in the spring and fall when the increase in airborne pollen can trigger symptoms.

Gut Reaction

"Many food intolerances result from a deficiency in the enzymes that aid digestion. For instance, the most common intolerance is lactose in cow's milk; it occurs when the enzyme lactase, which is required to break down lactose (a sugar), is absent from the body. In the genetic autoimmune disorder celiac disease, an examination of the intestine reveals destroyed villi. Those with gluten intolerance have intense difficulty digesting gluten, a natural component in wheat." Dr. Alessio Fasano, a researcher at the University of Maryland, estimates eighteen million Americans have some degree of gluten sensitivity.

- The gluten-free market is a $6.3 billion industry and is on the rise.
- An estimated eleven million Americans suffer from allergies, including to peanuts, various tree nuts, shellfish, and wheat.
- Two million children are allergic to peanuts.
- Researchers are working on a vaccine that will be both preventative and curative for allergies.
- Researchers at Washington State University have found that a compound in garlic is one hundred times more effective than two popular antibiotics at fighting the Campylobacter bacterium, one of the most common causes of intestinal illness. Their work was recently published in the *Journal of Antimicrobial Chemotherapy.*

Allergenic Foods

Peanuts and other nuts, fish and shellfish, wheat and cereals containing gluten, milk and other dairy products, eggs, onions, and garlic, sulfites in white wine, and even a brand of breath mint are a few allergens from among a considerably wider array that can cause breathing difficulties and irreversible harm. Allergies and food intolerances must be taken with the utmost seriousness. Anaphylactic shock can lead to death. Children and adults who have been diagnosed with a severe allergy customarily carry with them a specific antidote. All restaurant staff must be educated about food allergies and instructed to call 911 at the first sign of a problem.

Recommended Book

The Intolerant Gourmet: Glorious Food Without Gluten and Lactose by Barbara Kafka

FOOD JOB: *Anthropologist*

Sydney Mintz, the revered anthropologist, explains that, "If you take a bear from China and put it in a zoo in Seattle, it will continue to make bear sounds, it will eat the food bears eat and live to the same age as had it stayed in its native land. If you take a small boy from China and bring him to the US, he will immediately make new sounds: he will speak a different language. He will eat different foods. He will grow taller and die earlier as a result of an increased risk of coronary artery disease."

The Princeton Review explains, that "Anthropologists examine, analyze, report on, and compare different cultures and how they grow, develop, and interact. How people live offers insights into modern life and how significantly (or, more often, how little) we have changed and how similar we have remained in our basic systems of human interaction and communication."

Courses in anthropology are offered in colleges throughout the nation. It takes seven to eight years to earn a PhD in the subject.

• •

My Word: Dining With the Eskimos

Basically, the ability to obtain food can be seen through the lens of the conjugation of the verb "to eat"—I eat; you eat; we eat; or, heaven forbid, we are eaten. The original rationale for marriage was the formalization of a contract in which a man and woman together provided meat and two veggies for the family. Thus, the women foraged while the men, usually in comradely groups, preferred to hunt and kill for food (and maybe had a little fun too). Supermarkets rendered this model obsolete.

But.

Our earliest ancestors developed strategies for winning in much the same way that football players and the military still devise similar plans of action for winning. Thus, even in evolutionary theory, there is a quarterback and a team, a captain and his troops, or a queen bee.

This is the way it was with the Eskimos:

One man and his mates go out on a boat. They are hunting a whale. While they are gone, they entrust the care of their families to the community. (This is an ancient form of social security.) When the men return towing their trophy, a huge whale, there is a riotous celebration. Lamps are lit. Dances are danced, and songs are sung. There is one ritualistic song in which the hero (winner) is hoisted aloft, and it is revealed to all that it was *his* harpoon that felled the whale. Thus a star is born. The winner smiles and gives thanks, presidentially.

Whales are very big. There is far too much meat for one man or one family to eat, so it is cut into small pieces. Each portion is allotted according to the hierarchy of the society. This theory amounts to something like, "those who give now will receive their reward later in life." (This is an ancient form of the insurance business.)

In the meantime, the successful hunter is entitled to a leadership position in governance. He becomes the richest man, so he is also entitled to get the prettiest girl. (There is a long-held, though entirely wrong-headed, theory that the most beautiful girl will produce the healthiest boy babies.)

I mention these things just so that we may remind ourselves of baseball Hall-of-Famer Yogi Berra's observation, "It's déjà vu all over again."

• •

Anthropologists Think About These Things

Sir George Thomson, the British physicist and Nobel Prize winner, wrote in his book *The Foreseeable Future* that the nearest historic parallel with today is not the Industrial Revolution, but rather the invention of agriculture in the Neolithic age. So great have been the changes in the workplace in our lifetime that the kind of work many of us are engaged in today would be incomprehensible to our grandparents. As our work changes, so, too, do the working conditions. Whereas our grandparents and great-grandparents worked in the fields or on the factory floor, today, many toil cheek-by-jowl in small cubicles gazing at computer screens.

FOOD JOB: *Dietician*

"Imagine that you have been washed up on a desert island. There is fresh water available, but you can have only two other foods." Paul Rozin, professor of psychology at the University of Pennsylvania asked the following: "From this list which would keep you going until help arrives: corn, alfalfa sprouts, hot dogs, spinach, peaches, bananas, or milk chocolate? The correct answer is hot dogs and milk chocolate. They come closest to providing a diet of survival."

The researcher Anna Frost explains that:

> While they may not be the best everyday diet in normal life, hot dogs and milk chocolate both contain fat, protein, and, in the case of the hot dogs, a better amino acid balance, which give a human sufficient nutrition to survive for a year. Foods like bananas and peaches lack these precious nutrients: they are primarily composed of carbohydrates, water, vitamins, and minerals, and constitute only part of a complete diet. The point of this question is not to prepare people to reenact *Gilligan's Island*

with a year's supply of Hebrew National [hot dogs], but instead to consider how we stereotype foods as "good" or "bad."

Why Diets Don't Work

Deep inside the brain, within a tiny area of the hypothalamus, there is a gland that secretes neuropeptide Y. It is this chemical that stimulates appetite and controls our weight. Most scientists agree that it is neuropeptide Y which urges us to eat and that its direct opposite, cholecystokinin (CCK), tells us when we have had enough and suggests that we stop eating.

Raw Food Follies

Richard Wrangham, professor of Biological Anthropology at Harvard University, says that we are "cookivores." "We evolved to eat cooked foods," he declares. "Raw-food eating is never practiced systematically, anywhere in the world." Wrangham spent four years trying to disprove that last statement in a global investigation of current and historical cultures. He looked for the most extreme examples of people eating a pure raw-food diet but failed to find any, "except for people in urban settings who were philosophically committed to raw food," he says. One researcher studied several hundred German raw-foodists, who had access to food of "astonishingly high quality" relative to wild raw foods, says Wrangham. Nonetheless, 25 percent of this group was chronically underweight, and 50 percent of the females "were so low in energy that they stopped having menstrual periods," he says. So even under exceptionally good conditions of superb year-round food availability, people had low energy and were "biologically incapable of appropriate reproduction. From an evolutionary point of view, sterility gets you bounced from the gene pool."

Cooking transformed the human race, changed the size, brain, and body development that resulted in a greater number of babies. The chimpanzees nurse from their mothers for four years. Our human toddlers have teeth and jaws that can eat cooked food so mothers can have more babies. There is an inverse relationship between guts and brains. A small gut results in a larger brain: if the gut is efficient, it runs only three times a day. Humans have more calories available for the brain. Humans have only one hour of chewing a day, animals chew at maximum capacity all day. Animals have a large gut and small brain. The more frequently we eat, the more active is our gut, therefore there is lesser brain activity.

• •

My Word: Portions Are Big and Getting Bigger

We buy popcorn in a container that could double as a trash can. A "decent" size serving of mashed potatoes is one that has a crater of gravy deep enough to nestle in both buttocks. A serving of fish in a restaurant can cost as much as the monthly utilities bill. A steak can weigh as much (or even more than) thirty-six ounces. It is so huge you could sit at one end of it and carve it from the other.

"Big," of course, is the natural swing away from "small." Small was a concept that was briefly popular during the Nouvelle Cuisine era. Small was a fad (mercifully now faded) during which vegetables were miniaturized. We were confronted with one-bite cauliflowers, one-chew artichokes. Turnips, once as large as a small pumpkin, shrank to the size of a green (seedless) grape. Eggplants dwindled to the contour of an index finger and zucchini grew so small it appeared for a while as though it may disappear entirely or simply be painted on the plate as part of the pattern.

Many otherwise sensible folk have developed an unhealthy relationship to food and are treating the dinner hour as though we are visiting the emergency room in a hospital. My advice is to eat whatever makes you happy though a smaller slice of happiness may result in a longer life.

A standard serving of soda in the 1950s was a 6.5-ounce bottle. Today, the industry standard is a sixteen-ounce plastic container. Go to a movie and buy a thirty-two-ounce cup of soda and there will be enough liquid to fill a baby's bath.

One fifth of all the vegetables eaten in the United States are in the form of French fries and potato chips.

• •

Recommended Book

Catching Fire: How Cooking Made Us Human by Richard W. Wrangham

Eat More, Live Less

It is well known that human beings often lack the ability to control their appetites. Over time, the idea "Eat it because it is in front of you," gave way to, "Eat it because it is good for you." Now, the orders from on high insist that we eat as little as possible, because it is bad for us (whatever it may be).

In the laboratory, that would seem to be the beginning and the end of the matter, but it doesn't begin to explain why we think we are hungry so soon after eating Chinese food.

Perhaps this is because we don't feel the meal has ended properly because there is no dessert—the orange at the bottom of a bag of Chinese take-out is in no way equal to the slice of cheesecake we were rather hoping for.

When we are deprived of our regular pattern of eating, we become quite distressed and crave it all the more. We find ourselves opening the refrigerator door a dozen times with the faint hope that the cheesecake will somehow put in an appearance. It never does. This is why attempts to force changes in our diet are almost always doomed to failure.

If only we could get at the hypothalamus and turn it on or off like an electric lightbulb, we would be able to resist temptation.

But don't think for a moment that researchers aren't trying to discover ways to manipulate this little gland, this naughty neurotransmitter, which forces us to eat a carton of ice cream when what we "really" wanted was a tofu sandwich. So far, though, success at controlling our dietary desires has been elusive.

Using Your Culinary Knowledge for Good

Researchers discovered an eighty-eight-year-old man in a Colorado retirement home who had eaten twenty-five soft-boiled eggs a day for well over fifteen years as part of an otherwise sensible diet. In all this time he had maintained good health and a normal cholesterol level. One of his doctors discovered that his patient had extremely efficient compensatory mechanisms. His intestines were absorbing only a fraction of the cholesterol, and his liver manufactured double the normal levels of bile acids that break down cholesterol. So after eating close to 141,400 eggs in getting on for two decades, the old guy complained only of loneliness since his wife's death—and before too long, he joined her for that great banquet in the sky. It seems he had not died from eating a crazy diet, but from a broken heart. We should remember that eating healthfully is far more a question of balance than of abstinence.

Eating Chocolate, Cheese, and Body Parts

We can manage to nourish ourselves adequately whether or not our diets include foods like cheese, chocolate, milk, eggs, meat, poultry, or fish. To take just one example, some Asian peoples, having little or no access to milk products rich in calcium, nevertheless suffer no greater incidence of osteoporosis than those who eat high-dairy diets. Calcium, it turns out, is abundant in several green vegetables, and in tofu, which is made from soybeans.

Human beings eat every manner of body part, including brains (in black butter), cheeks, tongue, shoulder (of lamb), breasts (of chicken), bellies (of pork), feet (of calves), and fingers (of fish and ladies). This is the reason we are called omnivores. We also eat rocks (salt), fungi (mushrooms), and fermented foods and drinks including bread, wine, and beer.

▸▸ FOOD FOR THOUGHT ◂◂

If there were a pill that promised to make us thin and virile, prevent baldness, and grow long, thick eyelashes, we would rush out to buy it no matter the price and whether or not the FDA had approved it. We would take the pill whether or not its side effects included terrible rashes or a seizure once in a while. The drug Fen-Phen is a combination of fenfluramine hydrochloride and phentermine hydrochloride. These two stimulants promote weight loss by reducing appetite. Six million overweight people took this drug before it was withdrawn from the market for causing damage to heart valves. It then achieved robust sales on the black market.

What You Don't Eat Can Kill You Too

Every year, there an estimated 220,000 weight-loss operations performed in the United States. The number is increasing. The cost of these surgical procedures may (or may not) be covered by insurance. Lap-band surgery costs $21,500. It is not without risk for the patient.

It took the FDA thirteen years to approve Belviq, a new weight-loss pill available by prescription only.

FOOD JOB: *Food Behaviorist*

When the rights of the individual collide with the rights of society, it is almost always society who gets the upper hand. The economic toll and health consequences of drinking and driving and smoking led to legislation to demand that we buckle up and stop smoking in public places. Society can similarly be "persuaded" to lose weight through good (or better) eating practices in order to reduce the rapidly escalating cost of health care.

Appetite for More

Physiology and biochemistry are only two of the many factors that influence our appetites. Genetics is a key player as well. So is noise. Play loud music, and we eat faster. When seated in a noisy, brightly lit restaurant, we almost certainly will eat more. We eat more in the comfort and company of family and friends and less in the presence of strangers. Emotional trauma suppresses appetite; short-term tension, on the other hand, can make us ravenously hungry.

When women fall in love they tend to eat less. Men behave oppositely. Go figure.

Please Pass the Salt

Appetite is satisfied sooner when food is well seasoned. *The Harvard Health Letter* reports: "It seems unlikely that salt intake is a major influence on the development of hypertension in most of the world population." Nevertheless, every day thousands of people restrict salt in their diet without having any compelling medical reason to do so.

And Pepper

In *The Spice Cookbook*, Avanelle Day and Lillie Stuckey write that, "During the Middle Ages in Europe… pepper was almost priceless, counted out berry by berry, and worth taxes, tributes, dowries and rents. In medieval France a pound of pepper could buy could buy a serf his freedom. A pound of ginger bought a sheep; a pound of mace could be exchanged for three sheep or half a cow."

A Craving for Sugar

Hunger is not the same as appetite and has almost nothing to do with taste. Hunger relates to a drop in the level of blood sugar and the physical need for food. Appetite relates to the craving for food; taste is the ability to differentiate one food from another.

Smell This

The memoir *Season to Taste: How I Lost My Sense of Smell and Found My Way* is one of those astonishing and unexpected books that we may only be fortunate enough to stumble across by chance or on a word of recommendation. Its food vignettes invite us to think more carefully about what we eat and drink. In the course of the narrative, author Molly Birnbaum recounts her near total loss of the sense of taste as a result of a devastating car accident. The book relives the joy of her gradual recovery.

As Birnbaum explains:

> Every smell begins with a molecule. Whether it is a charcoal whiff of the smoke off a grill on a summer evening, the lemon dish soap in my mother's kitchen, or the acrid breeze that greets me at the garbage dump, every aroma is made up of invisible particles. A single scent can hold more than a hundred of them,

combining to create the complex aroma of Chanel No. 5, or ham roasting on Christmas Day, or the brined ocean shore in Maine.

Smell is the most direct of the senses. Aromas most literally enter the body before they can be consciously identified. With every inhalation, molecules travel the thin craggy pathways that begin at the nostrils and head toward the brain. They speed past the olfactory cleft, a narrow opening toward the top of the nose. They hit the olfactory receptors, which are housed on the hairline tips of the millions of neurons that peek through a gold-hued mucous membrane called the olfactory epithelium.

Every human has around 350 different types of these receptors, which are unique proteins... They connect to the smell molecules upon arrival, then transfer signals toward the brain by chemical impulse. Every human has between six and eight million neurons in the nose to do just that. These signals are fired rapidly by many neurons at a time, forming a pattern not unlike a line of musical notes or the HTML coding of a webpage. When combined, the brain interprets the signals as a smell—an "odor image."

Recommended Book

Season to Taste: How I Lost My Sense of Smell and Found My Way by Molly Birnbaum

Seeing is Believing

Television is a phenomenon that our ancestors didn't have to contend with. The excitement of seeing a pizza flashing on the screen alerts our appetite-control center, which in turn sends fast and furious messages to the salivary glands to get ready for the feast. "EAT?" is the question. "NOW" is the response. "NO" is not even an option. Desire is the consequence of the sighting of food, even if we have barely rested our forks from the previous meal.

FOOD JOB: *Flavor Maker*

A Google search will provide you with the names of several of the large companies that create flavors from a combination of elements, similar to the methods used by fashion perfumes. Among the leaders are Givaudan, a large multinational corporation that, "focuses on the challenges that food and beverage companies face as they go about growing their brands, and making products that consumers love."

Researchers can invent distinctive tastes for any processed food, whether for sea-salt potato chips; the deep, dark, woodland flavor of mushroom gravy; the sweet notes in fruit drinks, candy, and chewing gum; or the flavors in deli meats, cookies, or herbal teas. As the demand for low-fat and reduced-calorie foods and beverages surges ever upward, the demand for enhanced and artificially created tastes increases. If a processed food has a distinctive taste, it is highly likely it has received a boost from a laboratory. The interesting thing is that, given a choice, we often prefer what we have come to accept as the "real" tastes of artificial or synthetic flavors rather than the real flavors that they imitate or enhance.

►► FOOD FOR THOUGHT ◄◄

- Smell and taste are the most primitive and the least analytic of our senses. These twin senses are inextricably linked with our evolutionary history; they determine whether we are prepared to take the risk of accepting an unfamiliar food.

- Within the animal kingdom, each species thrives upon a distinct set of taste preferences. Natural selection has created strategies for exploiting every niche in nature's food supply. Some animals are omnivorous, while others eat so specifically that they risk extinction if their specific food becomes unavailable. Koala bears, for instance, survive for their entire lives solely on the leaves of a particular variety of eucalyptus tree. Cats, large and small—whether lions and tigers or house cats—cannot detect sweetness, whereas bears, being omnivores, love honey. Butterflies like sweets too; their taste organs are located in their front feet, so they taste a flower's nectar just by stepping in it.

- A so-called super-taster is a person who has around eight thousand taste buds. Fifty percent of the population has only five thousand taste buds, and another 25 percent has only two thousand taste buds.

- Taste buds regenerate every seven to ten days.

- Taste is influenced by climate, cultural preferences, age, medication, and stress.

What is Taste?

As I've mentioned, professional tasters are employed by dozens of companies. There are coffee and tea tasters, ice cream and cookie tasters, tasters who establish lifetime careers in all sectors of food service and food processing. But what exactly is taste?

It is a complex topic.

We can extend some of our senses—we can improve our vision with the help of eyeglasses, binoculars, and telescopes. We can increase our ability to hear with the help of hearing aids and stethoscopes. But we can't increase our senses of taste or smell. When one is gone, the other is diminished, though there is a possibility that the loss will not last forever.

It Tastes Like Chicken

Chicken tastes different when it is roasted, fried, poached, braised, broiled, or made into a stew. A free-range, locally raised chicken tastes different from one produced on a factory farm. Chicken tastes different in the United States, in France, India, or China. Geography changes the taste of chicken, because chickens' diets vary from country to country. And chicken tastes quite different from turkey, duck, quail, or pheasant, though it may be difficult to find the language to explain the variation.

A small quantity of exquisite-tasting food is more satisfying than a huge serving of bland food. Chutneys, salsas, and blow-your-head-off chilies spare the diner from the boredom of eating a steady diet of rice and beans.

Our taste buds can detect sweetness if one part in two hundred is sweet. We can detect saltiness in one part in four hundred. Sourness is perceived in one part in two hundred thousand. An odor can be detected even when diluted to one part in a trillion. A connoisseur can detect and taste and "nose" differences between hundreds of wine.

FOOD JOB: *Food Behavior Researcher*

If you're interested in becoming a food behavior researcher, check out employment opportunities at the Consumer Behavior program at Stanford University, the Tuck School of Business at Dartmouth College, the University of Illinois's Hospitality Management program, the Department of Nutritional Science at Pennsylvania State University, the College of Behavioral and Social Sciences at the University of Maryland, the eLab at Vanderbilt University, and the US Army's Natick Laboratories. This field is growing, so make sure to browse for more consumer-behavior research programs online.

Research and Ye Shall Find

Researchers gather together cheap cuts of meat: beef and pork hearts, lungs, and toe nails. They mix all of these undesirable, unwanted, unmentionable animal parts together and mince them finely. Then they wash them. Then they bleach them. Then they extrude them through the steel jaws of mighty machines, and what they end up with is a white—or more-or-less white—protein. With a little more tinkering, the result may be marketed as a banana snack. It may even be good for you. Even so, this and similar products are nothing more than mock food in a mock shape cooked by mock heat and designed to be a "tasty treat." The good news is that there are no dishes to wash. The bad news is unfathomable.

►► FOOD FOR THOUGHT ◄◄

- Geneticists have been able to breed chickens without feathers, but the birds became so neurotic about their nudity that they refused to lay any eggs. The experiment has been abandoned; the sky has stopped falling.
- Chickens were fitted with red contact lenses in an experiment reported by *Smithsonian* magazine. The idea was that rose-colored spectacles might reduce the hostility and pecking rampant among cooped chickens. It didn't.

Chicken Soup: Why It Works

A study conducted at the University of Nebraska Medical Center suggests that chicken soup contains biologically active substances capable of inhibiting neutrophil migration. This may account in part for its traditional use as a cold remedy. Chicken soup is also thought to be helpful in easing the pain of a broken heart.

FOOD JOB: *Label Designer*

Almost everyone agrees that food labeling is a good thing. But no sooner do we arrive at consensus than someone begins asking foolish questions and muddying an issue that had been perfectly clear.

It has been suggested that genetically modified food should be labeled. Whether or not this is so, a food label must fulfill three criteria:

- It must be truthful.
- It must be verifiable.
- It must be enforceable.

So here's the first problem: If the label on a genetically modified food is to be truthful, it must state that there is no evidence as to whether the food is safe to eat. In the interest of balanced scientific accuracy, it must also state that there is no evidence to suggest that it is unsafe to eat either. The only way to tell the truth is to declare on the label that the food may or may not be safe to eat.

The *verifiable* part also poses a bit of a dilemma. There is no practical and economical test that can measure the presence of a protein derived from a genetically modified ingredient. It is rather like asserting that a thing might be there, or it might not be there, but that, *if* it is there, it may or may not present a problem. In other words, the house may or may not be haunted, and if it is, the undetectable ghost may or may not be friendly.

The *enforceability* issue presents the biggest predicament of all. Up to this point, our label would say that a food may or may not be safe because of something that may or may not be there. In this case, we can't very well plead with a government agency to make or enforce a ruling on something that is undetectable and whose effects are unverifiable.

▸▸ FOOD FOR THOUGHT ◂◂

The Boston Globe reported:

> AGAR Supply Co. is partnering with Legal Sea Foods to launch a new traceability label. Legal Sea Foods's wholesale division, Nor'Easter, will supply nearly all of the fresh fish marketed under AGAR's Nautifish brand, including haddock, cod, salmon, and tuna. Nor'Easter will use new technology to create a bar code on each package that will include details such as when the seafood was caught, who caught the product, what region it was caught in, and when the seafood was prepared for packaging.

Corn Derivatives

Genetically modified corn derivatives are present in more than 3,000 grocery items. It may be more practical to label foods that do *not* contain corn or soy, additives or preservatives, artificial coloring, or, indeed, anything other than what the food clearly *is*. Even an onion, apple, or grain of rice may have been genetically modified.

If we decided to get rid of all these foods, where would we put them? Or, as the old nursery rhyme asks:

If all the trees were bread and cheese,
And all the seas were ink,
What would we have to drink?

▸▸ FOOD FOR THOUGHT ◂◂

There are fifty-six ingredients in a Pop-Tart. Should it therefore be defined as a food or a chemical? Should it be a controlled substance, and if so, should the government regulate it? These are questions asked by Kelly D. Brownell, Director of the Rudd Center for Food Policy and Obesity at Yale University.

What's Next?

The *Nation's Restaurant News* tells us, "The foodservice industry is taking steps to revamp kids' menus and [is] rethinking marketing efforts as government regulators and [wellness] activists weigh restaurants' role in the fight against childhood obesity."

▸▸ FOOD FOR THOUGHT ◂◂

Colleges and corporate dining rooms have adopted touch-screen technology to allow guests to place their orders before they find a table. When the food is ready, the buyer is alerted by cell phone. Every meal is made to order. The delivery time, from order placement to pickup, is six to seven minutes.

FOOD JOB: *Safety Inspector*

The news media is far more likely to criticize the "harmful" presence of food additives than to acknowledge their benefits. In fact, additives are used for all kinds of good and valid reasons: to extend a food's shelf-life, to improve its nutritional value, to make it taste good, and, yes, even to improve its looks. Without additives, food would spoil more rapidly, salt wouldn't pour, bugs would erupt in the flour, mayonnaise would separate, and ice cream would crystallize. Loud would be the wailing heard across the land if all the cookies softened overnight.

Harold McGee, author of *On Food and Cooking: The Science and Lore of the Kitchen*, sums up the issue in a nutshell: "Public debate about the proliferation of additives in our food is more likely to be constructive if we all recognize two basic facts: that our food has never been perfectly safe or free from additives and that consumers share the responsibility for whatever risk there may be in eating today."

Only in America is death considered optional. The National Safety Council reports that thirty-three thousand travelers die in automobile accidents every year in the United States. The Centers for Disease Control and Prevention estimates that each year, 48 million Americans get sick, 128,000 are hospitalized, and 3,000 die—all due to foodborne illnesses. The great majority of these illnesses are mild and cause symptoms that last for only a day or two. The most severe tend to occur in the very old, the very young, or in those with otherwise compromised immune systems, as well as in healthy people who have been exposed to very high doses of the harmful organisms.

Food safety is primarily the responsibility of food businesses, which suffer devastating economic consequences when a product is tainted. Federal, state, and local agencies issue regulations, but there can never be absolutely guaranteed safety, even with raw fruits and vegetables. It is not possible to achieve a totally risk-free environment.

Who Is at Risk?

Calling someone a swine is, figuratively speaking, far worse than calling him a pig. A swine is a disgusting, contemptible person. A pig isn't a nice person either, unless her name is Miss Piggy or one of those three little piggies that provide us with bacon for breakfast, a ham sandwich for lunch, and a nice pork chop for dinner. Perception, as you see, is reality. Thus we fear some things more than others.

Film director Alfred Hitchcock was a master at manipulating scariness: he knew a shadow at night is far more fearsome than a robber in daylight. Other terrifying things are:

- Mad cows—the possibility of contracting mad cow disease is one in ten billion. This doesn't mean the risk is zero, but it is perilously close.
- We are more likely to be sickened by our grandmother's potato salad that has been left out in the hot sun than to be bopped on the head by a crazed drug dealer.

- During an average year four swimmers are killed by sharks—the risk of being struck by lightning is thirty times greater than landing in the jaws of a shark.
- Killer bees are much more terrifying than regular bees.
- In the United States, 14,408 people are murdered in an average year, most of them by people who once loved them.
- Medical mistakes kill 120,000 a year. There are seventy thousand physicians in the United States. Accidental deaths per doctor is 0.71 according to the US Department of Health & Human Services.
- The number of gun owners in the United States is eighty million. The number of accidental deaths per gun owner is .0000188. Therefore doctors are approximately nine thousand times more dangerous than gun owners. We dwell in confusion.
- There are forty-three thousand car accidents on an average year. Squirrels (and deer) are responsible for twenty-six thousand injuries when drivers swerve to avoid hitting them.

Truly we live in perilous times. Apply to the US Food & Drug Administration (FDA) and the US Department of Agriculture (USDA) for government food safety jobs.

►► FOOD FOR THOUGHT ◄◄

We could prevent many hundreds of incidents of food poisoning per year if we simply irradiated our ground beef. The word *irradiation* is the hang-up here. If we renamed the technology "cosmic processing," it would be a wild success.

FOOD JOB: *Vegetarian Dietician*

Vegetarianism is becoming ever more mainstream. Millions of Americans have adopted this diet, and the converts increase in number daily. Even those who still enjoy meat are giving vegetarians greater respect, and although we may still find it difficult to imagine that a superstar athlete or former president (Bill Clinton) would opt for a vegan diet, stranger things have happened.

T. Colin Campbell, a retired professor of nutritional biochemistry at Cornell University, says it well:

> It's my guess that there's hardly another myth in nutrition so insidious yet so intractable as that which encourages us to believe that consuming lots of high-quality protein—basically the stuff of animal-based foods—makes for fitness, bigness, and strength of body. Rooted in antiquity, this myth began to sprout in the minds of men (especially men, it seems) long before protein was identified and named.
>
> The myth took root in the belief that we could get our strength, our agility, and our ability to soar to unimaginable heights only if we consumed the flesh and bodies of animals. Much later, in the early 19th century, when scientists identified protein as being more or less equivalent to the flesh of the animals they worshipped, it was heralded as *the* treasured nutrient. In the words of famous chemist Justus von Liebig, it was none other than the very "stuff of life itself."

A remarkable shift in perception is occurring. Choosing a vegetarian diet is now equated with having respect for one's own health and for the health of the planet. Chefs are building up a wide range of new vegetarian meals and taking fresh looks at classic meatless dishes from around the world. Innovative vegetarian dishes are appearing with increasing frequency on restaurant menus. If offered a summer garden of colorful vegetables and fresh pasta drizzled with fruity olive oil, a generous spoonful of Parmesan, and a handshake of freshly ground black pepper, who among us would feel deprived?

> *Former United Kingdom prime minister Margaret Thatcher is in a restaurant, dining with members of her cabinet. She orders a steak. The waiter inquires, "And the vegetables?" She replies, "They'll have steak too."*
>
> — Irena Chalmers

▸▸ FOOD FOR THOUGHT ◂◂

In industrialized Western countries there are more vegetarians than ever before—yet, in a parallel shift, there are more hamburgers eaten than ever before. It's also interesting to note that Eskimos, who eat a traditional diet consisting almost entirely of meat, have a very similar life expectancy to that of Indian Hindus, who are often strict vegetarians.

FOOD JOB: *Robotics Engineer*

Automation technology is a major component of the food business. Sensors use refracted light to test the sweetness of preserves. Machines measure ingredients with uncompromising accuracy and mix, stir, and knead dough and batter with precision so as to achieve the correct texture every time. Radio waves detect the crispness of cookies before they burn. Machines weave and extrude breakfast cereals from oats, wheat, corn, rice, and multigrain blends in a triumph of technology and food chemistry. Food technologists and engineers have their fingers in many pies. You have only to take a tour of any large food processing company to see the automation at every step, from the arrival of ingredients at the loading dock to the end of the line.

> *I like the idea that, if you have a party, the robot can recognize faces, take drink orders, go back to the kitchen, load up the tray and then go back, find those people, and deliver their drinks. I think that would be awesome.*
>
> —Colin Angle, CEO iRobot

FOOD JOB: *Vending Machine Engineer*

A vending machine has been perfected that, in a mere thirty-five seconds, will provide a single, sizzling serving of shoestring fries. A separate button dispenses a dollop of ketchup. Machines can now dispense dozens of choices, from complete dinners to assemble-it-yourself salads. Pizza, with your own selection of toppings, is baked in just a minute or two, and even ice cream sundaes can be dispensed the way you want them. Vending machine engineers and food scientists have a future in the future. Vending machines purveying fresh and healthy food will likely soon be showing up in schools, stadiums, hospitals, and on every street corner. Check FreshVending.com to see if there is an engineering or recipe development job waiting for you.

• •

My Word: Believe It or Not

We are undergoing a massive change in how we think about our food and in the ways we buy, cook, and eat it. Our opinions are influenced by activists protesting the pollution of the earth's soil, air, and water; the inhumane treatment of animals; and the presence of hormones, additives, and preservatives. Some of these concerns are amply justified; others have little or no basis in reality.

Our judgments are also molded—far more than we may be prepared to admit—by skillful advertising and by journalists and consumer advocates with axes to grind. Some who fear flounder genes in their strawberries are unworried about eating the vast confusion of genes served at Grant Achatz's restaurant, Alinea, on its twenty-course, $210-a-person tasting menu.

At the turn of the previous century, all farming was organic. There were fewer additives and preservatives in our food. The average woman had five children and spent five hours a day in the kitchen. She had no access to contraception and was unable to vote. The average income in 1900 was $3,000. Adjusted for inflation, this amounts to approximately $27,000 for a family of five, and would be deemed by today's standards to be at the poverty level. The average family had no access to indoor plumbing, electrical refrigeration, or air conditioning. They had no telephone and no car, no vacuum cleaner or electronic device of any kind. The people in the average family didn't have a high-school education. The average person ate one-fifth as much food as we do now. Life expectancy in 1900 was 46.3 years. There was minimal consumption of meat. More deaths were caused by infectious diseases, whereas today, more deaths are caused by lifestyle-related diseases.

• •

CHAPTER 6

promotion, publicity, advertising

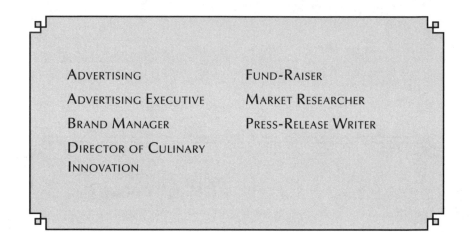

- Advertising
- Advertising Executive
- Brand Manager
- Director of Culinary Innovation
- Fund-Raiser
- Market Researcher
- Press-Release Writer

YOU MAY HAVE the best product, the most carefully researched cookbook, or the most inviting restaurant, but no enterprise can exist in a vacuum. You need customers, guests, readers, and viewers. This is where promotion, publicity, and marketing come into play. There is an art in getting the word out. Every business should have a plan for making sure its endeavors become part of public consciousness, whether locally or nationally. People who make promotion and publicity their career generally are forward-thinking and creative. It helps, too, if they enjoy socializing and the challenge of "selling" their clients.

►► FOOD FOR THOUGHT ◄◄

- According to BMO Capital Markets, food advertising is a $7.5 billion industry, second only to automobile advertising. The annual advertising budget of McDonald's is estimated to exceed $2 billion.

- If a TV commercial for one brand of cola is more appealing to a five-year-old child than another, the winning company may have created a loyal customer for eternity. Every year, the average American drinks fifty-three gallons of soda. In a lifetime, this adds up to a mighty river of profit.

- Sales of milk declined 3 percent last year.

- The average bottle of water costs five hundred to one thousand times more than the water from your kitchen faucet. While most bottled water is a good-quality product, the regulations for purity are actually tougher for tap water, and mandatory inspections in the United States are more rigorous.

- An article in the archives of *Pediatrics and Adolescent Medicine Studies* shows that children are much more likely to want to eat food that comes in branded packaging than food with no branding, even if it is the same product. For example, a study of three- to five-year-olds showed that 76.7 percent of children preferred French fries in McDonald's branded wrapping compared with 13.3 percent in plain packaging, when, in fact, the food was exactly the same.
- Perdue Farms had a great slogan: "It takes a tough man to make a tender chicken." The company's founder, Frank Perdue, knew more about chicken than anyone in the world and was doubly credible because he looked so much like a chicken. He was able to sell himself.

MARKETING GOALS

First, very carefully compose a mission statement that defines who you are and what you are trying to achieve, for example: "We are devoted to our guests. We are dedicated to providing great food prepared by great chefs. Our servers are knowledgeable, attentive, warm, and professional. We value our carefully selected food suppliers, recognizing that they play an important role in our success."

Then you can move on to the following:

- Define your target market (singles under thirty, college students, Frank Sinatra groupies ,etc.)
- Estimate the costs of your largest marketing expenditures. If you are opening a restaurant, this includes all complimentary meals and drinks. (For instance, if you know that a marriage proposal is in the offing, arrive after the proposal—not in advance or during—with complimentary champagne.)

- Estimate the cost of participating in charity functions. (The real cost is likely to bc double your estimate.) Have an explanation ready for all the events you must decline. It's good to pick two or three selected charities rather than to try to pollinate every flower in the garden.

- Be attentive to the media. For instance, if you have a restaurant, shower the writers and TV celebrities with desserts. You will reap dividends in free publicity.

- Factor in the cost of hiring a public relations professional. Decide on a strategy for covering advertising expenses. Engage a charming person to visit corporate headquarters whose task is to book direct sales. Offer to cater everything from coffee breaks and breakfast meetings to annual events and Christmas parties. Provide sample menus with prices. Write thank-you notes after events.

- Advertise in guide books, city magazines, and real estate publications. Use social media to connect prospective guests to special promotions (e.g., a Steak-and-Beer Festival, an Oysters-and-Champagne Festival, or an Arrival-of-Spring Festival).

- Maintain an active website.

- Establish a rewards program for frequent visitors to your business.

- Offer a special reward program to hotel concierges who recommend your restaurant.

- Reward your staff every day. Provide edible family meals.

Note: The marketing budget for a restaurant is 2.6 percent of estimated gross sales.

FOOD JOB: *Press-Release Writer*

The purpose of a press release is to provide information to the media in a form that is immediately useful and concise. A popular way to convey "news you can use" is to create a bulleted list. Following is an excerpt of the press release announcing the 1996 reopening of the Windows on the World restaurant—located in the 106th and 107th floors of the North Tower of The World Trade Center—after a $24 million restoration:

- Its 550 employees speak 25 languages.
- There are 52 cooks in the kitchen.
- Over 2,450 food items are ordered every week.
- 2,000 bottles of beer are on hand at any given time, in the Greatest Bar on Earth.
- There are over 20,000 bottles of wine in the Cellar in the Sky restaurant.
- 700 wines from around the world have made it to Windows's wine list.
- Over 27,000 bottles of champagne will be ordered in one year.
- Guests eat 51 pounds of caviar in one week.
- 1,000 calls or more are made to our Reservations office every day.

Windows reopened on the twentieth anniversary of its first incarnation and resumed its enviable position as the highest-grossing restaurant in the United States. Annual revenues hovered in the stratosphere—between $37 and $40 million.

How to Write a Press Release

Writing a press rclease is a fine art. The first objective must be to tempt the recipient to read it at all. There are a few very good ways to achieve this. The most important is to keep your release short and to get to the point quickly. This means using precious few, beautifully chosen and memorable words.

Make a plan. Make three points. Decide which is the first, second, and third point. Stick to your plan. Keep the press release to one page, use subheads and short, punchy paragraphs. Obtain the enthusiasm of the media to achieve this plan. Your objective is to attract more customers, increase sales, and make something or somebody look good.

FOOD JOB: *Fund-Raiser*

The ability to create novel and interesting ways to entice money to leave the pockets of benefactors is a gift beyond compare. For example, the New York Public Library introduced a magical fund-raiser called Tables of Contents. For this event, so-called celebrities "invited" guests over for dinner in their homes (or at their restaurants, or wherever). The guests paid real money to attend. I seem to remember that it was $1,500 each for this singular privilege.

At the time, I was living in the top two floors of a Manhattan brownstone, which had four fireplaces. I decorated the mantels with Scottish tartans, scattered candles of every shape and size around, and served a traditional Scottish/English dinner. At the moment the flaming plum pudding was brought to the dining table, there was a sound of Christmas bells. Children singing carols descended down the stairs while a chorus of adults simultaneously appeared from the floor below. The guests were delighted.

All were offered gingerbread men and mincemeat tarts. A small donation was made to the local church along with the larger one to the library.

• •

My Word: Respecting the Rules

What makes food acceptable in today's knowledge-based digital world depends on its having at least four of the following seven marketing attributes:

1. It must not drip or fall apart when eaten with one hand while driving, and it must be readily retrievable (without veering into oncoming traffic) in the event that a stray morsel should fall onto one's crotch.

2. It must be launched into our consciousness with energetic, amusing, and convincing advertising—preferably, all three—which, if possible, links the food to something extraordinary or mythical.

3. Its shape must be adaptable for service in fast-food outlets—whether as in a bun or in the shape of a finger (though not necessarily a fish finger), and it must not be accompanied by fresh vegetables, so that little children may be coaxed to eat it without unseemly public pressure. (See hot dogs and chicken nuggets or wings, etc.)

4. It must be wrapped. This refers both to the exterior and interior wrappings used to envelop and encase mystery proteins and thus add an all-important element of surprise.

5. It must be balanced, so that all basic food groups are included (e.g., it must be greasy, salty, sweet, and crunchy or crispy, and must have ultra-fast mouth-clearance).

6. It must be politically correct, so that every one—irrespective of age, ethnicity, religious affiliation, sexual preference,

income disparity, and dental maturity—will be rapturously happy (or, at least, not grumpy).

7. It must be cheap (or at least inexpensive) and yet must have a hearty heft in the hand. That is, it must deliver, and in quantities that cause the consumer, upon completion of her repast, to credibly announce, "Boy! I'm stuffed."

• •

THE PUBLICITY GAMES PEOPLE PLAY

The best publicity of all is word-of-mouth endorsement. Use a calendar to plot a strategy for organizing special events, for example, an oyster-shucking contest, a turkey-carving demonstration, a Bastille Day celebration, a single-malt scotch tasting.

It builds traffic to have a series of special events throughout the year: an asparagus and strawberry festival in the spring, a lobster festival in July, a harvest festival in the fall, and a Charles Dickens *Christmas Carol* dinner, along with some special holiday drinks like hot buttered rum and hot toddies in the winter. Add traditional Christmas gloggs and eggnogs to the bar offerings during winter, as well. During the holidays, surprise diners with the arrival of a group of bell ringers and choristers.

On tax day, a considerate host might offer a 10 percent "rebate" on every check.

On Thanksgiving Day, send your guests home with a beautifully arranged platter of "leftovers" and a homemade pie. This is a great way to guarantee repeat business, and it costs the restaurant relatively little.

Phil Romano, a brilliant Texas restaurateur, came up with the idea of pasting a sticker beneath one of the after-dinner cups of cappuccino or espresso. It entitled everyone at the table to the gift of a free dinner. Smiles all around.

Other promotional ideas include sending a limo for a guest of honor, mailing a dinner invitation to a newly engaged couple, or sending a baby gift when a birth announcement appears in the local newspaper.

On Mother's Day, announce that Mom's dinner is *complimentary*—on us! (Complimentary is a nicer-sounding word than "free.")

On Easter Sunday, the pastry chef could make hot cross bunnies, or chocolate Bugs Bunnies, or life-sized chocolate busts of Bunny and Clyde placed at the reception desk.

Keep records of guests' birthdays and of other special days, and send invitations to your guests from your restaurant the next year. Wedding-cake designers can acknowledge anniversaries (after first discreetly checking that the happy couple is still wed).

It's good to send dinner guests home with a muffin for their breakfast. It will remind them to come back, especially if the gift is packaged in an attractive container with the restaurant logo on it.

It's sweet to print the dessert menu in dark chocolate on a white chocolate tablet. The guest of honor can eat it.

At Christmas, auction a gingerbread house, with the funds going to charity. Guests are invited to choose the charity. The one with the most votes takes the cake (and the money).

In January, send the media a press release announcing a "white sale." All white foods are half-price, including herring in cream sauce, potato soup, scallops with white sauce, and vanilla ice cream.

Invite guests to sample different chocolate cakes and to "judge" which is best. Let them know that half the cost will be donated to charity.

It's particularly important to ask yourself, "What more can I give?"

FOOD JOB: *Advertising*

A thirteen-year-old boy received the ultimate present for his bar mitzvah. No, not a check for a modest sum of money. No, not the hottest new video game or electronic gadget. Instead, his uncle gave him a gift certificate with which to visit a brothel and pick a prostitute.

The lad's heart was pounding with excitement as he followed the madam up the staircase. When the she reached the top of the stairs, she looked back over her shoulder at the young boy, and remarked, "Sonny, enjoy the next couple of minutes. Anticipation is the best part."

A word of advice: Restaurant guests must always be greeted warmly. A welcoming gesture establishes the mood for anticipating a happy evening.

How to Get Started in Advertising

If you like to sell, and you are fascinated by market trends and ideas, you might want to try your hand at advertising. There are several avenues from which to approach employment: you can apply for a job at a traditional advertising agency, where you can work your way up as you learn the business. Or you can look into smaller, boutique agencies, where your tasks may be more varied.

Here are a few areas to explore if you are thinking about entering this arena:

- Identify the differences between advertising and public relations.
- Examine the influence of the media on all aspects of the hospitality industry.
- Define the differences between consumer and trade advertising and publicity.

- Research the impact of commodity boards and trade associations on food reporting.
- Look into the roles of radio, the Food Network, Bravo, the Discovery Channel, PBS, and other media on restaurant and hotel operations.
- Research the role of social media, blogs, and other websites on restaurant publicity, reviews, and reservations.
- Define the role of consumer-advocacy groups in shaping public opinion.

FOOD JOB: *Advertising Executive*

In his book, *Getting into Advertising*, David Laskin notes that trying to describe what you do is the biggest joke in the industry. He quotes David Ogilvy's book, *Ogilvy on Advertising*, about a conversation overheard on an airplane:

> "What business are you in?"
> "Engineer. You?"
> "I'm an account executive in an ad agency."
> "You write ads?"
> "No, copywriters do that."
> "That must be a fun job?"
> "It's not that easy. We do a lot of research."
> "You do the research?"
> "No, we have research people for that."
> "Do you bring in the new clients?"
> "That's not my job."
> "Forgive me, but what is *your* job?"
> "Marketing."

"You do the marketing for the clients?"

"No, they do it themselves."

"Are you in management?"

"No, but I soon will be."

▸▸ FOOD FOR THOUGHT ◂◂

When President Ronald Reagan deregulated advertising targeted at children, food-company budgets increased from $4 million to $42 million.

Greatest Ad Lines

Carolyn Wyman, the author of *I'm a Spam Fan: America's Best-Loved Foods* and *Better Than Homemade: Amazing Foods That Changed the Way We Eat*, has uncovered the origins of many ad lines of our favorite foods:

> Elmer Taggart was the vice president of the Taggart Baking Company [, which] introduced Wonder Bread, the first bread to be available sliced, an innovation that gave rise to the expression, "the greatest thing since sliced bread." For the wrapper, the designer was inspired [by] looking at the sky near his house in Indianapolis as it filled with the colorful balloons that were competing in the International Balloon Race. To him, the balloons embodied wonder. That's how packages of the bread ended up featuring red, blue and yellow balls.
>
> Wheaties, "the breakfast of champions." Early endorsers were the actor who played Tarzan, boxer James Dempsey, and Babe Ruth (the man not the candy).
>
> Rice Krispies: Snap! Crackle! And Pop!
>
> "Plop, plop; fizz, fizz" was another wildly successful advertising slogan from the same era (this time, for an antacid).

Selecting the right name and the right words can spell success or failure for many a business and ad slogan.

Kit Kat candy bars, Cap'n Crunch cereal, and Coca-Cola have that cheery, clickety-clackety, crispy, crunchy, crackle that we all crave. The very sound and rhythm of these repeated "k" sounds go a long way to contributing to the popularity of the brands.

The makers of Heinz tomato ketchup knew all about the thrill of anticipation. The company used Carly Simon's song "Anticipation" in the late 1970s to associate the plop of ketchup with the irresistible seduction of French fries.

Reprinted courtesy of Carolyn Wyman, www.carolynwyman.com.

Recipe for Success: Ketchup-Container Creator

In his article "Top-Down Approach Rekindles Our Love Affair with Ketchup," Frank Greve reported the following in the *Seattle Times* on June 27, 2007:

> Ketchup's modern revolution began in 1991 in a small precision-molding shop wedged between a scrap yard and a saloon in Midland, Michigan. The key prop in the dingy scene was a molding press that was meant to turn injections of liquid silicone into flexible, one-piece precision valves.
>
> It wasn't working quite right, however. Paul Brown, the shop's stocky, bullheaded owner, spent his days sitting before the press on a four-legged stool, chain-smoking and rethinking the valves' design.
>
> "I would pretend I was silicone and, if I was injected into a mold, what I would do," recalled Brown, a computer-phobic, intuition-guided shop technician.

His vision was a dispensing valve for a new kind of shampoo bottle that could be stored upside down on, say, a tub's edge. The valve had to open easily when squeezed and shut securely when the squeezing stopped. No drips. No leaks—ever.

To that end, Brown, then 48, and his mold-maker, Tim Socier, came up with a valve that's a little silicone dome with right-angled slits cut in its top. When the bottle's sides were pressed, the dome's slits opened like flower petals and released the contents. When the pressing stopped, the air sucked back into the dome, causing it to retract and the slits to close.

Brown sat back in his chair and said: "Holy cow, I just hit the jackpot."

He was right. The shampoo customer bought in. Eventually, so did baby food maker Gerber, which uses a version of the valve in its sippy cups. So did NASA's space program when it needed a leak-proof drinking-water system for spacewalking astronauts. So did other package makers. Years later, so did Heinz and Hunt's, Heinz's main competitor, for their top-down ketchup bottles.

Brown sold his company in 1995 for about $13 million.

▸▸ FOOD FOR THOUGHT ◂◂

The objective of advertisers is to arouse the will to buy a product by connecting it with a positive or persuasive emotion. They target every segment of the market, and their aim is spot-on. They have figured out that the food of the well-heeled is line-caught, organically grown, humanely reared, grass-fed, home-smoked, char-grilled, blackened, pan-seared, wind-dried, sun-dried, oven-roasted, slow-cooked, free-range, artisanal, local, and seasonal.

A little lower down the economic ladder, the food is convenient and easy to prepare.

Words such as "hand-dipped" and "country fresh" have a nice ring to them when you live in a crowded city. Packaging margarine in a mud-colored plastic tub and saying it's "country fresh" has a charming pastoral connotation to it, even though in our hearts we surely know that it is manufactured from chemicals in a factory in a city.

The Jolly Green Giant is a powerful association of ideas, particularly when being jolly is a distant emotion for far too many consumers during painful economic times.

FOOD JOB: *Market Researcher*

According to the *Packer*, the business newspaper of the produce industry, market researchers have learned the following:

- That the most likely buyers of peaches are consumers earning more than $100,000 a year, while shoppers age twenty-three to thirty-nine are those least likely to buy fruit with a stone or pit in it.
- That married consumers are 30 percent more likely to buy fruits with a stone—plums, pears, nectarines, apricots, cherries, and mangos—than unmarried shoppers.
- That only 30 percent of single, divorced, or widowed consumers buy fresh pears. Forty-two percent of this group prefer Bartlett pears, 18 percent choose Anjou, and 11 percent buy Bosc pears.

"When some customers are going through a major life event, like graduating from college or getting a new job or moving to a new town, their shopping habits become flexible in ways that are both predictable and a potential gold mines for retailers. A study found that when someone marries, he or she is more likely to start buying a new type of coffee. When a couple moves into a

new house, they're more apt to purchase a different kind of cereal. When they divorce there's an increased chance they'll start buying a different brand of beer."

—Charles Duhigg, *The New York Times*, "How Companies Learn Your Secrets," February 16, 2012. His book, *The Power of Habit: Why We Do What We Do in Life and Business*, further explores these findings.

▸▸ FOOD FOR THOUGHT ◂◂

Do you remember what Jean Anthelme Brillat-Savarin said? "Tell me what you eat, and I'll tell you who you are." Advertisers can figure out who you are by identifying five items in your supermarket cart. For example Pampers, Hamburger Helper, a frozen diet dinner, a bar of chocolate, matzo ball soup, a five-pound bag of rice, barbecue sauce, imported cheese, and organic granola are all dead giveaways. They provide clues to your age, income level, weight, marital status, gender, ethnic origin, and philosophical leanings.

Focus Grouping

Successful restaurants constantly reevaluate their mission as they consider trends that will impact their business. Focus groups work best when organized by a professional leader or moderator who carefully guides the proceedings and records the opinions of all the participants. Here are a few actual questions that were posed at a recent focus group, which included several levels of management:

- What makes a restaurant a great restaurant? (This question is so all-encompassing it could easily overtake the entire session.)
- What steps can be taken to establish (our restaurant) to become a leader?

- What is the basis for the authority we are seizing to establish ourselves as experts in this subject?
- How do we give our restaurant substance and meaning?
- How do we reach potential guests?
- How shall we describe our purpose?
- Is there more to our search than defining or reinterpreting apple pie?
- How do you make an old dish new again?
- What is our meat heritage and how is it interpreted today?
- What are the impressions we want to convey to local, regional, national, and international guests?
- What references can be used to describe New American cuisine?
- Can great food and great wine be had at a great price? How can we provide it without going broke?
- How do we express American Cuisine in our philosophy, on the menu, and how do we convey our core values in our marketing and publicity planning?
- Does the food of the earliest settlers have any bearing on our current search for definition?
- What has been the contribution of the immigrant tradition?
- Who will be cooking in the kitchen?

Romano's Macaroni Grill

The best advertising for a restaurant begins with its name. To my mind, one of the cleverest is Romano's Macaroni Grill. It describes itself on its website as "a casually elegant Italian restaurant serving handcrafted pastas, craveable entrees, and a diverse wine list." Bingo! Every "Yes, please!" knee-jerk response box is checked. Everyone loves the words "macaroni" and "grill."

Dunkin' Donuts—even though (or perhaps because) the name is spelled informally—triggers a surefire association with hard-working, blue-collar folk who may, in fact, not actually dunk donuts in coffee or anything at all.

Recipe for Success: Dunkin' Donuts Researcher

Mat Schaffer wrote the following in the March 3, 2010, issue of the *Boston Globe*:

> Stan Frankenthaler oversees a 10,000-square-foot lab with twelve working kitchens at Dunkin's Canton, Massachusetts, headquarters. He heads up an eighteen-person culinary team, divided into four groups: beverages, savory, baking, and ice cream.
>
> "I've got chefs, food scientists, school-of-hard-knocks bakers, and people who have dual degrees in culinary and marketing," he said. "We created flatbread sandwiches, the egg-white omelet. We took all the flavored cream cheeses and reduced the fat. We created the multigrain bagel. We did smoothies, we did Orange Coolatta. We tinker until we get it right, and then we have to put some science into it so that we can repeat the recipe in the 7,000 stores. If we can get you to pause for just one second and say, 'Wow, that tastes great!' we've really done what we set out to do."

FOOD JOB: *Director of Culinary Innovation*

Chef Dan Coudreaut is director of culinary innovation for the McDonald's Corporation at the company's Oak Brook, Illinois, headquarters. He develops new menu items for McDonald's 13,700 restaurants in the United States, and his contributions include fruit and walnut salad, the premium chicken sandwich line, Asian salad, chicken tortilla snack wrap, Southwest salad, and the McSkillet burrito.

Like so many other distinguished culinarians, he started his career as a dishwasher. Then he went to culinary school, graduated at the top of his class, worked as a sous-chef in several grand restaurants, and migrated into product development at Ponderosa and Bonanza steakhouses.

FOOD JOB: *Brand Manager*

When we think of Ben and Jerry, we think of caring philanthropists who produce super ice cream. We think of Starbucks as earth-friendly folk who generously provide health benefits to their employees, started the Create Jobs for USA initiative, and make high-priced coffee sold in a paper cup.

These images are creations of marketing experts. A culinary brand manager understands the demographic profiles of food-television viewers, analyzes food trends, researches packaging innovations, and coordinates the strategies of advertisers and marketers.

The brand manager invents novel or traditional products to be endorsed or manufactured by food celebrities and distributed to any consumer eager to buy. The goal of a culinary personality brand manager is to create a unique, instantly recognizable, and endearing personality for the brand. He may be inclined to encourage brand stakeholders to repeat such words as "bam," "EVOO," and "y'all" in order to further his ultimate objective, which is to make heaps of money for the brand. This objective holds true whether the brand is Emeril (Lagasse), Rachael (Ray), or Paula (Deen). "How easy is that?" Ina Garten, the Barefooted One might well ask.

What Is a Brand?

By definition, a brand is a distinctive product, service, or concept. Branding is the process of creating and disseminating the brand name. Branding can be applied to the entire corporate identity as well as to individual product and service names. Sometimes the name of the restaurant is more commercially important than the name of the chef. For instance, the Four Seasons restaurant in New York City has greater celebrity than the name of its former chef, Seppi Rengli. The Windows on the World restaurant once had more immediate name recognition than its former chef Michael Lomonoco, and guests of Disney's restaurants are attracted by the fame of Mickey Mouse. Few give a fig about the identity of the cooks in the kitchen.

▸▸ FOOD FOR THOUGHT ◂◂

Martha Stewart, Anthony Bourdain, Gordon Ramsay, Wolfgang Puck, Emeril Lagasse, and other highly visible personages in the food world had meteoric rises to fame. They shared a single objective. They monetized themselves by marketing their considerable talents, and in so doing, became brand names on par with Chanel, Juicy Fruit, Fendi, Tommy Hilfiger, Versace, Mrs. Fields, Mrs. Butterworth, and Betty Crocker. In effect, they became universally recognizable. It has been quite a long time since the only chef whose name we recognized was Chef Boyardee.

• •

My Word: In the Beginning

What a long way we have come since Marie-Antonin Carême and Auguste Escoffier toiled in their dark, satanic kitchens. What a long way we have come since the only way you could get your name in the history books was to commit suicide on the job.

It was Paul Bocuse who pioneered the concept of the brand-name chef. It all began at his restaurant, Bocuse d'Or, in Collonges-au-Mont-d'Or outside Lyon, France. He was awarded the first of his three Michelin stars in 1958. His fame and name eventually became attached to restaurants in Australia, Hong Kong, Tokyo, and (briefly) in the United States. A new restaurant at the Culinary Institute of America now bears his name. He endorsed a line of fancy foods and a brand of champagne. He created signature dishes for the president of France—salmon in a pastry crust with scallop mousse and sauce Choron, followed by poulet de Bresse encompassed in a creamy sauce of morels and spinach. The guests at these meals were respectful and as aged and distinguished as the wine. Every meal was concluded with a murmured chorus of well-bred amens.

• •

Do I Know You?

About.com reports, "Getting your name known and receiving press coverage for your work isn't just an ego trip. It keeps restaurant seats filled and tables turning. Name recognition makes buyers beg for whatever you are offering for sale.

"Brand managers are results-oriented and highly creative innovators who can talk to anyone and everyone. They have well-developed communication and analytical skills, and entrepreneurial leanings."

▶▶ FOOD FOR THOUGHT ◀◀

A CNN reporter places the average brand manager's salary at $76,100, though this figure can rise to $90,000 or higher for a senior executive.

Education and Experience Requirements

Being a brand manager often requires a bachelor's degree and four years of field experience. (For culinary brand managers, it helps to have culinary training, but it isn't crucial.) An interview is like a dance. Listen first to the "music" in the room, then try to follow the leader's steps. Following are some sample interview questions for an applicant to this field, written in *HR Management Report*:

1. Describe a time when you went above and beyond for a customer.
2. What would you do to maximize the brand image in this region?
3. A new competitor is entering the market. How do you protect your market share?
4. Tell me about a brand that does not compete in your current category that is not performing well and why.
5. Walk me through your résumé—tell me why you're qualified.
6. Give me an example in which you have led a team successfully to accomplish a task
7. Why should we hire you as opposed to someone else?
8. In trying to market a product, how do you differentiate one brand of product from another.

How to Get Started

To get started and gain insights, check out the Center for Brand and Product Management at the University of Wisconsin School of

Business, as well as the top ten brand-management blogs. You could also consider planning special events for one of the many culinary schools that seek student enrollment. They could perhaps use someone to help organize tours for conference attendees or media junkets for international tourist offices or on-site events for trade associations promoting their products.

CHAPTER 7

history and culture

Culture evokes images of grand opera and Gothic architecture, of Shakespearean sonnets and Rembrandt portraits; in fact the term has a simpler meaning. Scientists define it as behavior, skills, or knowledge—a way of life—that you share with and acquire from others of your species, but that differs from the way of life practiced by those of your kind living elsewhere. It's what we mean when we say Japanese culture is different from Brazilian.

—NICHOLAS WADE, *THE NEW YORK TIMES*

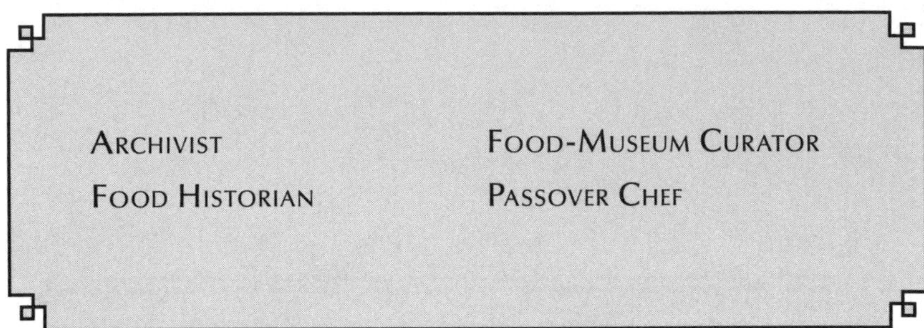
Archivist
Food-Museum Curator
Food Historian
Passover Chef

NOTHING—ABSOLUTELY NOTHING—IN THE food world "just happens." Everything happens for a reason, even if we don't yet know precisely what that reason was or is. What we do know is that the food we eat is central in the politics and economics of our time.

Jobs related to food history and culture are popular career paths among many who are interested in the ways that the social sciences define our own and other cultures. An understanding of the culinary history of a region will enhance the adventurous traveler's experience.

As food historian Sandra Oliver explains, "Every ingredient contains fascinating stories about its origins, uses, and travels over the earth and throughout time. So does every recipe we read, every dish we produce, and every utensil and cooking method we employ."

FOOD JOB: *Passover Chef*

More Jews celebrate Passover than they do any other event in their liturgical calendar. It is the oldest of the Jewish holy days and has been observed for more than three thousand years. It commemorates the Exodus, the story of the flight of their ancestors from slavery in Egypt after the angel of death was sent by God to kill the firstborn of every family, sparing only the families of the Israelites. In the story, because the Jews had to leave their homes so quickly, the bread did not have time to rise. Matzoh, a flat, unleavened bread, is the only bread that is kosher at this time.

The Seder is the traditional meal that is Passover's high point. It is prepared at home on the evening before the first day of Passover. A book called the *Haggadah* guides diners through the meal, which includes symbolic food and drink such as salt water, bitter herbs (usually horseradish), greens, wine, and haroseth, a tasty paste of fruit and nuts. The meal also includes some of the best in traditional Jewish cooking—gefilte fish, matzoh-ball soup, and beef brisket—though roasted chicken may be served instead of beef. Singing, ritual readings, and a hide-and-seek game involving a stolen piece of matzoh are integral to the occasion.

Cholent (Beef Brisket)

Because Orthodox Jews do not cook after sundown on the Sabbath, cholent, a beef brisket with several hours' cooking time, has long been a favorite dish. Traditionally, it is put into a heavy pot in a very low oven before sundown and left to simmer very slowly all night. After services at the synagogue, the hot meal is ready to eat right away.

Seder Menu

There are no unbreakable rules for the Seder dinner, though certain dishes are customarily served. One of the best things about the meal is that, usually, there is far too much food, so there are plenty of leftovers. You can, of course, buy everything from the store, but many families enjoy the ritual of preparing the food at home. The only cautionary note is to remember the old saying, "Too many cooks spoil the broth." So by all means, ask relatives and friends to contribute a dish, but try to persuade them to stay out of the kitchen. Kosher wine does contain alcohol, though Manischewitz, a widely known brand, is so sweet that you might not detect it. If you are going to depart from tradition, buy a wine everyone will enjoy.

Recommended Books

Joan Nathan's Jewish Holiday Cookbook by Joan Nathan
Encyclopedia of Jewish Food by Rabbi Gil Marks

FOOD JOB: *Archivist*

As Richard Pearce-Moses wrote, "Archivists keep records that have enduring value as reliable memories of the past, and they help people find and understand the information they need in those records."

Suppose you are an avid researcher. Suppose you decided to write a proposal for developing an archive for a famous restaurant to provide a historical record of its operations. Suppose the CEO of a famous restaurant, say The Rainbow Room, thinks that this is a marvelous idea.

When it reopened in 1987, the CEO of the Rainbow Room did indeed think just that, and he commissioned my small publishing group to create the Rainbow Room Archive. Eventually, it came to occupy more than a dozen large filing cabinets. The archive for the Rainbow Room—which originally opened in 1939, during the height of the Great Depression—is now housed in tax-deductible splendor and available to credentialed scholarly researchers.

If this were your new job, you would methodically immerse yourself in a research library—such as the main branch of the New York Public Library—and you would comb through old newspapers and magazines—even video—and seek out interviews of figures affiliated with the organization. This would include everyone from the building contractor to the architect, from the graphic designer or florist to the public relations person and any other staff.

The archive would have alphabetically arranged folders containing biographies of the executives and of other key personnel. Also included would be press releases, reviews of significant parties, and reservations made by celebrity guests. There would be a great many menus included. There would be wine lists and transcripts of anecdotes concerning the bar. The archive would contain records of special occasions and provide details of holidays, including Christmas, Easter, Mother's Day, and Thanksgiving Day. There would be reproductions of advertisements, documents from charity benefits, profit-and-loss statements, newsletters, and other promotion and publicity pieces—even records of gifts given to the staff. For example, one Rainbow Room staff member was given the gift of a red jeep that he had mentioned he coveted! (I, too, once received an especially memorable gift. One day, when I was in bed with a cold, I heard the bell ring. I opened the door to find a Rainbow Room waiter in full uniform, carrying a tray containing a hot lunch and bottle of wine!)

As you can see, assembling an archive is a huge task, but it is one that can be happily undertaken for a food company, cooking school, restaurant, or virtually any other culinary enterprise. Things rarely happen for the first time, so an archive can provide guidance to an organization when it reviews how similar events were handled previously.

Archive Anecdotes

Any archive is enriched by the inclusion of small anecdotes. Take the following examples:

- Sir Edmund Hillary was the first Western climber to reach the summit of Mount Everest. Upon arriving at Rockefeller Center with a reservation for dinner at the Rainbow Room (located on the 64th floor), he nervously commented: "I do hope they have an elevator here."
- A celebrity guest suddenly realized one of her diamond earrings was missing. After searching the table and the floor beneath the table, she imperiously accused the waiter of

stealing it. She raised a huge fuss. The general manager was summoned, and the dishwasher drained. Every garbage receptacle was examined. The earring was nowhere to be found. Arriving with the bad news, the manager glanced down at the guest's cleavage and detected a sparkling object. He did not attempt to retrieve it but did, tactfully, reveal its location.

How to Become Your Own Archivist

If you made an archive of your own life, it could reveal some precious clues about your character and serve as a guide to help map your future culinary career. Here are a few questions to ask:

- What are the three most significant things that have happened to me? What have I learned from these experiences?
- Which people have had the greatest impact on my life? Why do I admire, fear, or hate them?
- What is my most memorable meal?
- If I had a choice, would I prefer to be rich or famous, both or neither?
- What are my three strongest talents?
- What makes me different from everyone else?
- Describe yourself in three words.

To embark on a successful career, you must evaluate your own unique knowledge and life experiences and use them as a springboard. Now that you know yourself, listen to your heart and let it lead you to a joyful destination, whether as an archivist or in any other profession or intellectual challenge.

Surprisingly the most difficult thing to do is to identify which path to take from among the many options.

Once you know what you want to do, you must ask for help. No one arrives at his or her destination alone.

FOOD JOB: *Food Historian*

What is a historian? Betty Fussell is a historian. The subject of her PhD thesis was English tragicomedy in the Renaissance. She offered to let her landlord read it in lieu of rent, but he was a heartless man who said he'd prefer cold hard cash. So Betty left home. She went to live in France and in England. She traveled to the Near East, the Middle East, and the Far East. She journeyed through Pakistan and Afghanistan. She visited Africa, India, China, Russia, Latin America, and Southeast Asia. And everywhere she went, she ate breakfast, lunch, and dinner and wrote about her adventures in dozens of the world's most distinguished magazines. She wrote books and articles and essays. One of her studies was titled "On Murdering Eels and Laundering Swine."

She also wrote a book that incorporated history, geography, economics, politics, theology, mythology, and a tiny bit of pornography. It is *The Story of Corn* and is considered the definitive work on the subject.

Betty Fussell has lectured at the Smithsonian, the Metropolitan Museum of Art, Princeton University, Cornell, Dartmouth, and dozens of prestigious institutions of learning. You too can make a living as a historian. It helps a lot if you are also a great writer.

What Food Historians Do

The job of food historian was described by panelists at the 2012 Roger Smith Cookbook Conference in New York City:

> Food historians uncover, record, and reproduce food stories, recipes, and dishes. They search literary texts and nonfiction

> works, including old cookbooks, for hints of daily diet and culinary customs, so [as] to get a clearer picture of what the average person—not just the wealthy and privileged—ate at any given time and place. They search for new sources, studying kitchen inventories, trade and taxation records, and ancient cave carvings, drawings, menus, and then look around for ways to use their knowledge. Their information may be combined with a job in travel, teaching, or writing.

Culinary libraries need the help of historians, as do academic journals and publishers. So too do modern moviemakers and producers of TV series. Directors must make sure their characters—be they gladiators, or characters from *Braveheart*, Jane Austin, or *Downton Abbey*—eat the food of their period in history.

Trend predictors rely on historical patterns, too, because it is imperative to understand the past in order to grasp what is happening now and what is likely to occur in the future.

The history of what we eat provides a geographic destiny and social history of the nation. Food puts everything into a living, ever-evolving frame of reference comprised of everything from paintings and photographs to diaries and oral histories.

Very often, historians simply study their subject for the love of it.

Food Historian Andrew F. Smith

Andrew F. Smith teaches food studies at the New School in New York City. He has written about food extensively and was editor of *The Oxford Encyclopedia of Food and Drink in America*. The promotional copy for his book *Drinking History 15 Points in the Making of American Beverages* is as follows:

The author recounts—in delicious detail—the creation of contemporary American cuisine. The diet of the modern American wasn't always as corporate, conglomerated, and corn-rich as it is today, and the style of American cooking, along with the ingredients that compose it, has never been fixed. With a cast of characters including bold inventors, savvy restaurateurs, ruthless advertisers, mad scientists, adventurous entrepreneurs, celebrity chefs, and relentless health nuts, Smith pins down the truly crackerjack history behind the way America eats.

Smith's story opens with early America, an agriculturally independent nation where most citizens grew and consumed their own food. Over the next two hundred years, however, Americans would cultivate an entirely different approach to crops and consumption. Advances in food processing, transportation, regulation, nutrition, and science introduced highly complex and mechanized methods of production. The proliferation of cookbooks, cooking shows, and professionally designed kitchens made meals more commercially, politically, and culturally potent. To better understand these trends, Andrew Smith delves deeply and humorously into their creation. Ultimately he shows how, by revisiting this history, we can reclaim the independent, locally sustainable roots of American food.

Recommended Books

Eating History: Thirty Turning Points in the Making of American Cuisine by Andrew F. Smith

Pancake: A Global History by Ken Albala

The Migrant's Table: Meals and Memories in Bengali-American Households by Krishnendu Ray

Apple Pie: An American Story by John T. Edge

Fried Chicken: An American Story by John T. Edge

Donuts: An American Story by John T. Edge

Truck Food Cookbook: 150 Recipes and Ramblings from America's Best Restaurants on Wheels by John T. Edge

Food Historian Paul H. Freedman

Paul H. Freedman is Chester D. Tripp Professor of Medieval History at Yale University. He specializes in medieval social history, the history of Spain, comparative studies of the peasantry, trade in luxury products, and the history of cuisine. He also is the author of *Out of the East: Spices and the Medieval Imagination* and is editor of *Food: The History of Taste*, which has been translated into nine languages. How did he get to be a historian? He earned a master's degree in Library and Information Studies. He studied at the University of California at Berkeley before ascending to his exalted position at Yale.

CUISINES IN HISTORY

Diets have evolved, changed, and adapted throughout the course of human history. Who eats what depends on what will grow where and what cooking implements and fuels are available.

The wok is recognized as among the most useful of all cooking utensils. Its convex base was designed to hold it firmly between three stones containing the fire. To conserve fuel for fires, the wok, with its rounded base and flaring sides, was designed to provide the maximum heated surface area for cooking. Ingredients were cut into small pieces so the food would cook quickly.

Dietary patterns are rooted in geography and in religion. Butter, cheese, milk, cream, and ice cream are eaten in temperate climates where dairy cattle graze. Orthodox Jews don't eat pork. Hindus don't eat beef.

To be truly virtuous, some Buddhists comply with their religious ban on killing animals by getting someone else to act on their behalf. Because an egg may contain the beginnings of a new life, those who are devout ask their servants to break their eggs. In this way, the master escapes blame because he didn't do the killing, and the servant avoids responsibility because he was ordered to crack the shells. Helpful shopkeepers may keep a supply of eggs that have been "accidentally" cracked. There is much to be commended in Eastern philosophy.

Some strict vegetarians eat net-caught fish, rationalizing that a fish caught in a net is not killed exactly, but merely taken from the water. A semantic difference perhaps, but protein is sometimes more important than doctrine.

Asians consume as much as two hundred pounds of rice per person per year, compared with only eight pounds per person in North America. Some Asians eat as much rice in two weeks as most Americans eat in a year. Asian people who don't drink milk have a considerably lower incidence of osteoporosis than those around these parts who eat a lot of dairy. This is because those who live in the Far East eat much more calcium than Westerners; calcium is found in the green leafy vegetables and soy-based foods that make up a major part of their diet.

What we choose to eat depends largely on what we believe, but our beliefs are fraught with fear and with cultural and religious taboos. Few dare raise a voice to oppose conventional wisdom. Woe betide the member of the tribe who announces that he would rather eat macaroni than missionaries. Woe betide those who insist we must re-invent agriculture because this view is wildly unpopular amongst the pastoralists.

In the Darker Ages

As the anthropologist Peter Farb wrote:

> The ancient Romans distinguished between foods, not as proteins versus carbohydrates, or even meat versus vegetables, but as cultivated versus wild. Farmed animals were a more civilized food than game. Wine and bread, because they were created by man, were symbols of cultured living. Only barbarians ate wild plants. Only the poorest peasants ate black bread dipped in olive oil. Any risk of a return to rural conditions was a sign of social regression.

Taboos and Prejudices

Three missionaries are boiling in a pot. A gathering of scantily clad cannibals surrounds them. Standing nearby are several bottles of Romanée-Conti, 1937. The corks are drawn so that the wine can breathe in the warm jungle air. One missionary sighs mournfully as he observes, "You can tell they are heathens. They are going to drink red wine with white meat."

Throw Another Virgin in the Pot

Change occurs only when people are willing to accept it. When we look back on our distant history, the "progress" has been staggering. Think how far we have come since the days when it was thought the only way of ensuring a bountiful harvest was to offer a virgin as a sacrifice to the gods.

For thousands of years, human beings have adapted to the elements and the natural world. We have hunted and gathered, sowed and reaped, and toiled from dawn to dusk—just to get enough food to eat. And when, finally, we are on our own at the supermarket, and can choose virtually any food in the universe, what do we want to eat more than anything?

Diet Coke is the most frequently bought item in the supermarket.

Customers become very angry if they have to wait more than three minutes to lay their hands on their fast food. If it takes longer than three minutes to "cook" dinner in a microwave, forgeddaboutid. Some people are weird.

Not us.

Recommended Books

The Sociology of the Meal by Roy C. Wood.

The Sacred Cow and the Abominable Pig: Riddles of Food and Culture by Marvin Harris

The Magic Harvest: Food, Folklore, and Society by Piero Camporesi

Why We Eat What We Eat: How Columbus Changed the Way the World Eats by Raymond Sokolov

Consuming Passions: The Anthropology of Eating by Peter Farb and George Armelagos.

▶▶ FOOD FOR THOUGHT ◀◀

- The earliest artifacts of our history reveal that, eons ago, we were stomping grapes to make wine. The recent discovery of an ancient, grape-juice-stained sandal proves the point. The miraculous turning of water into wine is now thought to be less miraculous than the use of a porous clay amphora in which wine was stored and transported. (How refreshing it must have been on blazing hot day in the desert, many centuries ago, to quaff a drink of cool, cool water flavored with the dregs of the wine remaining in the vessel.)
- Proof of the existence of olive oil dates back five thousand years.

Lunch Money

Most of the world's population uses money to exchange for food. It is not surprising then that many terms for money are actually words for food. See "small potatoes," "dough," "bread," "gravy," "nest egg," "chicken feed," "bread and butter," and "peanuts."

The Romans exchanged salt for work, and from this origin is derived our word "salary." Bartering goods for services, or exchanging one commodity for another, has always been a popular way of avoiding the tax collectors. Among the many popular items for barter have been: rattlesnake rattles, dried salt cod, and tobacco. In Hawaii, in early times, a fishhook commanded a higher trading value if it was sunk into a just-caught fish.

Old Wives' Tales

Cherries, they say, help to relieve the pain of gout and arthritis. Perhaps the old wives are remembering the days when they were young wives, "with lips like cherries."

Russians say that a poultice of hot oatmeal and dry mustard will ward off pneumonia. In Switzerland, people smear a paste of oats on painful chilblains. And in Germany, those who have drunk too deeply swear that eating a bowl of oatmeal topped with fried onions helps alleviate the agony of a hangover. (In fact, the best cure for a hangover is a bowl of cold spaghetti and a fizzy soda.)

Old wives put a lot of faith in hazelnuts. They say the nut cures chronic coughing if it is pounded with honey, and that, when mixed with pepper, it will get rid of the common cold. Better yet, if it is burned and mashed with suet and smeared on the head, it will cure baldness.

Would-be medieval magicians used to put celery seeds in their shoes, hoping this would help them fly. It didn't.

As a psychoanalytic folklorist, my professional goals are to make sense of nonsense, find a rationale for the irrational and seek to make the unconscious conscious.

—Alan Dundes, *Bloody Mary in the Mirror: Essays in Psychoanalytic Folkloristics*

The Folklore Program at UC Berkeley

To enroll in the Folklore Program, contact the University of California at Berkeley at Folklore.Berkeley.edu/contact.php. Following is an extract from the program's overview from their website:

> The Folklore Program at the University of California, Berkeley trains intellectual leaders in folkloristics for the twenty-first century. We seek to provide a deep, critical, and theoretically informed reading of folklore scholarship from the seventeenth century through the present. We urge students to develop a particular field of expertise in folkloristics. At the same time, we advise our graduate students to develop strong grounding in another discipline or multidisciplinary perspective, such as race and ethnic studies, performance studies, science studies, rhetoric, narrative theory, ethnomusicology, materiality, women's and queer theory, and others, in order to bring new perspectives to their work in folkloristics.

Fairy Tales, Myths, and Fables

The fairy tales we are told as children remain deep in our unconscious. They are not lost, nor are they entirely forgotten. You undoubtedly remember the stories about Jack and the beanstalk (and his poor, hungry mother, who got to eat the beans), Hansel and Gretel (and the gingerbread house and the wicked witch), Little Red Riding Hood (and the Big Bad Wolf who gobbled her up), and Snow White (and the poisoned apple).

Running through these and dozens of other myths and fables are three food threads: the fear that there won't be enough to eat, the fear that the food we have will be snatched away from us, and the fear that we will be poisoned. This is pretty much the point at which we have arrived in the great debate about agricultural biotechnology.

Fear of "messing about" with our food supply is rooted in scary Frankenstein's monster that was an 1823 invention of Mary Shelley. She was a writer of fiction who created a fictional character that becomes the terrifying, fictional scientist inventor. It is this vivid imagery that masquerades as the "truth" and personifies (if this is the correct word) the widespread opposition to dread GMOs (genetically modified organisms.)

Matter of Fairy-Tale Fiction

Some little girls imagine Cinderella was a blonde, blue-eyed girl. She wasn't; she was an imaginary Chinese princess. She had long black hair. And black eyes. And her feet were small because they had been bound, as was traditional with girls from noble families.

It is suggested by the British-American author and journalist Christopher Hitchens, that Harry Potter was another variation on this ancient tale, in which a young mother dies in childbirth and the father marries a woman with healthy children who hate the infant (see *Sleeping Beauty*, etc.).

But no matter the origin, our fantasies remain unchanged: the poor girl (or boy) always ends up with the sweetheart and the real estate. He or she becomes a prince or princess among men. We love royalty and castles and big houses, which show that some people are superior to others but that we can become so if we learn how to climb the ladder.

Deeper meaning resides in the fairy tales told to me in my childhood than in the truth that is taught by life.

—Friedrich von Schiller, *The Piccolomini*

Recommended Book

The Uses of Enchantment: The Meaning and Importance of Fairy Tales by Bruno Bettelheim

Myths and "Mythstakes"

- Marco Polo did not introduce the Italians to Chinese noodles, nor were they responsible for the emergence of pasta.
- Catherine de' Medici did not introduce the French to Italian cooking, which then became the base for the French gastronomic advances in the eighteen century.
- Robert Gibbon Johnson did not introduce the tomato into the American culinary repertoire.
- African-American scientist George Washington Carver did not invent peanut butter and neither did John Harvey Kellogg.

WHAT WE DRINK

A History of the World in Six Glasses is a brilliant story of drinking, traced from the Stone Age to today. Author Tom Standage identifies the brews that changed our lives. They were beer, wine, spirits, coffee, tea, and cola. I'll quote from the book jacket:

> Beer, which originated in the Fertile Crescent, was so important to the first civilizations of Mesopotamia and Egypt that it

was used to pay wages. The golden age of ancient Greece was also the age of wine, which became the main export of Greece's vast seaborne trade. Spirits such as brandy and rum fortified sailors on long voyages during the Age of Exploration and oiled the pernicious slave trade. Although coffee originated in the Arab world, it stoked revolutionary thought in Europe during the Age of Reason, when coffee houses became centers of intellectual exchange. And hundreds of years after the Chinese began drinking tea, it became so popular in Britain that it started to dictate British foreign policy at the height of the British Empire. Carbonated beverages were invented in Europe in the late eighteenth century, but became a twentieth-century phenomenon, with Coca-Cola becoming the leading symbol of globalization.

Courtesy of Tom Standage, British journalist and author of A History in the World in 6 Glasses

Recipe for Success: Tea Taster

Noble Fleming was a tea taster par excellence. He said he got into the business purely by chance, when a friend of his family offered to take him on as a nineteen-year-old apprentice. Anxious to leave the dreary wet weather of England, he leapt at the opportunity to work in India. Eventually, he became one of a handful of tea masters.

The New York Times obituary noted with admiration that during his seven decades working for Thomas J. Lipton's Tea Company, "Mr. Fleming traveled to tea estates of 1,000 acres or more—primarily in India, Sri Lanka and East Africa—searching for varieties with specific tastes in the way an oenologist knows a château wine. Based on soil, elevation, rainfall, temperature, and how the estate was managed, he would make an initial assessment of the tea's quality." Fleming's evaluations determined what was subsequently bought at auction.

▶▶ FOOD FOR THOUGHT ◀◀

The average markup for an iced tea runs a whopping 4,400 percent. Just don't assume you'll always get a lemon wedge with it. At about ten cents a slice, the lemon costs about twice what the drink itself does.

TEA: SAMPLE DESCRIPTIONS

African Nectar: African Rooibos Leaves teeming with Tropical Fruit and Blossoms, Antioxidant Rich

Chamomile Citrus: A Tea to Curl Up With, Soothing Chamomile with Subtle Slices of Citrus

Rainforest Mind: A Lush Brew of Rich Black Tea, Provencal Mint and Other Herbs, with Tropical Fruit

Source: Mighty Leaf Tea

THAT WAS THEN; THIS IS NOW

Nouvelle cuisine is a culinary concept that has changed the way we think about food. With its near total reliance on foods in season and emphasis on good health, the "new" movement was embraced by a generation of multi-starred French chefs who broke free from the rigidity of the classic cuisine of Escoffier. Alice Lane notes in her essay "Auguste Escoffier: A Legend in a Chef Jacket" that the chef was "dismissed from his job at London's Savoy Hotel in 1897 along with his associate, César Ritz, who was accused of stealing over £3,000 in spirits and wine." She goes on to say that "Escoffier was not implicated in this theft but was accused of receiving gifts from the Savoy's vendors." Tut, tut.

Master Chef Paul Bocuse was the general of the nouvelle cuisine's benevolent uprising. Bocuse was described by *Newsweek* magazine as the Frank Sinatra of the nouvelle cuisine "Rat Pack," whose members included brothers Jean and Pierre Troisgros, Raymond Oliver, Alain Chapel, and Roger Vergé. But it was Frédy Girardet who was revered as the most accomplished chef of them all and whose restaurant in Lausanne, Switzerland, was considered by many disciples to be the most distinguished. He is credited with creating the acclaimed cuisine minceur (literally "slimming cooking") that inspired other lesser mortals, many of whom, like he, were also once students of the legendary chef Fernand Point.

Michel Guérard was also considered to be among the most influential among this generation of French chef idealists. Guérard created celestial marvels, little duets with vegetables and herb gardens and Asian influences.

Thus we begin to see a logical procession, as one generation of chefs holds hands, or at least influences the palate, of the next.

• •

My Word: Wizards of Godz

I watched Heston Blumenthal, chef of the Fat Duck restaurant, give a cooking demonstration at the International Chefs Congress in Manhattan. It was mind-boggling. It's one thing to read about Heston Blumenthal and his work and quite an astonishment to actually see him in action. "Eating is a multisensory experience," he says. And, by George, he's right. Heston also says that his cooking "is all about contrasts of texture and flavor. It's based on knowledge: knowledge of anatomy and physiology and psychology and magic."

In the brain the centers for taste and memory are anatomically very close together. Heston knows that. He also knows that our own personal taboos, prejudices, and experiences have a profound influence on our food preferences.

Heston created a seafood composition in a shadow box, a kind of deep picture frame. In went a base of sand—tapioca (or was it semolina?)—and on it he carefully placed three kinds of seaweed, an oyster, a razor clam, a sea urchin, and a coverlet of ethereal white frothy seafood foam. There's a garnish of artfully arranged crystallized and fried anchovies. OK, sound good?

Sound is the operative word. To experience the full impact, the diner wears seashell-shaped headphones. While savoring every tiny morsel, the conscious mind is enveloped in the cries of seagulls and the sounds of waves crashing on the beach. Incredible! Transported to the seashore, the fish leaps from the icy waters and leaves a faint brine hovering in the air—and in the mouth.

What is fascinating about this is borne out by an experiment in which the same seafood dish was accompanied, not with the sounds of the ocean, but with the grunting of pigs and the clucking of chickens. Everyone hated the food. Some diners even spat it out. But the same folk loved the bacon and egg ice cream with the farmyard symphony resonating in their heads! Similarly, if you eat a potato chip listening to loud cracking sounds through headphones, it makes it seem wonderfully crispy.

Chef Blumenthal engages experts from many fields to help him achieve the singular sensations he seeks. For a Christmas dinner, his objective was to re-create the innermost essence of the moment, not just the taste and the smells of Christmas, but the feeling of his family on Christmas Day, a day on which his father always gave his mother a bunch of roses. Heston Blumenthal was seeking the essence of Christmas, the emotion of Christmas, the memory of Christmas. Where to begin?

Why, in the Middle East of course, to procure gold, frankincense, and myrrh, and then on to Siberia to get a bucket of reindeer milk! Then it was on to a consultation with Christophe, the Parisian perfume expert, who analyzed the molecular structure of each component. And then the real task began.

How to incorporate the other flavors of the season: nutmeg, roasting chestnuts, orange, whiskey, and how to serve the composition?

Why, in the form of a sorbet encased in a contained tabletop fire, over which a bouquet of roses is suspended to release their fragrance? The sights, sounds, and smells of Christmas are concentrated in the sorbet and served from a wooden teaspoon—carved from the myrrh tree of course. Why did no one think of such a thing before? The miniature scoop of sorbet dissolves in slow ecstasy in the mouth.

• •

PAST IS PROLOGUE TO THE FUTURE

It is interesting to see several disparate approaches to dining occur at the same time. We can secretly crave a Big Mac or Kentucky Fried Chicken. At the same time, we can gasp at the scholarship of Dr. Nathan Myhrvold, who was the first chief technology officer at Microsoft before "retiring" to devote himself to his five-volume masterwork, *Modernist Cuisine: The Art and Science of Cooking.* (It was $650 on Amazon, recently reduced to $450; a collectors edition is available for $840.) Myhrvold shows the reader how to see inside the food as it cooks and to examine the anatomy of a bubble.

Recommended Book

The Fat Duck Cookbook by Heston Blumenthal

FOOD JOB: *Food-Museum Curator*

A short list of food museums (and there are many more):

Idaho Potato Museum in Blackfoot, Idaho

Washington Banana Museum in Auburn, Washington

Shinyokohama Ramen Noodle Museum in Yokohama, Japan

The National Museum of Pasta in Rome, Italy

Wyandot Popcorn Museum in Marion, Idaho

Jell-O Gallery in Leroy, NY

Museum of Culinary History and Alimentation (MoCHA) in London, England

The Museum of the American Cocktail in New Orleans, Louisiana

The Museum of Burnt Food in Arlington, Massachusetts

CHAPTER 8

from farm to table

It's difficult to remember that only fifty years ago all farming was organic—and sustainable. There were no pesticides and "factory farming" was a concept that was unimagined. Even beef was brought to market in season, like asparagus, shad roe, soft shell crabs, and summer corn and tomatoes.

—BILL NIMAN, FOUNDER OF NIMAN RANCH

Farm-Related Jobs

Agriculture Researcher

Apple Farmer

Beekeeper

Cheese Maker

Coffee Magnate

Farm to Table

Farmers' Market Manager

Forager

Garlic Grower

Human Plant Pollinator

Mushroom Farmer

Plant Scientist

Seed Scientist

Truffle Farmer

Fish Jobs

Caviar Connoisseur

Crab Fisherman

Fish Farmer

Water Expert

SUSTAINABLE FARMING IS a form of agriculture that will last forever, because it meets the needs of the present without compromising the food supplies of future generations. This is a concept that was practiced effectively for thousands of years; it can be just as viable a model for us today.

Human beings naturally revere nature and the natural order. American biologist, theorist, naturalist, and author Edward O. Wilson makes a compelling case that this affinity for nature, "biophilia" he calls it, "is an innate epigenetic program handed down to us by way of natural selection."

However it got here, the idea that natural things are good for you—and its corollary, "don't muck about with nature"—is widespread and fiercely held. It accounts for much of the avidity for "organically" grown versus insecticide-laden foods and for the preference for herbal supplements and other "natural" remedies over those concocted by scientists working in laboratories.

SOME ENCHANTED ISLAND

A brewery on a tropical island is dumping tons of carbohydrate-rich black sludge into the clear blue waters of the harbor, destroying the fabulous coral reefs on which the local population depends for tourism and endangering the coastal marine life. Fish essential to the daily diet are dying in alarming numbers.

Then someone has a brilliant idea.

The sludge from the brewery becomes an ideal medium for growing mushrooms. After the mushrooms are harvested, the sludge-soil residue is mixed with rice and used to feed chickens and other farm animals. The animal manure is collected and put through a liquefaction and heating process—which produces the gasoline substitute methane as a byproduct—and can then be used as an agricultural fertilizer and as fish meal for an aquaculture farm.

In the farm's ponds, the filtered liquid from the manure processing supports six species of fish, ranging from top to bottom feeders, and including carp, crabs, prawns, and various forms of plankton. This natural environment sustains itself, requiring no further cleansing or costly antibiotics to protect the health of the fish.

The project is still in the experimental stages, but its planners are already dreaming of planting the ponds with fruits, vegetables, and flowers in a hydroponic system where their roots absorb nutrients from the suspended microscopic particles of fish waste.

A negative has been turned into an inspirational positive: the coral reefs have been preserved; there is food to eat and beer to drink. There is a surplus of produce to sell, and new jobs have been created. What's more, the entire system is eminently sustainable—provided that everyone does their part in drinking the beer that creates the sludge.

This example gives us just a glimpse of how many threads there are to sustainable cuisine—the brewery, the coral reef, the worries about the vanishing tourists, the dirty water that posed a threat to people's livelihoods—and all the sensible and practical solutions that turned everything around.

Before you get too excited about this fairy tale, I must tell you, the whole thing is a myth. Nevertheless, this magical island was described in *World Watch* magazine as an example, in microcosm, of the problems we face and the opportunities that are available to us and to others who search a sustainable cuisine.

> *Poisoned in his paved cities, blindfolded by his impulses and necessities, man tends to disregard the system of nature in which he stands. It is only at infrequent moments when he finds himself beneath the*

stars, at sea perhaps, or in a moonlit meadow or on a foreign shore, that he contemplates the natural world—and he wonders.

—Samuel Taylor Coleridge, "Hymn to the Earth"

▸▸ FOOD FOR THOUGHT ◂◂

Chicken has become cheap. In 1900, it took four months for a chick to grow into a two-pound chicken. Now it takes a mere seven weeks to produce a four-pound roaster. Today, it is not uncommon to have ten million chickens under one roof. This will produce over half a million dozen eggs a day. One tenth of a cent drop in the per-egg production cost increases the daily gross profit of six thousand dollars or over $2 million a year.

• •

My Word: The Great Food Revolution

In 1968, the Democratic National Convention in Chicago changed the way we eat today. When Mayor Richard J. Daley's security forces beat up the students who were protesting the war in Vietnam, images of the televised chaos on the floor of the convention hall crashed into every home in the nation. Mayor Daley had thrown a stone into deeply troubled waters that continue to ripple right onto our dinner plates today.

In the blink of an eye, we lost our faith in government and big business. In its place we discovered virtue in brown rice, whole wheat flour, and fair trade. Millions became vegetarians. Suddenly we supported animal rights and organic and local farming. A gathering force demanded an end to the use of pesticides, antibiotics, and hormones in beef. We were strenuously lobbying for minimal packaging, recycling, and no more plastic bags. The entire world was going green. The climate was changing.

A small group of protestors had grown into a huge political movement, with advocates of their core beliefs echoing throughout the world. A few small voices had become a mighty roar.

We can see both the trend back to nature and its direct opposite, extreme technology, continue to march in tandem. One sector urges its children to grow their own food, while the other becomes increasingly disconnected from the ways in which food is produced.

But, just a thought: If we insist on eating locally, we will have to forego coffee, tea, sugar, chocolate, spices, salt, pepper, and cork for wine bottles.

• •

WHAT IS SUSTAINABLE CUISINE?

Sustainable cuisine is a way of eating joyfully, in the knowledge that what we eat is good for us and good for the world around us too. It doesn't rest on nutrient profiles or mathematical speculation. It doesn't focus on any single ingredient or put its faith in magic bullets. There's a place for chocolate cake as well as black bean soup. It excludes nothing, though it does include a balance of fats, grains, fruits, and vegetables—and above all, taste. It can even mean saying yes to steak for dinner and butter on our bread and boiled eggs for breakfast and hot fudge sundaes . . . just not every day.

A sustainable cuisine is wonderfully simple regimen to adopt. The basic idea is to put fresh vegetables and grains in the center of the plate and consider meat as a side dish instead of the other way around. Or you can eliminate meat entirely if you choose to. It involves making rational, sensible, balanced food choices, but it by no means requires giving up the foods that make us exclaim, "Mmm! Yum!"

A GLIMPSE OF (EARTHLY) PARADISE

At the end of the summer, a group of restaurateurs near Washington, DC, hosted a Farm Dinner Festival in association with the American Farmland Trust, a national organization dedicated to helping organic farmers. The giant picnic was a glorious example of a sustainable farm-to-table concept in action.

Everyone was welcome, and more than 2,000 people wearing casual clothes and huge smiles came to enjoy a splendid meal at a moderate price. Families, friends, and strangers sat together at trestle tables and were invited to eat as much as they wished.

The foods were beautifully arranged on large platters, china and terra-cotta serving dishes, and in colorful bowls.

The produce, harvested at the peak of the season, came from small farms in neighboring states, and everything was prepared and served by the restaurant chefs. The feast was composed mainly of fruits, vegetables, and grains, but in true sustainable-cuisine style, small portions of meat, chicken, and fish had a place on the plate too.

Here's just a small sampling of the foods and desserts served at the feast:

- Three-bean salad with roasted peppers
- Five-star Idaho country potato salad
- Zucchini pickles
- Long Island deli potato salad
- Sweet and sour cabbage
- Virginia green-bean salad

- Organic mesclun salad
- Oven-roasted vegetable salad
- Vegetable short stack
- Roasted beet and watercress salad
- Yukon gold potatoes with garlic and herbs
- Traditional corn on the cob with Amish sweet butter
- Grilled salmon with peach chutney

And for dessert:

- Swedish cream
- Blackberry cobbler
- Peach bread pudding with double raspberry sauce
- Berry trifle
- Peach upside-down cake
- Panna cotta with fresh berries
- Peach cobbler
- Blackberry oatmeal bars
- Peach raspberry pie
- Homemade peach ice cream
- Assorted shortcakes
- Sweet ripe melons, peaches, and berries
- Blackberry sorbet

Almost all of these dishes—and there are hundreds more that fit comfortably into the palette of a sustainable cuisine—are simple and quick to prepare at home. They are also increasingly seen on restaurant menus and everywhere chefs can create their own food festivals.

Old and New

For a party at the Rainbow Room, street vendors' carts were re-created from old etchings. Actors were hired to call the street cries accompanying displays of cockles and mussels: "Alive, alive, O!" Alongside fruits and vegetables were little plates of hors d'oeuvres prepared from whichever ingredient the hawker called out. (For example, there were indeed fresh oysters, but also a contemporary version of oysters Rockefeller.) Fresh peaches were offered—and poached with a touch of aged Balsamic vinegar and a sprinkling of Madagascar pepper. The idea was a rapturous success—one you could duplicate with your own imaginative twist.

Recipe for Success

Elinor Ostrom was the first woman to receive the Nobel Prize in economics. Her expertise is in sustainability. She researched fisheries worldwide and discovered that the most sustainable way to manage fish stocks is to let the fisheries determine how to share resources. She proved that privatizing public resources—allowing one body to make decisions about the use of resources—is inferior to letting a diverse group of bodies make collective decisions. Similarly, unconventional farmers tend to make the right decisions when they rationally manage their natural resources in conserving the soil, finding new ways to manage crops without excessive irrigation, and putting livestock on the land that sustains it most efficiently.

FARMING IN OTHER LANDS

Chinese farmers are feeding a billion people, 22 percent of the world's population, on only 7 percent of the earth's arable land. Over an agricultural history spanning seven thousand years, the Chinese have developed practices of intensive organic farming so sound that fields cultivated during the Han dynasty are still fertile after twenty centuries of continuous use. Soil fertility is maintained year after year through composting and through rotating food crops with green manure crops grown specifically to be turned under, adding natural nitrogen and organic matter to the soil. All resources and waste materials are carefully managed and everything used is reused and then used again.

In Mexico, archaeologists have discovered that as early as 2000 BC, the people were eating corn, amaranth, beans, squash, avocados, and chilies. This is a well-balanced, sustainable cuisine. The grains provided carbohydrates, the beans and squash supplied protein and other nutrients, avocados added fats and oils, and the chili peppers delivered vitamins and gave thunderbolts of flavor to a meatless and otherwise monotonous diet.

Many generations ago, Mexicans grew beans, squash, and corn together, copying the way they grew in the wild, and their descendants called the plants "the three sisters of life" because they brought good harvests each year. It is interesting to note that they also developed the skill of soaking the corn kernels in lime water, which released a boost of calcium that was essential to a community that had no access to dairy foods.

Around 1500 BC, on the other side of the world, Egyptian farmers also planted beans, squash, and corn in the same manner, encouraging both the bean and squash plants to support themselves by climbing the strong cornstalks. We now know how it was that these crops kept the soil fertile from one harvest to the next—by fixing nitrogen in the land.

That was then. What about now? What about us? The principles of sustainable agriculture may be all very well on a small scale, but how are we going to feed the rapidly expanding world population on lofty idealism?

Maybe the question we should be asking ourselves is how are we going to continue to feed the world *unless* we make changes in the current system? This doesn't mean turning back the clock, but blending the best of ancient wisdom with the best of our new scientific ideas. For instance, instead of thinking in terms of maximum yield, we must start thinking about the maximum *sustainable* yield, for the long haul.

According to the US Department of Agriculture, thirty-eight million people in our nation—13.9 million of them children—live in households that suffer from hunger or live on the edge of hunger. This hunger and "food insecurity" are far too widespread in our wealthy society. Hunger in the United States is a problem that can be solved.

Another report from the US Department of Agriculture reveals that we waste ninety-six billion pounds of food in America each year. A recent study from the University of Arizona at Tucson discloses that almost half the food in the country goes to waste—a statistic that should alarm an industry that is struggling to achieve greater efficiency in order to salvage profits.

►► FOOD FOR THOUGHT ◄◄

- Americans, on average, throw away thirty-three pounds of food per month, said experts at the Reuters Food and Agriculture Summit. This astonishing figure adds up to almost 400 pounds a year. A high percentage of the tossed fare is produce, which causes concern, since fruits and vegetables take the most resources to get from farm to table.

- In 2012, thirty million Americans were receiving food stamps.
- It took hundreds of thousands of years to put one billion people on the planet, but only 120 years to add the second billion. Forty years after that, there was a third billion, and the fourth, fifth, and sixth billions were added in just thirteen years each. The projection is for this rate of growth to slow slightly in the new millennium. But, by the year 2050, we will have well over nine billion people on planet earth. Demographers have estimated that the maximum population the Earth can sustain is twelve billion.

FOOD JOB: *Agriculture Researcher*

Cornell University, the University of California Davis, Texas A&M University, and many colleges in the Midwest and throughout the country offer programs and courses in agricultural research and development. The University of Illinois's website lists 5,913 post-secondary institutions in the United States that offer campus-based programs. All of these institutions are accredited by the US Department of Education. You can also research accredited degrees offered online in that section of their site or in its student resources section. If you want some guidance or advice about what it's like to be an online student, you should use the eLearners Advisor.

> *If you can't feed a hundred people, then just feed one. Together we can offer a gift of hope. And give and receive a warm hug.*
>
> —Mother Theresa

▸▸ FOOD FOR THOUGHT ◂◂

Ismail Serageldin, Chairman of the Conference on Overcoming Global Hunger, said the following: "In the nineteenth century some people declared that slavery was unconscionable and unacceptable, that it degraded the free as well as the slaves, and that it must be abolished. They were called abolitionists. Today hunger associated with extreme poverty in a world that has the means to feed its people is unconscionable and unacceptable. We must become the new abolitionists."

FOOD JOB: *Farm to Table*

If we were to analyze the future food-jobs market, among the most fertile fields would certainly be the principles of farm-to-table dining. This vast arena involves small- and large-scale farming as well as low- and high-tech farming principles and technologies. Field-to-fork wisdom encompasses seed science, innovations in insect control, and advances in efficient irrigation methods. It includes the study of meteorology, economics, and politics; of buying and selling, storage and transportation, preservation and nutrition,;and yes, of cooking and eating.

Going forward, what we choose to eat will undergo greater scrutiny than ever before. We are only just beginning to accept the irrefutable conclusion that our daily diets have profound effects on our long-term personal and planetary well-being. Eating for life opens a floodgate of career opportunities for everyone from tillers of the soil to ethicists wrestling with new spheres of morality.

How to Get Started

The website FarmtoCollege.org lists more than one hundred college-based farm-buying programs, with such participants as Harvard University, Ohio University, University of California, Vassar, and Skidmore, among many others. Former Secretary of State Hillary Rodham Clinton calls these farm-to-college programs a crucial part of the strategy for creating new markets for farmers.

Would you consider becoming the food buyer for a college or corporate cafeteria? Google, Facebook, and many other companies employ chefs twenty-four hours a day. They often have large budgets. Chefs decide what they want to cook and frequently buy ingredients from local farms. This involves traveling and talking to many different producers, from egg suppliers to herb growers.

▶▶ FOOD FOR THOUGHT ◀◀

Paul Wigsten, produce buyer for the Culinary Institute of America, says that he spends upwards of $750,000 annually buying local fruits, vegetables, eggs, dairy, honey, and meat from thirty Hudson Valley farms, all of which are within thirty-five miles of the Hyde Park, New York, campus. That figure continues to grow each year.

A 1959 Shopping List for the Four Seasons Restaurant

The shopping list for the Four Seasons included thrushes, ortolans, turbots, morels, twenty-two types of olives, and crayfish and wild strawberries from France. There was smoked salmon, Dover sole, and Colchester oysters from England; venison from Norway; grapes, fresh grape leaves, and peaches from Belgium; rabbits, salmon, trout, and Malpeque oysters from Canada; truffles from Italy and France; and Mediterranean fish from Marseille. This represented an astonishing leap in gastronomy at a time when most considered that they had had a great meal if it consisted of a hefty steak, a baked potato, frozen string beans, iceberg lettuce with green goddess dressing, and cheesecake or apple pie for dessert.

▶▶ FOOD FOR THOUGHT ◀◀

Every week, 330 farmers leave their land. As a result, there are now nearly five million fewer farms in the United States than there were in the 1930s.

Of the two million remaining farms, only 565,000 are family operations. Paradoxically, farmers' markets are flourishing.

FOOD JOB: *Farmers' Market Manager*

Here is a dream job for anyone who wants to work both indoors and out. It is a job for any visionary accountant, planner, marketer, lawyer, negotiator, city planner, or politician who is environmentally friendly but a cold-hearted entrepreneur. It's a job for a person who wants to look out for the financial interests of farmers.

Every business needs bones, blood and guts, and willing hands. It is the farmer who fills this role. The manager controls the purse strings, ensuring that there will be a profit at the end of the day when all the bills are paid. The manager copes with the nuts and bolts of zoning, parking, food-safety issues, and each of the myriad details that can be controlled.

For information about the vitally important details of managing a market, check these sites:

FarmersMarketCoalition.org/managerfaqs

FarmersMarketCoalition.org/fmfny-manual

Mass.gov/agr/markets/farmersmarkets/resources_managers.htm

NYFarmersMarket.com/NYFM_Training_Manual.pdf

NourishedKitchen.com/farmers-market-tips

FoothillsFarmersMarket.com

SimplyHired.com/a/salary/search/q-farmers+market+manager

The meaning of the word "fresh" is becoming blurred. Food in the US typically travels between 1,500 and 3,500 miles from field to fork. When a head of lettuce with little nutrient value and high water content grown in the Salinas Valley is shipped more than 3,100 miles to the East Coast, it requires thirty-six times more fossil-fuel energy for transport than it provides in caloric energy when eaten.

Young Farmers Conference: Reviving the Culture of Agriculture

Each December, Stone Barns Center for Food and Agriculture in New York hosts the National Young Farmers Conference, an event which brings together over 300 young and beginning farmers from across the country for intensive workshops, demonstrations, conversations, and networking as part of the Center's Growing Farmers Initiative. The conference is unique in scope and reach, convening thought leaders and creative practitioners in the sustainable agriculture movement with farmers eager for ideas, information, and connection.

The Center's Growing Farmers Initiative trains beginning farmers (10 years experience or less) in resilient, restorative farming techniques and seeks to increase the number of sustainable small and mid-size farms.

It attracts farmers, young and young in spirit, who are eager to be part of a movement with shared values about sustainable agriculture. They are ambitious and innovative. They are both back-to-the-land and high-tech. Feet on the ground, head in the sky, they live simply but want to change the world.

Stone Barns Center (www.stonebarnscenter.org) is a nonprofit working farm and education center with a mission to improve the way America eats and farms. The Center's many programs—its year-round workshops, paid farm apprenticeships, annual National Young Farmers Conference, and Virtual Grange (www.virtualgarage.org)—seeks to equip young farmers with the knowledge, tools, networks and hands-on experience to grow better-tasting, healthier food and become responsible stewards of the land.

Farm-to-Table Internship Opportunity

Following is a real posting for an internship/apprentice position, excerpted from GoodFoodJobs.com. Perhaps it will help inspire you to develop your own program:

> Growing Gardens unites the Boulder County community through urban agricultural projects, such as: The Cultiva Youth Project (Ages 12–19), The Children's Peace Garden (Ages 4–10), Horticultural Therapy (Seniors and People with Disabilities), Fresh Food Families & Fitness, and The Community Gardens (General Public). Growing Gardens' mission is to enrich the lives of our community through sustainable urban agriculture. The Environmental Education Instructor will work in each of our programs.
>
> *Courtesy of Growing Gardens of Boulder, CO*

Farm-to-table-related opportunities are at the top of many popular culinary careers, but there are several paths to these destinations. A little research will reveal the keys needed to open these doors. Use Google to locate the top farm-to-table-related employment opportunities in your area, or perhaps in an area of the country in which you'd like to live.

There are many benefits to internships or employment with a community garden before venturing into the kitchen to cook. Here are just a few, as quoted from the Growing Gardens organization of Portland, Oregon:

- Hands-on experience making a positive impact in the lives of children, teens and adults.
- Friendly, relaxed environment.
- Good experience; develops marketable teaching and group leading skills.

- Classroom training offered through Growing Gardens classes.
- Access to a wide variety of organic seeds and plant starts.
- Share of vegetable production as garden permits.
- Garden is located with easy access to public transportation.
- Monthly stipend of $400.

• •

My Word: Sex and the Single Cow

Let's talk about the birds and the bees.

Farmers have been messing about with Mother Nature since the beginning of time, tinkering with breeding techniques, trying to grow a better ear of corn, chickens that laid more eggs, or cows that produced more milk. (As Sir Oliver St. John once asked, "If a queen bee were crossed with a Friesian bull, would not the land flow with milk and honey?") In many ways, it is such painstaking breeding techniques that have provided us with such an abundance of, not only milk and honey, but a vast array of good things to eat and drink. It certainly isn't chance. For centuries, poultry and animal breeders have been responding to consumer demand for more red meat and white meat (and the other white meat, pork). Modern turkeys' breasts have become so big that they can't get close enough to mate. All are artificially inseminated. Old-fashioned animal husbandry is no longer what it once was. Selling semen from prize bulls has become big business.

We are told that cattle were among the first animals that human beings domesticated. And in fact, the establishment of farms on which plants and animals were bred and contained was the first step in the establishment of modern society. Some researchers believe that organized farming began throughout Europe and Asia roughly 8,500 years ago.

Cloning is the newest tool in the toolbox of progress. What began in 1996 in Scotland with the birth of Dolly the sheep has continued at an accelerated rate. The fact that this research is happening without the same press uproar as it once created doesn't mean it isn't happening.

Jim Greenwood, president of the Biotechnology Industry Organization, characterizes the agricultural benefits of cloning as follows: "Take a steer, prized for the quality of its lean meat, and use a swab to remove one cell from inside its cheek. (Every cell contains an exact copy of an individual's unique DNA sequence.) The DNA is removed from the egg of another cow. Marry them and transplant the 'fertilized' egg into a mother embryo. Wait. A calf is born that is identical to the donor. This is the latest way of transferring the best available genetic qualities from one generation to the next."

Is it safe? Nothing is completely safe, though the US Food and Drug Administration believes that cloning is safe, as does the National Academy of Sciences. For the consumer, however, the safety of cloned livestock (and its milk) is not yet an issue, as it will be ten to fifteen years before it becomes commercially available. After the first cloned calf is born, the next generation will be bred normally, as will the next generation, and the next. It will be several generations down the road before we will be buying the meat.

There are an estimated one hundred million cattle in the United States, and as few as a hundred or two hundred cloned animals. It costs $15,000–$20,000 to produce a clone, so it would be far too costly to eat it. It is used only for breeding stock.

The purpose of animal biotechnology is to improve the health of the animals, to develop more nutritious food, to conserve the environment, and to improve human health. It is important to know that cloning doesn't involve genetic engineering. It is a process of *in vitro* fertilization, a more precise method of breeding than the age-old techniques used to produce thoroughbred horses and purebred dogs and cats.

Mark E. Westhusin, director of the Reproductive Sciences Laboratory at Texas A&M's College of Veterinary Medicine, says that cloning "is just an assisted reproductive technology. We're not trying to resurrect animals or get deceased animals back." As Dr. Larisa Rudenko, director of an Animal Biotechnology Interdisciplinary Group at the FDA, points out, "Clones are biological copies of normal animals." She compares them to identical twins born a generation apart.

Why bother, you might ask? We've got plenty of meat and too much milk. Indeed, but what about developing countries that could benefit mightily from disease-resistant cattle that efficiently convert smaller quantities of feed into food for the hungry? If we know how to improve the efficiency of animal metabolism and its ability to convert food into meat and milk, should we utilize this knowledge? If we can preserve our forests, instead of cutting them down to increase the acreage for grazing cattle, should we use our knowledge? If we can improve the nutrient profiles of milk and meat, should we use this knowledge? If we could prevent ground-water contamination by breeding enviro-pigs with 30–40 percent less phosphorus in their waste (and less toxic manure) should we support these new technologies? Some say no.

After all, it took ages to accept that the fact pasteurization of milk reduces the incidence of tuberculosis. We believe what we want to believe.

There are many courses offered at universities and community colleges for those interested in the development of new technologies on the farm.

• •

▶▶ FOOD FOR THOUGHT ◀◀

The European Society of Human Reproduction and Embryology reports that approximately 350,000 babies conceived in petri dishes are now *born* every year, adding to a grand total of more than five million live babies worldwide since the birth of the first human embryo fertilized in vitro in 1978.

FOOD JOB: *Apple Farmer*

They say that Adam and Eve were the only couple truly made for each other, but then there was that unfortunate misunderstanding about the apple in the Garden of Eden. Now, apples grow throughout the world, in every temperate climate. We get misty-eyed about apple pie. And while we may say that a thing is "as American as apple pie," truth be told, way back in 1590, Robert Green, an English poet, whispered to his beloved, "Thy breath is like the steame of apple pyes."

Apples are similar to human beings. They have the same mentality as we do about incest. Nature has made the reproductive organs from both the male and female mature at different times. In essence, an apple cannot reproduce with itself. It must find another breed of apple to mate with. Which is why apples have so many varieties.

Apple Facts

In 2010, an Italian-led consortium announced that they had decoded the complete genome of the tree producing the golden delicious variety of apple. It had about 57,000 genes—the highest number of any plant studied to date—and more genes than the human genome (which has about 30,000).

Apples are grown commercially to be precisely three inches in diameter. This is the optimum size that can be stacked within a square foot of supermarket display space.

Scientists have bred a new apple that doesn't discolor when it is cut.

Apples are eaten with honey at the Jewish New Year of Rosh Hashanah to symbolize a sweet new year.

Cornell University offers a degree course in pomology (the study of apples).

Twenty-eight professors and alumni from Cornell have received Nobel prizes. None were granted for their apple pies.

FOOD JOB: *Beekeeper*

Experts are at a loss to account for what the *Economist* magazine called the "big buzz off." Undeniably, honey bees are vanishing at an alarming rate. This is a deadly serious matter. One third of our food comes from pollinated crops. Three-quarters of all flowering plants rely on insects, bees, and other creatures, large and small, to carry pollen from male to female plants. The reproduction of almost all of our fruits, vegetables, and nuts relies on this.

Without bees there would be little beef to eat; bees are needed to pollinate the alfalfa and clover that is used for cattle feed. Without bees, there wouldn't any ketchup for our burgers or mustard for our hot dogs, either; bees pollinate tomato and mustard plants. The world as we know it is teetering on the brink. As Hannah Nordhaus of *High Country News* points out, "Bees are the glue that hold agriculture together." Just one example: 580,000 acres of almonds flower simultaneously in California's Central Valley. Without bees to pollinate the crop, the yield would be barely forty pounds of almonds instead of the 2,400 pounds now harvested thanks entirely to the buzzing of innumerable bees. Almond Joy indeed.

▸▸ FOOD FOR THOUGHT ◂◂

The average worker bee flies fifteen miles an hour and produces one-twelfth of a teaspoon of honey during its entire lifetime.

To produce a pound of honey, a bee colony will visit two million flowers and fly 55,000 miles.

The *Obama Foodorama* blog posted some interesting news on its site: "The White House Beehive, the first to ever be on the grounds, has been expanded from when it was first installed on the south lawn beside First Lady Michelle Obama's kitchen garden in 2009. More bee boxes have been added, to increase the output of honey. In 2011, the hive produced 243 pounds of honey, up from 164 pounds in 2010 and 124 pounds in 2009. (Yes, there is an official Beekeeper in Chief. His name is Charlie Brandts. He is a sweet guy.)"

If the bees disappeared from the surface of the globe then man would only have four years of life left. No more bees, no more pollination, no more plants, no more animals, no more man.

—Albert Einstein

Alarm Bells Ring

Since the first whispers of the crisis began to appear in November 2006, twenty-four states have reported up to 90 percent plunges in bee populations. Echoes of similar losses have been heard in several European countries. No one knows for sure what's going on. Are the bees suffering from something they ate? Could blight, a parasite, or a deadly mite cause the fatalities? Is blame to be laid on pesticides, ringing mobile phones, or whirling wind turbines that disorient the bees?

Two things are infinite: the universe and human stupidity; and I'm not sure about the universe.

—Unknown

The Flight of the Bumble Bee

A beekeeper may own up to 70,000 hives. Even an average-sized beekeeping operation may have 13,000 hives holding close to 300 million bees. These specialists say that they've lost nearly half or even more of their bee population. Worker bees are wandering off and disappearing, like drunken drones. They seem to have lost their ability to navigate.

When a hive needs food, a scout bee is sent to look for it. When she returns, she performs a dance that is effectively a set of directions pointing the way to the pollen source.

Follower bees in the hive read these instructions with their antennae. After millions of years, this honeybee language is so refined that the follower bees can interpret the scout's message flawlessly, even if the conditions of their flight aren't exactly those of the reenacted flight. For example, the scout bee conveys direction in terms of the position of the sun. As that changes, the follower bees adjust the directions.

They do the same for wind and distance, which the scout expresses in terms of energy (honey) needed to get to the food source. Scientists have even discovered that if the follower bee is younger than the scout, she knows that she will need less fuel to reach the nectar.

Solutions in Science

Entomologists have unraveled the bee language by gluing a miniature bar-code device onto the backs of bees. The standard bar code can differentiate between as many as a million items, but postage-stamp size is far too big and heavy to suit a bee. So apiarists turned to a scanner engineer, who developed a bee bar code just a tenth of an inch wide. A scanner installed at the entrance to the hive monitors the bees' comings and goings and reports on the vital role that bees play in pollinating crops.

FOOD JOB: *Human Plant-Pollinator*

If a solution to the bee crisis is not soon discovered, we may have to resort to the methods of the *palmeros*. Sincc the date palm's male and female flowers grow on separate trees, and since the female flower emits no scent to attract bees, palmeros, the elite workers of the date industry, climb up the six-foot-high male trees to collect pollen. Each male tree produces enough pollen for forty-nine female trees. The palmeros then climb to the tops of the female trees, carefully blow the pollen onto the pods, and slip a paper bag over each to generate heat and ensure that the precious pollen isn't blown away.

▶▶ FOOD FOR THOUGHT ◀◀

The Beekeepers Association says that fruit growers usually pay from between thirty to forty dollars to have a hive placed among their plants in the spring, with the hive's owner keeping the honey. Now the price has risen to one hundred dollars a hive. With one hive required for each acre of almond trees, that can add up fast. No wonder many are taking up beekeeping as a hobby. Fortunate are those who can sell their honey at farmers' markets, retail stores, and online.

FOOD JOB: *Garlic Grower*

Farmers sometimes make fortunes when they specialize in a single crop, garlic for example. We have been fascinated with the powers of garlic, pretty much forever:

- Garlic was included in the rations of Roman soldiers, who chewed it before battle with the hope that it would give them courage (and perhaps scare off their enemies?).
- The philosopher Pliny claimed that garlic prevented madness, repelled snakes, and could counteract the power of the devil.

- Indonesians believed that garlic had the power to enable them to communicate with the dead.
- Western superstitions, heavily influenced by Bram Stoker's 1897 novel *Dracula*, suppose that garlic wards off vampires.
- Louis Pasteur first described the antibacterial effect of garlic and onion juices… Garlic is effective even against antibiotic-resistant strains.

My final considered judgment is that the hardy garlic bulb blesses and ennobles everything it touches, with the possible exception, ice cream and pie.

—Angelo Pellegrini, *The Unprejudiced Palate: Thoughts on Food and the Good Life*

FOOD JOB: *Mushroom Farmer*

Kendall Morrison rescues dead oak logs. He bores inch-deep holes in them, in which he plants shiitake mushroom spawn. (He orders the spawn online from Fungi Perfecti at Fungi.com.) Morrison claims to harvest about a pound of mushrooms per log. (No word on the length of the log.) Profits are mushrooming. Kits are freely available, and you can even grow mushrooms in your basement.

►► FOOD FOR THOUGHT ◄◄

Dried mushrooms such as morels sell steadily (though not briskly). Prices vary from high to very high. Thieves may be better off going for the fungi and forgetting about the cash register.

FOOD JOB: *Plant Scientist*

The scientists and engineers who have walked into our kitchen have gone out to fields too. Have you noticed that berries are the only crop that has their seeds on the surface? All other plants have them on the inside, except seedless grapes, which have given up their seeds completely. Rumor has it that growers are trying to producc "pitless" avocadoes.

It is not known whether consumers are demanding peppers in a rainbow of colors or why it became necessary to grow a black tomato, but where there's a will there almost always is a way.

FOOD JOB: *Seed Scientist*

Plants and their pollinators are mutually dependent, and each cannot survive without the other. Every flower vies for the attention of its pollinators by developing unique colors and scents. Insecticides are formulated to target only specific, harmful species.

RARE FOOD JOB: *Truffle Farmer*

As Ted Burnham has written in *The Salt*, NPR's food blog:

> "As orchards go, truffle orchards are upside-down and backwards." So says Tom Michaels, owner of Tennessee Truffles. "The magic," he says, "happens not on the branches of oak and hazel trees, but beneath them, where a richly flavored mushroom sprouts from fungal colonies laced around the trees' roots. This cultivated variety is the black périgord truffle, or *Tuber melanosporum.*
>
> These truffles are notoriously hard to farm, even in France, where périgords originate. Now, in the rolling hills and clay soils of eastern Tennessee and western North Carolina, a growing

number of farmers are hoping to establish southern Appalachia as the new truffle capital of the world.

Michaels says he was the first American to grow périgords commercially in 2007, from trees inoculated with *melanosporum* fungus using a relatively new French technique. He claims that about 200 orchards are now in development in the US, but because it takes years before truffles appear, few are producing yet. "The next few years are the moment of truth" for the burgeoning industry," he says.

▸▸ FOOD FOR THOUGHT ◂◂

There are an estimated 6,000 professional truffle hunters in the world. They are assisted in their work by trained dogs and pregnant pigs. The specific gene that attracts a pregnant pig has been identified: the identical gene has been recognized in male underarm sweat.

FISH

FOOD JOB: *Caviar Producer*

Interestingly, the state of Idaho has become a center for the production of caviar. Farm raised sturgeon are cultivated in climate-controlled conditions that are a pure reflection of a Russian winter. The female reaches maturity when she reaches her fifth birthday. Her life expectancy in captivity is fifty years. Every eighteen months, she is "milked" and relieved of a little over one pound of eggs—caviar!

Caviar is made by extracting the roe sac from the fish. The eggs are separated, washed, drained, salted, and shaken in fine sieves to dry them. They are then packed in specially made tins and stored at, or slightly below, freezing.

FOOD JOB: *Caviar Connoisseur*

Types of Caviar

Beluga is the most highly prized and highly priced caviar, and has the largest eggs. It comes from the beluga sturgeon, which lives in the Caspian Sea.

Osetra and sevruga both come from smaller sturgeon than the beluga. Their eggs are smaller, too, but they are preferred by some caviar connoisseurs.

Malassol caviar may come from either the beluga, osetra, or sevruga sturgeon. The word itself, translated from the Russian, means "lightly salted" and usually designates a shipper's highest grade of caviar.

Salmon (red) caviar of superb quality is processed in Alaska, mostly by Japanese workers. The bulk of the supply is shipped to Japan, where it is held in high esteem.

Whitefish (golden) caviar, comes mostly from the Great Lakes, it was hugely popular until we realized that it tastes of more or less nothing at all.

Lumpfish caviar is comprised of hard little eggs whose black dye weeps, like mascara after a good cry.

> *There is more simplicity in the man who eats caviar on impulse than in the man who eats grape-nuts on principle.*
>
> —G. K. Chesterton, *Heretics*

A few words on caviar from Ludwig Bemelmans, a prince among food writers:

> Caviar is to dining what a sable coat is to a girl in evening dress. As a young man I had a cozy picture about caviar production. In my mind's eye I saw the broad mouth of a river, which I comfortably called the Malassol; in it a lot of big Russkies were singing

> boat songs and wading and carefully lifting immense sturgeons out of the water while relieving them gently of their eggs with a soft, sluicy swish and putting them back again, like milked cows let out to pasture.

How elegant the process was, in his mind, how civilized. Not a bit like the reality. After the collapse of the Soviet Union, everyone began to fight with everyone else. Sturgeon became endangered as a result of illegal poaching, black-market sales, water pollution, and dams. The sturgeon population plummeted 99 percent. Russia imposed an export ban, and the United States and Europe instituted a compulsory import ban, in hopes that the species would eventually recover.

▶▶ FOOD FOR THOUGHT ◀◀

- Idaho is known as the land of potatoes, but with its flourishing fish farms, perhaps the state will consider changing its motto to "Land of fish and chips."
- In addition to the United States and Russia, caviar is produced in China, the United Arab Emirates, Spain, and Finland, among other places.
- The FDA allows only salted sturgeon roe to be sold as caviar. Others must prefix the name—for example, salmon caviar, lumpfish caviar, or whitefish caviar.
- The wholesale price of caviar is approximately $600 a pound.

Recipe for Success: Something Fishy

Born in Bremgarten near Zurich, Albert Stockli took over housekeeping after his mother's death, when he was nine years old. His education was absorbed from an uncle, who was a chef in a hotel. Albert soaked up knowledge, and he grew in every way. By the time he was seventeen, he was well over six feet, a height extended at least another foot by the ever-present white toque that, it was rumored, he wore to bed and bath.

He rose to become the director of the Restaurant Associates company and its president's, Joe Baum's, nurtured genius. For the Forum of the Twelve Caesars restaurant, he invented such dishes as Flaming Snow Mountain, which Joe insisted on setting on fire because, as he wryly pointed out, "It doesn't hurt the food much, and you can charge an extra buck for the show."

Albert had an irascible nature, and when he demanded fresh, fresh was what he got. Fish were delivered to his Stonehenge Inn and Restaurant, in Connecticut, literally at dawn. The trout, for his dish *la truite au bleu*, were delivered live. (To prepare, stun the trout with a single blow on the back of the fish's neck. Clean and gut thoroughly, leaving on its head and tail, and place in cold water. Bring to a gentle simmer. The trout will curl, cradling its tail in its mouth—and will turn blue. Serve with a beurre blanc sauce.)

Albert bought Stonehenge with his then partner, Leon Lianides, after "retiring" in a huff following a rip-roaring "discussion" with Joe Baum in the dining room of the Four Seasons, shortly after the last guest had left.

Albert claimed to the end that he preferred living in the country, where he could yodel whenever he wanted to. (He was, after all, a native of Switzerland.)

He did things his way, ritualistically. Early each morning, dressed in his whites, wearing his tall toque, he strode through the kitchen into the adjoining garden to gather bouquets of herbs, which he laid out in neat bunches along the length of the chopping block. Next, he arranged one of each type of fish in military formation, heads forward, and tails to the rear.

Then the work began. Stooping over his fish, he confronted them, eyeball to gleaming eyeball. Hands bent on chubby knees, he smelled each fish and each herb. Then, slowly and thoughtfully, he selected one herb from this bunch and one from that and chopped them into myriads of combinations. He put a little tarragon in this group, a touch of sorrel in another, and a few curls of parsley here and there. The gentle, soothing rhythm of chopping continued until each herb was so fine it could dance an arabesque on the tip of his knife. Each combination of herbs was then matched to each fish, until the parade was flanked with small mounds of fragrance.

Then the inspection began again. The chef picked up the first fish in line, rubbed a pinch of herbs onto its shiny skin, sniffed it delicately, smiled smugly to himself, wiped his hands on his clean white apron, and proceed to the next. By the time he reached the end of the line, he was supremely content. His apron was green with sweet-smelling herbs and ever-so-slightly fishy.

One memorable night, the youngest cook stole the master's apron, which by now had become a historical record of the day's activities. He dropped the flavored apron into a broth and simmered it gently for twenty minutes. The result was a gloriously nuanced fish soup.

Albert yodeled.

FOOD JOB: *Fish Farmer*

A well-managed farm is a place where the advantages of aquaculture can be most clearly seen.

At fish farms, experts decide when the fish have reached the desirable size and weight. At that precise moment, thousands of identical fish are channeled into a filleting factory, where they are cleaned and sent on their way to market. The fish farmers can go home for lunch and never need to invest in a sou'wester or even a pair of waterproof boots. And the fish are delivered, clean and safe to eat, on a predictable schedule and at a predictable price.

Fish farming is one the world's fastest-growing businesses. Annual global sales are already approaching the $78 billion mark and will continue to escalate as the stocks of wild fish decline. Close to a quarter of the entire world supply of fish now comes from aquacultured sources, and the percentage increases every year driven by the urgent need to provide affordable protein to feed the growing world population.

Think of aquaculture as the aquatic counterpart to agriculture. Culturally, we have evolved from hunter-gatherers to farmers, and just as we decided to cultivate food rather than venture out for wild game, a parallel can be drawn here with those who farm fish rather than brave stormy seas in search of wild ones.

An added bonus of fish farming is that each species is raised separately, without needlessly catching and destroying other unwanted species.

> *If nothing prevented hatching of every egg from every cod it would take three years to fill the sea and you would be able to walk across the Atlantic dry shod on the backs of the fish.*
>
> —Alexandre Dumas

Gone Fishing

Overfishing is a global crisis. Forty-mile-long drift nets were banned—and replaced with eighty-mile lines baited with 1,000 hooks. Schools of fish are located using GPS technology, radio beacons, strobe lights, and radar. The lines are then dropped to a depth of a mile using anchors.

Fish are caught faster than they can reproduce. Too many boats, many of them subsidized by governments, are chasing too few fish.

They are also capturing and killing the juveniles of commercially important fish through what is known as "by-catch." This is like having flocks of chicken and throwing all the little chicks to the wolves.

We are eating our golden geese and failing to invest in an abundant fish supply for the future.

Recommended Books

Song for the Blue Ocean: Encounters Along the World's Coasts and Beneath the Seas by Carl Safina

Four Fish: The Future of the Last Wild Food by Paul Greenberg

Cod: A Biography of the Fish that Changed the World by Mark Kurlansky

►► FOOD FOR THOUGHT ◄◄

- Fish farming has been practiced in China for an estimated 4,000 to 8,000 years.
- Ken Stier, writing in *Time* magazine, estimates that "close to 40 percent of the seafood we eat nowadays comes from aquaculture." He continues, saying: "The $78 billion industry has grown nine percent a year since 1975, making it the fastest-growing food group, and global demand has doubled since that time."

I know human beings and fish can coexist peacefully.

—George W. Bush

►► FOOD FOR THOUGHT ◄◄

- Close to three-quarters of the world's commercially important fish are now overexploited or depleted.

- Salmon is now farmed in nearly every country that has a cold, deep-water coastline. Half of the salmon eaten in the United States comes from fish farms.
- More workers die at sea than in coal mines.

GETTING STARTED IN FISH FARMING

Entry-level positions at fish farms involve assisting with the growing and cultivation of the fish and the maintenance of fish farm premises and equipment.

Fish farm hands may be employed in either fin fish farming or shellfish farming. Employees usually work outside, either on or in the water or at shore-based facilities located in sheltered waters. Some employers also require a diving qualification and/or a license to operate a barge. It is not a requirement to be able to swim.

Sounding the Alarm

In her book *Diet for a Small Planet*, Frances Moore Lappe argues that grain-fed cattle are essentially "reverse protein factories"—they require many pounds of plant protein to produce one pound of flesh. Now, there is a similar dynamic in the global aquaculture industry as it strains to satisfy consumers' voracious appetites for carnivorous, top-of-the-food-chain fish such as salmon and tuna.

▶▶ FOOD FOR THOUGHT ◀◀

In the late nineteenth century, one hundred million pounds of oysters (more than 45,000 metric tons) were harvested from the Chesapeake Bay. Today the haul is fewer than 250,000 pounds.

FOOD JOB: *Crab Fisherman*

To be a crab fisherman in Alaska, you have to have a love of hard, physical, outdoor work. And it helps to have an entrepreneurial spirit—or the soul of a gambler. A crew of four or five crab fishermen signs on for a ten-day voyage, after which each receives a percentage of the take, when boat expenses have been paid. Using this system, a fisherman can earn anywhere from a little in six months to a lot in a week depending on the catch. For more information, visit: www.Alaskafishingjobs.com and www.alaskajobfinder.com.

FOOD JOB: *Water Expert*

Nearly half of the world's population is facing a water shortage. More than 97 percent of all the water on planet earth is seawater. Less than 1 percent of the supply of fresh water is available for human use. Seventy percent of all the water used in the United States is used for irrigation. More than half is wasted and never reaches the crops.

Water Works

Here's some astonishing news: A small town in Australia has voted to get rid of water. Bottled water, that is. The riled-up community has declared that all the bottled water, on all the shelves, in all the places that it is sold, has got to go.

This declaration may be the beginning of another great rethinking of our priorities. What's starting as a tiny trickle could become a tidal wave, a just-in-time return to common sense. The cause of getting rid of plastic bags began much like this, with a few voices and several fingers pointing to its environmental impact.

My Word: Water

Why should anyone be surprised to learn that the latest new culinary specialist is the so-called "water sommelier"—or glacéau—whose job entails pairing the right bottled water with a given dish? This is surely among the most curious of all food fads.

▶▶ FOOD FOR THOUGHT ◀◀

In a number of small communities in the mountains of Chile and Ecuador, and in the Middle East, frequent dense fogs provide a unique way of obtaining clean water. The fog-water collectors resemble oversized volley ball nets and are made of polypropylene mesh. Each net is stretched between two posts and is suspended a few feet from the ground. As fog passes through it, beads of water form on the mesh and gradually drip down, joining with other drops like water on a windowpane. Eventually, the drops fall into gutters placed beneath the nets, which drain into a reservoir. From there, a pipeline carries the water down the hillside. Farmers use the water for irrigating crops and making deserts bloom.

▶▶ FOOD FOR THOUGHT ◀◀

The United Nations is playing a vital role—through the International Law Commission's Committee on Natural Resources—in developing guidelines for shared watercourses. One of the most promising developments is the trade of "virtual water," which basically means the trading of water as a staple product to water-scarce regions. The World Bank, too, is calling for more appropriate water pricing.

★ RARE FOOD JOB: *Coffee Magnate*

Robert Stiller, founder, president, and CEO of Green Mountain Coffee Roasters, says, "Coffee farming has been passed on through generations of families. It is not surprising that the tough life is driving people to abandon their crops for work in the cities. To insure high-quality beans, Stiller's company has supported producer-initiated projects to improve the quality of life in farming communities. He supports organizations like Coffee Kids, Grounds for Health, and the Rainforest Alliance. Green Mountain Coffee Roasters offers a line of certified organic and Fair Trade coffees.

▶▶ FOOD FOR THOUGHT ◀◀

Coffee, chocolate, and vanilla are three varieties of seeds consumed by people all over the world. These crops are remarkably similar in the location of their cultivation and processing. All three have been prized since ancient times:

- Each is grown within twenty degrees north and south of the equator.
- Each needs shade from overgrowth, which tends to be located in remote areas of the forests.
- Eighty percent of these crops are grown by small farmers, whose families have been farming for many generations.
- All require intensive manual labor; they are hand picked at perfect ripeness, sorted, fermented, and then dried.
- Almost all are grown organically, because few farmers have the resources to buy fertilizers or pesticides.
- Few small farmers can afford to pay the fees to obtain organic certification.

Good coffee should be black like the devil, hot like hell, and sweet like a kiss.

—Charles Maurice de Talleyrand

THE FAIR-TRADE LABEL

by Fareez Dossani

The fair-trade certification indicates that in the developing world, farmers of crops like coffee, cocoa, fruit, and to a lesser extent, vegetables, are treated well and paid fairly.

Workers are joining co-ops that help growers get higher prices for their beans if they meet certain environmental and other requirements. These are set by inspectors, who establish that the certification standards are met. To earn certification, growers must show that they are protecting the environment and investing in community projects.

In the past, workers have cut trees and switched to cattle ranching or growing corn to make more money. That is changing now that coffee crops can bring in higher prices and now that forests are under greater protection. The most important element of fair-trade policy is that it sets a fixed price for coffee, which holds even when the market fluctuates.

The prices paid for these commodities both at the wholesale and consumer levels, are higher than those fetched by their uncertified equivalents.

There is increasing pressure on large companies from green and labor interests to adopt fair-trade practices. Some major food companies have made the adoption official. These include Starbucks, McDonald's, Dunkin' Donuts, and Kraft subsidiary Maxwell House Coffee, the second largest buyer of coffee.

The rush to certify coffee is now drawing an expanding list of players, including giant plantations and multinational traders, something that seemed unimaginable just a few years ago.

Fareez Dossani was a student at the Culinary Institute of America.

On bended knee, the black slaves of the Ambassador, arrayed in the most gorgeous Oriental costumes served the choicest mocha coffee in tiny cups of egg-shell porcelain, hot strong and fragrant, poured out in saucers of gold and silver, placed on embroidered silk doilies fringed with gold bullion, to the grand dames, who fluttered their faces with many grimaces, bending their piquant faces, rouged, powdered and patched, over the new and steaming beverage.

—Isaac d'Israeli on the popularity of coffee in France, *Curiosities of Literature*, 1817

▸▸ FOOD FOR THOUGHT ◂◂

Howard Schultz, founder and CEO of Starbucks Coffee, recalls that he was once incredulously asked, "You mean you're going to sell *coffee* for a dollar in a *paper cup*?"

Recommended Book

Onward: How Starbucks Fought for Its Life Without Losing Its Soul by Howard Schultz and Joanne Gordon

▸▸ FOOD FOR THOUGHT ◂◂

Sumatran coffee plantation workers have tracked a discerning, catlike creature, the civet, which, in the wild, is believed to eat only the most flavorful coffee beans. What the animal excretes ultimately becomes *kopi luwak* coffee, the world's rarest and most expensive coffee, costing, most recently, $450 a pound. (It is not customarily served in a paper cup.)

FOOD JOB: *Forager*

The chef's art of sourcing ingredients and of having them grown or produced to exacting specifications began in Manhattan at the Four Seasons restaurant in 1959. Later, chef Larry Forgione took up the mantle at the River Café and An American Place, as did Alice Waters at Chez Panisse in Berkeley, California, who partnered with her farmer friend, Tom Chino. He brought her magical vegetables in rainbows of never-before-seen color.

They say that this idea of foraging—as practiced by farmers, beekeepers, herbalists, wild-game enthusiasts, artisanal bacon and fish smokers, maple syrup tappers, and dedicated bread bakers—is something new. What they say is not exactly true. Since the time of the Neanderthals, and undoubtedly, even earlier, our ancient ancestors foraged for food. They were prepared to eat almost anything that didn't eat them first.

> *I believe if ever I had to practice cannibalism, I might manage if there was enough tarragon around.*
>
> —James Beard

▶▶ FOOD FOR THOUGHT ◀◀

Generally speaking, it is one thing to kill one's sworn enemy, but it is considered awfully bad manners to eat him. Further research reveals that even cannibals shrink from eating women. It is men only in this "dog eat dog world."

Living off the Land

In a sense, all restaurant chefs are foragers. They explore; they taste; and, sometimes, they commission farmers to grow crops according to very specific guidelines. (As a practical matter, producers must be located relatively closely to buyers, or the cost of delivery becomes prohibitive.)

Here's a food job for you if you have a small truck. You could travel from farm to farm, picking up the harvest and delivering it (you guessed) right from farm to table.

FOOD JOB: *Cheese Maker*

It's fair to say that the New American Cuisine was based on charismatic goat cheese. We are still eating our way through mountains of it. It is served warm, with a flourish of baby lettuces. It is rolled in fruitwood ash and floated upon sea-green virgin olive oil. It is sliced into medallions and garnished with nasturtium petals. Goat cheese is turning up in omelets. It is topping fancy pizzas. It is crumbled into pricey salads and molded onto crisp baguette slices to accompany ultra-cool chardonnays and fumé blancs.

It is not as though these darlings of the ultra-chic are particularly good for us. A single ounce of fresh goat cheese is chocablock with calories (eighty-two), and yet there is mounting evidence of our new enthusiasm for goat's milk yogurt, goat's milk ice cream, goat's milk fudge, and, astonishingly, even goat's milk itself.

Recipe for Success: Steven Jenkins, Le Grand Fromage

I'm sixty-one years old. I've lived in New York City for thirty-nine years, since 1973, when I was just a twenty-two-year-old kid. In the late summer of 1975, I got a much-needed job—in a cheese shop, at 92nd street and Madison Avenue. It could have been a pet shop in Greenwich Village, an East Side antique shop owned by some oddball, or another kite store, such as the one not far away at which I had been working previously. I didn't care. Cheese had nothing to do with it. I had decided that I liked getting a regular paycheck and having something to do all day, so I resolved to do my very best to hold the job and pay the rent on my studio apartment, and not be a burden on my then girlfriend (to whom I have now been married for thirty years).

I became a *maître fromager.* That is, in 1980, I became the first French-certified, practicing master cheesemonger in North America. For all the years since then, I've been up to my elbows and eyeballs in cheese and cheese-related substances. It is said that I know whereof I speak. Last year, I was given a lifetime achievement award by the American Cheese Society. I belabor my qualifications to state the following: Liz Thorpe has written *The Cheese Chronicles*, a book about American cheese, and it is the best book about cheese you'll ever read. I recommend it highly.

—*Steven Jenkins*

Recommended Book

Cheese Primer by Steven Jenkins

CHAPTER 9

education

Lots of people limit their possibilities by giving up easily. Never tell yourself this is too much for me. It's no use. I can't go on. If you do you're licked, and by your own thinking too. Keep believing and keep on keeping on.

—NORMAN VINCENT PEALE

Chef Instructors

Culinary Librarian

Educator

Food-Writing Teacher

Front-of-House Trainer

Mentor

Recruiter

Scholar

Union Organizer

FOOD JOB: *Chef Instructors*

CHEF INSTRUCTORS AT cooking schools are responsible for training students and for providing continuing education for experienced working chefs. Teachers provide practical, hands-on instruction, not only in cooking, but also in purchasing, cost control, budgeting, menu development, product utilization, time management, and in ethics and professionalism. The job entails developing curricula, writing lesson plans, grading homework and class assignments, administrating examinations, and evaluating students' performances.

Classically trained chef instructors draw from their own practical experience to teach others. A minimum of five years' experience working as an executive chef in a restaurant kitchen, bakery, catering company, or other branch of the hospitality industry is usually a condition of employment. As part of the interview process, prospective instructors may be asked to prepare several dishes and to demonstrate their teaching abilities. They may have no formal academic qualifications, although people entering the field now generally do.

A successful chef instructor must be able to solve problems and maintain discipline in the classroom. As with all teachers, chef instructors acknowledge that classes vary, one from another. A significant indication of instructor competencc lies in the ability to transform the bad or bruised apples into polished chefs, not just to make the already shiny ones shinier. In other words, a teacher combines the attributes of saintliness with the benign affection of motherhood.

THE ACADEMICS

The academic sector is among the fastest growing areas of culinary education. Many professional schools are offering classes in everything from hospitality law, finance, and economics, to interpersonal communications, food culture, and languages.

Students can learn a great deal about the domestic and political lives of nations by studying the food heritage to which they feel viscerally connected. (I grew up in England and Scotland, where—it is said—there are only three vegetables, and two of them are Brussels sprouts. It is also said that France is a nation of one religion and a hundred cheeses. Britain has a hundred religions and one cheese: Stilton.)

WHAT IS GASTRONOMY?

Gastronomy is among the newest and (to my mind, the most fascinating) subjects that have lately gained interest both among students and teachers. But what is gastronomy?

The Pioneers of Gastronomy

Jacques Pépin was just thirteen when he began his culinary apprenticeship. Surely he couldn't have imagined then that he would achieve such fame as a chef, television star, and writer. His acclaimed books *La Technique* and *La Methode* describe the principles of culinary technique and artistry and have earned him a Lifetime Achievement Award. This is an honor bestowed each year on an author whose contributions to food literature have had a substantial and enduring impact on the American kitchen.

Jacques is not only a beloved teacher but also a dedicated student. He studied at Columbia University, where, in 1972, he was awarded an MA degree in eighteenth-century French literature. His résumé lists many accomplishments, but perhaps his enduring legacy will be as a founder of Boston University's master's program in gastronomy.

Darra Goldstein didn't study gastronomy, though she is the founder of *Gastronomica: The Journal of Food and Culture*. She earned a PhD in Slavic languages and literature from Stanford University, and then became a restaurant consultant, cookbook author, and curator of an exhibition at the Smithsonian's national design museum called *Feeding Desire: Design and the Tools of the Table*. I mention her many qualifications in order to underscore the fact that she is also a professor at Williams College. She teaches Russian through the prism of that country's literature, culture, art, food, and drink.

The late Alan Dundes was professor of anthropology and folklore at the University of California, Berkeley, where, according to his obituary, "He gained an international reputation for his Freudian deconstruction (and reconstruction) of everything from fairy tales to football to the Book of Genesis." He and his devoted students believe that food and eating are serious subjects that deal with the essence of life. "Cultures are defined by their food customs," he said. His students studied the allure of violent sports, holiday traditions, and even the mystique of the vampire.

Clearly, the material for gastronomy classes varies widely (and wildly), and is subject to interpretation by each instructor. A writer from the *New York Times* reported on a class that was delving into the importance of Friday night pizza parties for parent-child bonding and discussions. Other courses delve into such questions as, "Why are Jewish immigrants from Eastern Europe drawn to Chinese restaurants for Sunday supper?"

For one instructor, gastronomy means an in-depth study of classical French culinary traditions: nouvelle cuisine, modern and postmodern cuisine, and recently and soon-to-be deceased trail-blazing French chefs. Another teacher peers into the ethics of food production, scrutinizes the protocols of fine dining, and explores and speculates on the evolving role of the contemporary chef. Yet another lecturer ponders the phenomena of the biggest days of the food year: Thanksgiving Day dinner and Super Bowl Sunday.

Gastronomy Comes of Age

Participants at a conference at the New School in New York City, dissected the complex interrelationships between people and their food in the following manner:

> What we eat and why we choose the foods that make up our daily diets; the ceremonies that surround food; how it underscores our sameness and differences; its mythic and symbolic importance; the joy of plenty; the fear of famine and deprivation—all are occasions for reflections on the human condition. Why do we tolerate the prevalence of widespread hunger in a world of abundance? What roles do culturally determined food preferences or the power of science, politics, or global trade play in determining who will be well fed and who will starve?

Clearly, culinary education is no longer limited to peas, beans, and carrots.

FOOD BECOMES THE FOCUS OF INTERDISCIPLINARY LEARNING

The evening meal offers us a unique opportunity to learn about our past, present, and future. Imagine a menu consisting of Malpeque oysters garnished with sevruga caviar followed by roast beef, or Chilean sea bass in a ginger-saffron broth. The salad course is locally grown, organic mixed greens followed by a cheese platter and for dessert, flourless chocolate cake. One dinner can be the framework for discussing the history of oysters, trade issues involving the banning of imported caviar, carnivorous and vegetarian diets, the role of chefs in boycotting endangered fish, or the discovery of fire and its role in the evolution of the human race. The chocolate cake for dessert provides an opportunity to talk about food fads and trends—and there is still time to talk about fair-trade issues as they relate to tea and coffee or the impact of stock-market gyrations on reservations at uptown restaurants.

Then there are the politics of organic farming and GMOs to consider, along with the ecclesiastical symbolism of olive oil, the history of the spice trade in general, and salt and pepper in particular.

Here too is an opportunity to talk about the physiology of taste and the long-term effects of chronic hunger. We could then dwell on the economics and politics of obesity and the impending water crisis. This could lead to an investigation of tipping, of the slow food movement, or of our affection for goat cheese versus our rejection of goat meat.

MASTER OF LIBERAL ARTS IN GASTRONOMY

Here's some information from Boston University web site:

> Co-founded by Jacques Pépin and Julia Child, the Master of Liberal Arts (MLA) in Gastronomy is a unique, multidisciplinary program that encompasses the arts, the humanities, and the natural and social sciences. Students in the program examine the role of food in historical and contemporary societies from a variety of perspectives—gaining a holistic view of the impact of food, food science, and nutrition on world civilization.
>
> The Gastronomy Program promotes scholarship about food by drawing from the diverse resources and expertise of a variety of Boston University faculty members, academic departments, visiting faculty, and industry professionals. The program offers

> special emphasis on experiential learning and sensory training through hands-on culinary arts laboratories and wine studies courses. The interplay of reading, research, and writing about food—as well as exploring food through the senses—offers exceptional range and depth to food studies at Boston University.

The education of those interested in food bears little resemblance to the apprenticeship system of bygone days, though it still exists, as every culinary student who has spent several months as an unpaid extern will agree. Advanced degrees in food studies are all the rage.

Success Story: An Adventure Leads to a Life as a Teacher

I recently met an interesting woman named Gina Stipo. She told me of her culinary adventure and the evolution of her career. Her story began with a trip to Italy. Well … let me ask Gina to tell you her story in her own words:

> About ten years ago, I was driving down a two-lane road through some of the most beautiful scenery in Tuscany. It was a road I knew well, for I'd driven it every day over the past two years. It led from the small rural town where I live to the medieval city of Siena. Looking at the golden rays of the setting sun pouring over the green fields of winter wheat, I shook my head in disbelief, exclaiming out loud, "Holy Cow! I'm actually living my dream."
>
> I live and work in Tuscany, teaching cooking classes, leading culinary and wine tours, and sharing what I've learned about regional Italian cuisine with visitors from all over the world.
>
> If I had gone to the library to consult a book on "How to Live and Work in Italy," I'd still be sitting there, frozen under the avalanche of information on work permits and visas

requirements. But I followed a path and, like Alice, fell down a hole into Wonderland.

My passion for good food prepared with loving care and shared in a convivial setting was instilled at an early age. I grew up in an Italian-American family on the East Coast of the United States. We also lived in Verona, Italy, for four years. I went to college; I worked in corporate America. The excellent salary I made went toward traveling, throwing dinner parties, eating in top restaurants, and drinking fine wines. But it wasn't enough.

When I was 36, I received a small inheritance from an aunt—enough to pursue a dream and change my life. I wasn't in a serious relationship, and I didn't have kids. "If not now, when?" I wondered.

I quit my job, sold my house, put my stuff in storage, and took off to Italy for six months. After attending cooking school in Bologna, I traveled around Italy, watching the seasons change. I was blown away by the elegant simplicity of the food and how the dishes changed as the months went by. The cuisine of northern and central Italy was unlike anything I'd experienced in my southern Italian family upbringing.

I was fortunate enough to spend the last two months of my sojourn on a rural estate, Spannocchia, where I worked in the kitchen in exchange for room and board. Situated deep in the wooded hills south of Siena, it was my first exposure to Tuscan cuisine.

I loved the simplicity of the dishes: the strong flavors of rosemary and sage; the reliance on what was growing in the garden in the late fall; the celebration of harvest, wine, and new olive oil. I worked with the estate's Tuscan cook to formulate her recipes in English.

When I returned to America, I enrolled in culinary school at the Institute of Culinary Education (ICE) in New York. An internship with Odette Fada at the San Domenico restaurant continued my education in regional Italian cuisine. I worked in restaurants, making eight dollars an hour. It was a pittance of what I'd made in my corporate job, but I was so much more fulfilled.

In the spring of 2000, I returned to Spannocchia for a visit. The owners, who by now were my friends, asked me to stay for the season. I jumped at the chance, planning to return to the "real world" at the end of the year.

Immersing myself in Tuscan culture and traditions, eager to learn as much as possible, I yearned to share my experiences with people who shared my passion. Foreign visitors to the estate were the perfect test cases. At the end of the year, rather than move back to the United States, I stayed and found my own apartment in town.

Never before had anything felt so right. I learned that when you encounter road blocks, you don't beat your head and work harder to overcome them; you look for the road that is wide open and sunny, and walk down it.

In 2001, I built a website, choosing the name Ecco La Cucina, which means "here's the kitchen" in Italian.

I applied for and received a visa and went through the bureaucratic nightmare of filing every year to renew my permit to stay. I am now a permanent resident.

What began as simple classes teaching pasta has grown to include wineries, market visits, culinary workshops on Tuscan cuisine, and week-long culinary tours throughout Italy. My sister has become my partner in the US, and we make a great team.

By showing up, working hard, developing relationships, and giving people value for their vacation dollars, I've built a solid reputation and a strong business. Life in a foreign country wasn't always easy, but what I've learned is immeasurable.

If you would like to know more about Gina, perhaps attend her next week-long Tuscany classes and culinary tours in June. You can visit her website and plan your trip now! www.eccolacucina.com

FOOD JOB: *Educator*

If you have an idea for a course you would like to teach, you must write a formal proposal—don't try to describe it orally or it may be misunderstood or misinterpreted. You have only one opportunity to sell your idea, so you have to make sure you have thought through every detail.

Write an introduction to your course and establish clear grading criteria. Your own qualifications may or may not include having attended culinary school. Give your proposed class a good title. You will need to provide student learning objectives.

TEACHING TEACHERS

Cooking Matters is a cooking-based nutrition education course designed to teach low-income families how to prepare healthy, tasty meals on a limited budget. Professional chefs and nutrition educators volunteer their time and expertise to lead hands-on courses that show adults, teens, and children how to purchase and prepare nutritious foods in healthful, safe, and tasty ways.

This can mean the difference between feeding families for just one night and making sure they have the knowledge, skills, and resources to prepare healthy meals for a lifetime.

FOOD JOB: *Mentor*

There are surely few more satisfying "jobs" in the world than being a mentor. This can be a formal or informal role. In a formal capacity, a mentor is part of a team of advisers that works within the framework of an institution of learning, with career services or alumni affairs. Otherwise, some folk set up their own business as career-change and career-advancement advisers.

The role of mentor involves a serious commitment to hearing and listening, and to understanding that the words a mentee speaks are not necessarily a direct reflection of what he or she is seeking.

A mentor draws on past experiences and up-to-date information to make connections between present practical realities and future ambitions and goals. A mentor can smooth the path to a career by making suggestions about jobs that may not have been previously considered, or even known to exist. She must also be willing to review cover letters and résumés, make introductions, and stay in contact with her mentee over the long haul.

Her task is to encourage, support, and guide—and to back off and change tactics if her approach to problem solving is not achieving the desired objective. As Holly Humphrey, dean for medical education at the University of Chicago explains, "In serving as a mentor, one has the privilege of sharing knowledge, expertise, insight, and experience ... which can ultimately affect generations far beyond the most immediate recipient."

FOOD JOB: *Recruiter*

Every business has its own unique head-hunting specialists. Recruiters for executives in the food industry are no exception. Those who work in this field will of course benefit from possessing culinary knowledge.

It is also helpful to understand psychology and to know what's new and who's who in the food industry. For more information look into food and beverage recruiters here, CareersInFood.com.

FOOD JOB: *Union Organizer*

Consider, too, a career as a union organizer or labor arbitrator. During a strike or other labor dispute, both sides agree to the selection of an arbitrator. This role is similar to that of a peacemaker—a fair-minded judge and conciliator. His or her task is to persuade, cajole, and find an acceptable compromise in a previously irresolvable labor crisis. A legal background is essential, and culinary knowledge is invaluable. The opinion of the arbitrator is almost always final.

FOOD JOB: *Front-of-House Trainer*

Who needs a trainer? Everyone does—every athlete, every debater, everyone in every field needs guidance, coaching, and teaching in order to become proficient and accomplished. An athletic trainer must have the same skills as a restaurant's front-of-house trainer.

The qualifications require demonstrable in-depth knowledge of the field, the ability to communicate effectively, the power to inspire, and the strength to simultaneously carry a big stick and a cold beer.

FOOD JOB: *Food-Writing Teacher*

This is a wonderful food job. I teach a course titled Professional Food Writing. There are surely many ways to approach this subject. One way is to instruct students about the rules of grammar and composition. Require readings in textbooks. Analyze the content. Schedule quizzes that test comprehension and the ability to spell and construct coherent sentences. I confess that I don't do all these things. Instead, I put together a series of topics that the students will surely confront as food professionals.

The classes include such subjects as: how to write a letter of apology; how to write a recipe, menu, or press release; how to write an editorial for a trade magazine; how to organize your material; how to write a restaurant or book review; how to write a personal profile or obituary; how to write a proposal for a cookbook or magazine article; and, lastly, how to write and position blog content.

If this is a field that appeals to you, I suggest you contact a school, college, or university and ask for their course guidelines. Follow the directions with utmost care. Each institution will vary, one from another. You may be asked to write a synopsis of your proposed course, along with the students' learning objectives and a paragraph detailing your curriculum. Likewise, you will probably be asked to provide your grading criteria.

I try to be neither strongly opinionated nor judgmental and instead, encourage all to try their best.

The ability to write clearly, concisely, evocatively, provocatively, humorously, and informatively are skills that can provide you with a lifetime of delight—perhaps even a steady income. I encourage my students to appreciate the art and craftsmanship of others' work and to be proud of their own.

Applying for a job as a writing teacher may be an opportunity for you to transfer your practical experience in the hospitality industry into a wonderfully satisfying new life.

Your Future as a Writer or Writing Teacher

No matter whether you end up writing menus, memos, recipes, ad copy, press kits, cookbooks, or restaurant reviews—no matter if you become a science writer, food historian, researcher, broadcaster, script writer, marketer, public-relations specialist, feature writer, news reporter, columnist, or consumer advocate—you will need to know how to make your words persuade, charm, inform, and inspire action.

Writing, of Course

In the first session of my food-writing seminar, every student is given $16 million (imaginary) dollars to create a proposal for a restaurant or other business venture. This exercise provides the context for all the lessons that follow. Thus, the student becomes a celebrated chef or other entrepreneur. He or she writes a menu for an imagined restaurant and provides a few sample recipes. The student writes an article for a consumer magazine and a different one for a trade magazine. He or she writes a restaurant review, a cookbook review, a press release, and receives a contract for a cookbook. The student also writes a letter of apology according to the scenario that one of his or her servers has spilled red wine on the bride's gown during a wedding reception.

Students learn how track and take advantage of food trends.

Students assemble a complete portfolio of their work by the end of the semester. The final grade is based not only their written material, but also on their verbal participation in class discussions. The ability to communicate well verbally transcends the medium of the written word.

Question: Do writing courses stifle writers?
Answer: I wish it would stifle more of them.

—Anonymous

FOOD JOB: *Advocate*

The Jones family has been farming in Huron, Ohio, for six generations. In 1983, a hailstorm destroyed twelve hundred acres of their peppers, cabbage, and sweet corn. They became bankrupt and lost not only their farm, but even their home. Farmer Lee Jones credits restaurateur Charlie Trotter for getting him started on the road to micro-scale success in the mid-1990s. Jones and his son started over and began tending just six acres of farmland.

Today Jones is acknowledged as an expert on sustainable agriculture and on its influence on the culinary industry. His Chef's Garden farm supplies restaurants with top-quality produce. His biography reveals that he travels nationwide speaking about sustainability, at seminars and culinary events like the International Chefs Congress and the James Beard Foundation Awards. In addition, he frequently participates in panel discussions as an agricultural expert, including at the Women Chefs and Restaurateurs National Conference in 2007 and at Chef Raymond Blanc's American Food Revolution in Oxford, England, in 2004. He currently sits on the board of *Chef* magazine.

The family established "Veggie U," a national not-for-profit organization that offers an Earth to Table science curriculum to fourth-grade and special needs classrooms. "Their goal is to place this exciting hands-on curriculum in all ninety-three thousand fourth-grade classrooms nationwide in an effort to decrease childhood disease and increase youth awareness of healthy food options and the importance of sustainable agriculture. Healthy kids also learn better and become more active contributing members to their families and communities. Veggie U has delivered more than eighteen hundred classroom kits across twenty-six states." To enroll or to apply for other work at the Chef's Garden, contact VeggieU.org/index.php.

An ideal education combines classroom learning with experiential learning to demonstrate how to put theory into practice. Classroom learning cannot supplant the importance of on-the-job training, nor can on-the-job training alone prepare students for success. Thus, the best internships are those that teach students key skills, offer hands-on experience and take place in an atmosphere in which they can ask questions, and even make mistakes while continuing to learn.

—Megan Meyer, National Restaurant Association Education Foundation

A CULINARY INTERN SPEAKS

By John E. Kelly IV

Blue Hill at Stone Barns is a restaurant specializing in local and sustainable food located in Pocantico Hills, New York. Virtually all of the food served in the restaurant is grown on the Stone Barns property or on the main farm in the Berkshires. The remainder is all sourced from within a 250-mile radius. Everything from local liquors to hybrid tomatoes developed by Cornell agronomists augments the offerings. The farm also serves as a classroom and recreational area for food professionals and tourists. The chefs have farm duties designed to strengthen their bond with the food. Interns help keep the farm running and are a source of knowledge for improving the food that is served in the restaurant.

New menus at Blue Hill are created every day, based entirely on the day's harvest. The food is unpretentious yet elegant, and is served on white china and dark stone slabs.

Recipe for Success: Dan Barber

Dan Barber is chef and owner of Blue Hill restaurant and the Center for Food and Agriculture at Stone Barns. He earned a BA in English from Tufts University in 1992, and the following year, attended the French Culinary Institute in New York City. He apprenticed at Chez Panisse and worked on the line at the Campanile restaurant in Los Angeles. He traveled to France before working at Bouley.

With his brother and sister, he opened the Blue Hill restaurant in Manhattan. David Rockefeller funded the restaurant. In 2006, Barber received the Best Chef, NYC, award from the James Beard Foundation, and the following year, he was named Outstanding Chef by the organization. In 2009, he was named one of the world's most influential people in *Time*'s annual "*Time* 100" list.

Chef Barber's efforts to create a consciousness around our everyday food choices led him to the World Economic Forum's 2010 annual meeting in Davos, Switzerland, as well as to the 2010 Technology Entertainment Design (TED) conference, where he looked toward a new ecological approach to cuisine. His writings continue to appear in many influential publications.

Reprinted with Permission from The James Beard Foundation that compiled this biography prior to his nomination as member of the Who's Who of Food & Beverage in America.

FOOD JOB: *Culinary Librarian*

Rebecca Federman is the culinary librarian at the New York Public Library. She describes her work in the following manner:

My official title is social sciences bibliographer, which means I order books and keep on top of trends and publications within the social sciences: women's studies, political science, history, and other disciplines. But I also spend a lot of time working with the Library's culinary collection—both the cookbooks and the historic restaurant menu collection. That's one of my favorite aspects of the job: reading through menus from the mid-nineteenth century to the present, helping researchers, and meeting people. It's a job where one wears a lot of hats and is never bored.

HOW TO GET STARTED AS A CULINARY LIBRARIAN

by Kimberly Beeman, Library Director, The International Culinary Center

I graduated from college with a degree in English and American literature. I love working with books, and I love working with food. I've spent most of my working life in kitchens and libraries. My cooking experience includes a half year as a student prep cook at the Harvard Faculty Club; two years at Burdick Chocolate, where I boxed up bonbons and first made pastry cream; six months at the worker-owned collective Black Bear Bakery in St. Louis, where I learned that working with anarchists is more fun in theory than in practice; and a brief job as a pastry cook at Mesa Grill and Bolo, two of Bobby Flay's restaurants in New York City.

I have worked at a total of five libraries: Widener and Houghton at Harvard; the Special Collections department at Boise State University; the lower and middle school library at Sacred Heart (an all-girls school in New York); and the French Culinary Institute. Clearly, I was destined to become a cookbook librarian. Or at least, that's what I tell myself.

Culinary Collections and Libraries

A Selective Guide to Culinary Library Collections in the United States, **compiled by The Culinary Historians of New York.**

Peacock-Harper Culinary Collection, Virginia Tech University Libraries
You can find nearly two centuries of historical information about the domestic sciences, including customs, eating behaviors, food choices and habits, social and economic history, and scientific and technological progress. To identify titles in the Culinary History Collection, search the library's online catalog, Addison, by doing a combination word search for "Culinary Collection." To locate images digitized from the Collection, browse the available categories or search the VT ImageBase.

Schlesinger Library Culinary Collection
This special collection of the Schlesinger Library supports research in culinary history, history of domestic life, and the role of food in history and culture. A guide to culinary holdings is available on this website. The books, which date from the sixteenth century to the present, represent the cuisines of all nations.

Conrad N. Hilton Library
This site links to the Culinary Institute of America's library catalog, Internet resources, and resource guides on culinary topics. The Culinary Institute of America's Conrad N. Hilton Library houses an outstanding collection of nearly 86,000 volumes, 4,500 DVDs and videos, and approximately 280 current periodical titles. Although there is a strong specialization in the culinary field, the collection also has a liberal arts listing supporting the college's ever-expanding educational programs. The library maintains the CIA's archives and special collections of menus and rare books. Services offered to the college community include reference assistance, Internet and database searching, and interlibrary loan.

Husted Culinary Collection: Penrose Library, University of Denver
The Husted Special Collection is one of several large culinary collections in the United States. Although the collection is international in scope, most of the volumes represent regional cuisines of the United States. The breadth of the collection provides a unique resource for researchers interested in the history of American domestic and culinary practices over the past few centuries

Los Angeles Public Library Menu Collection
This is a database of menus stored in the Rare Book Room of the Central Library. Images of the actual menus can be viewed. You may search by keyword, restaurant name, type of cuisine, and date.

The Menu Collection of the New York Public Library
As part of its extensive resources related to cookery, food, beverages, and culinary history, the New York Public Library owns one of the world's largest historical collections of menus—over twenty-five thousand.

Nestle Library, Cornell
The Hotel School, Hospitality and Management Department at Cornell University houses one of the largest hospitality libraries in the world. The library capabilities extend beyond Cornell to the hospitality industry through the fee-based research service Hotline.

FOOD JOB: *Scholar*

As Ken Albala writes, "Scholars are born; they do not become what they are not. They are willing, indeed eager, to delve deeply, penetrate purposefully, and provide endless detailed footnotes (that only other scholars read)."

He notes: "There is an insatiable hunger for food. Though publishing has long been recognized as an essential step on the track to tenure, only recently has food been accepted as a subject worthy of academic recognition."

The ability to convey information in a way a reader will accept it is a skill beyond compare. Too many learned treatises are impenetrably boring.

Peer scholars review other scholars' manuscripts. Peer reviewing is sometimes painful, often subjective, and frequently suspected of being tinged with unfriendliness. Fees are miniscule and customarily paid with extreme reluctance. Winning a triathlon is nothing compared with the exultant triumph of publishing an article in *Gastronomica* magazine or by a university press (though once bitten by the bug, it is tempting to reenter the lion's den immediately).

THE CHARMED LIFE OF A SCHOLAR

By Ken Albala

Lest you suspect that I was ordained from birth to a life in academia, let me assure you that in my youth I was a mediocre student at best, attracted more to the stage than books. Extraordinary teachers in college turned me around completely. These were intelligent, passionate professors across a range of disciplines, which led me to a love of learning and an abiding interest in the Renaissance that continues unabated to this day.

My career in food, however, happened more surreptitiously. My advisor in graduate school, Eugene Rice, one day informed me that the deadline to pick a dissertation topic had arrived and I honestly hadn't a clue where to begin. He counseled me to walk across the park (Central Park, that is) and check out the New York Academy of Medicine on the Upper East Side. The suggestion seemed totally random to me so I asked "why?"

His answer: "They have comfortable chairs."

Having never expressed an interest in the history of medicine, the idea still seemed capricious, but I made an appointment at the rare book room and dove into the card catalogues. These were the days before computers. Therein I stumbled on an entire drawer devoted to nutritional theory, everything ever written between 1450 and 1650, in half a dozen languages, collected by Margaret Barclay Wilson early in the 20th century and thereafter donated to the academy. With my usual enthusiastic aplomb and unusual habit of deciding life's course without deliberation, I picked these as the subject of the next three years' work. Armed with paper and a sturdy pencil for note taking, I soon began to understand the comment about comfortable chairs.

In retrospect, I think it was an excellent choice. In fact, the best advice I could give to anyone writing a dissertation is that you better really love your topic. Coming from a family obsessed with food, this was a logical choice for me. At the time I didn't realize that this opportunity to focus on a single subject for several years without any other distractions apart from teaching one class, was a luxury I would never again enjoy as a scholar. That's to say, the academic life is mostly about good juggling many research and writing projects at once, teaching, service and an unfathomable number of small annoying tasks.

When I completed my dissertation, the job market was terrible. I spent a year away from academia, in some ways a seriously deserved break, as a museum guard at the Metropolitan Museum of Art and as an apprentice at a pottery studio. I recall the very first day I arrived on campus, another more senior graduate student told me that to be an academic you have to get used to odd jobs. Little did I know that included after graduation. The next hiring season I did land a job, at the University of the Pacific in Stockton, California—it might as well have been a foreign country. After living here nearly 20 years I still find the place perplexing.

The next several years as an assistant professor I spent teaching classes and serving on committees, not thinking much about writing, until the promotion and tenure deadline began to loom. I revised my dissertation, which was published in 2002 by the University of California Press in their new food series as *Eating Right in the Renaissance*.

At the time Food Studies was just emerging and little did I know that the next decade would be spent basically riding the wave as it slowly gained academic respectability. One writing opportunity led to another. Then an editing opportunity with my own *Food Cultures Around the World* series for Greenwood Press. Apparently unable to say no to anything, I began to spend more and more time writing, some academic monographs like

The Banquet, some popular works like *Beans: A History*, some reference works, a textbook (*Three World Cuisines: Italian, Mexican, Chinese*) and even some cookbooks (*The Lost Art of Real Cooking* and *The Lost Arts of Hearth and Home*).

I did a lot of editing as well, encyclopedias, essay collections, and eventually a journal—*Food Culture and Society*. As the years passed I had more and more speaking engagements too.

It hadn't dawned on me until recently that I was among the first generation of scholars who began writing about food without coming from some other field. Food was the only thing I'd ever written about and while years ago I had to explain what I was doing, pretending not to notice suppressed giggles, now food has a permanent solid footing in higher education. Food had of course become a hot topic everywhere. Sixteen published books later and another half dozen in the works; neither food studies nor I show any signs of slowing.

It may seem a little monomaniacal since I write about food, teach about food, read about food, and cook as often as I can, but I wouldn't trade this profession for any other. My advice to those interested in becoming food scholars: find a nice quiet place to read with comfortable chairs.

Recommended Book

The Cookbook Library: Four Centuries of the Cooks, Writers, and Recipes That Made the Modern Cookbook by Anne Willan, Mark Cherniavsky, and Kyri Claflin

CHAPTER 10

relief work, lobbying, advocacy

If you think you are too small to be effective, you have never been in the dark with a mosquito.

—BETTY REESE

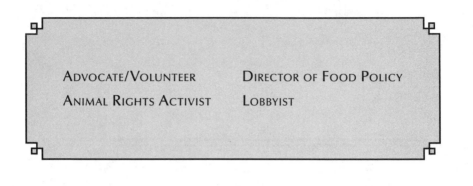

Advocate/Volunteer

Animal Rights Activist

Director of Food Policy

Lobbyist

THE CONSEQUENCES OF hunger are infinitely greater than the immediate problems of not having enough to eat. Being unable to find adequate amounts of food quickly leads to irreversible deterioration of mental as well as physical health.

A. A. Milne, the beloved author of *Winnie the Pooh*, said, "In the quiet hours when we are alone and there is nobody to tell us what fine fellows we are, we come sometimes upon a moment in which we wonder, not how much money we are earning, not how famous we have become, but what good we are doing."

Many chefs these days *are* fine fellows: they do well by being good neighbors. They volunteer at local food banks, the Feeding America hunger-relief charity, and with other organizations. Mario Batali is one among many who have created their own philanthropies. His is called the Mario Batali Foundation. As Batali has said, "Those of us who are fortunate enough to make a living feeding people have a very clear view of those who cannot afford to eat."

Cat Cora's foundation, Chefs for Humanity, is an alliance of culinary professionals and educators working with US and global organizations. It provides nutrition education, hunger relief, and emergency and humanitarian aid to reduce hunger across the world. She and her coworkers personify President Ronald Reagan's philosophy when he said, "We can't help everyone, but everyone can help someone."

Share Our Strength is a national organization whose mission is to make sure that no child in America grows up hungry. The country's leading hunger-fighting organizations—Meals on Wheels, City Harvest, Feeding America Entertainment Council, and food banks—weave together networks of community groups, activists, and food programs in hundreds of communities in order to supply children and adults facing hunger with nutritious food where they live, learn, and play.

Chefs and restaurateurs Charlie Trotter and Marcus Samuelsson are two more among the fine fellows I mentioned. They have spent innumerable hours supporting nutrition education and hunger relief organizations.

Almost all major fast food chains have established charitable foundations as well. One of the most visible programs is the Ronald McDonald House for parents of children in hospitals. The PepsiCo Foundation, too, focuses on health and wellness, youth development, and higher education.

Other soft drink companies have established company foundations as well. The Coca-Cola Foundation, for instance, also concentrates its energies on education. Its programs include a scholars program that gives two-year college scholarships to high school seniors and provides extensive funding for many other causes. Most large fast food chains, junk food manufacturers, and soda makers give to or have started philanthropies.

The Arby's Foundation, established in 1986, has focused on Big Brothers and Big Sisters of America, which has helped children from primarily single-parent homes by matching them with adult volunteers. Domino's Pizza supports the Make-A-Wish Foundation, which grants the wishes of children with terminal medical conditions. The Ingram- White Castle Foundation gives scholarships to college students.

In the soft drink world, Claude A. Hatcher, founder of Royal Crown Cola, established the Pichett-Hatcher Education Fund in 1933. By 1968, this fund had assets of almost $5 million and was one of the largest student loan funds of its kind in America.

Ben Cohen and Jerry Greenfield were trailblazers in the food industry. They funded their foundation in 1985, with an endowment of Ben & Jerry's stock. Their employee-based community action teams lead the foundation and distribute grants to surrounding communities.

Ben & Jerry's has always held certain values, and these have permeated every aspect of their business. Their brilliant Heifer International Foundation enables even those who have little to give to offer a living gift that truly keeps on giving. The gift of a cow costs $500, but anyone can contribute just $50.00 for a cow share. The foundation helps children and families around the world receive the nutrients, training, and supplies they need to live more self-reliant lives. When, for example, a family receives a heifer, every morning there's a glass of fresh, rich milk for the children to drink before heading off to school.

Likewise, through Heifer International, one can buy a whole goat for $120 or contribute $10 for a share. Goats provide up to a gallon of rich, nutritious milk each day and don't need large tracts of land for grazing. Sheep as well can be gifted for $120 each. Their wool can be used to make clothes and their manure turned into fertilizer. Finally, their mutton may provide a good dinner, while two sheep will produce even more little lambs.

There are still more animals available through Heifer International. Chickens require little, but give a lot. They don't take up much space and can thrive on food scraps. A flock of little chicks costs just twenty dollars. Three rabbits cost sixty dollars, or ten dollars a share—and they breed, well, like rabbits. A pig, too, might make a perfect present. And it is also possible to donate funds for a pair of ducks, a beehive, or the "Noah's Ark" gift package ($5,000), which is a true farmyard of fifteen lady and gentleman pairs of food-producing animals and a hive of bees. Heifer International's animals are like living savings accounts for struggling families.

All these organizations welcome full and part-time paid workers and volunteers to help with marketing, event planning, accounting, and other management skills. Learning about the many opportunities to help those in need is like discovering a Hansel and Gretel trail of crumbs; a foodie fairy tale with a happy ending. Small crumbs are transformed into loaves and fishes that feed many thousands.

FOOD JOB: *Advocate/Volunteer*

▶▶ FOOD FOR THOUGHT ◀◀

"FoodCorps places motivated leaders in limited-resource communities for a year of public service." Explore the possibilities at FoodCorps.org.

Success Story

As a twenty-one-year-old, Wendy Kopp raised $2.5 million of start-up funding, hired a skeleton staff, and launched a grassroots recruitment campaign. During Teach For America's first year in 1990, five hundred men and women began teaching in six low-income communities across the country. TeachForAmerica.org.

We make a living by what we get, we make a life by what we give.

—Winston Churchill

★ RARE FOOD JOB: *Director of Food Policy*

Edith Murname is a chef operating out of the Boston mayor's office. Her job? She was named as the first ever Director of Food Policy. Chef Murname creates and coordinates policy impacting every food-related area—from the food served in schools, to farmers' markets, to anti-obesity programs and food charities. The position was funded by a gift from a philanthropist. She hopes to increase access to free ingredients and to expand opportunities for urban farming. As Chef Murname says, "Fresh food is really important to both the city's physical and economic health."

FOOD JOB: *Animal Rights Activist*

The issue of animal rights arouses powerful emotions in the people who call for the nurturing and humane treatment of domesticated animals. Antagonism runs deep between action groups representing the interests of animals and meat and poultry producers whose job it is to bring safe and abundant meat to market at the lowest possible cost.

Why has this become such a contentious issue? When America was still largely a farming nation, most people knew firsthand how cattle, pigs, and chickens lived and died. Times were hard then, for people as well as animals, and it was understood—by the people anyway—that an animal's sole purpose in life was to provide them with a living. Well-treated cows had healthier calves; well-fed hogs fetched higher prices; chickens that pecked in the yard tasted better than those that were cooped up; but very few believed that livestock had an inalienable right to a certain quality of life.

Now that both human and animal populations have increased hugely, and now that farming has become industrialized, we buy our meats already cut and packaged. All the dirty work—and there's plenty of it—occurs out of our view, and we welcome this distance between what was once a living creature and the food on our plates.

FOOD JOB: *Lobbyist*

The Restaurant Association is just one among literally hundreds of special-interest advocates operating in Washington, DC. These include lobbyists for agricultural and fishery industries, food processors, and every other corner of the big business of food. The American League of Lobbyists says, "We want people, young people, to enter government affairs and to be part of the great American political process."

CHAPTER 11

job hunting

First try to evaluate what's in you before looking for what's out there.

—DICK BOLLES

JOB HUNTING

AS A FIRST step, it is essential to resolve these three questions:

1. What do I want to do?
2. Who do I want to work with?
3. Where do I want to work?

Try to think about the next three to five years. Hardly anyone can anticipate the long-term future, so it's probably best to try something new and just see how it goes. The possibility of working for a single organization for one's entire career and of being provided with benefits and a pension upon retirement rarely exists in this country. That time has gone. Each of us is totally responsible for the trajectory of his or her own career. The choices we make must be for ourselves, not for parents, loved ones, or the perceived expectations of others.

▶▶ FOOD FOR THOUGHT ◀◀

Working for a jerk is not worth the emotional pain. You are offering your time and expertise in exchange for cash. A good salary is not worth anything if you are unhappy.

My Word

Visualize the house where you want to live. It may be a huge estate; it may be a small cottage. It may be in your neighborhood, or you may have glimpsed it during a faraway journey. Imagine driving up to that house ... getting out of the car ... ringing the doorbell ... and telling the owners you would like to live with them. You would find it interesting. And would the owner please pay you to live with him? You'd like some benefits, too, and perhaps moving expenses.

This may not be what job seekers actually do or say, but this is the sort of attitude that many of their applications convey, unfortunately.

Companies are in the business of making money; they are not responsible for your health and happiness. You will be hired only if the employer thinks that you are bringing something of value to the table. It is your task to convince the employer that you are better equipped than any competitor to fill the position in question.

How do you do that?

Be prepared.

"Spectacular achievement is always preceded by spectacular preparation."

—Robert H. Schuller, televangelist

A Cover Letter Winner

A culinary student recently asked me to look at a cover letter he was about to send concerning an externship at a famous farm-to-table restaurant. He wanted it more than anything in the world.

Before he showed me the letter, he spoke of his grandfather's small farm. He described the excitement of getting outside after the long winter and planting new seeds. He described how he felt with the earth between his fingers. His faccd glowed as he spoke of the first green shoots peeking through the soil, the flowering of the fruit trees, the gathering of vegetables, and of cooking dinner using the foods he had grown and picked.

He beamed.

He handed me the cover letter, addressed to the owner of the restaurant.

His salutation read: "To Whom It May Concern." (Such greetings should usually be reserved for the lost luggage departments of airlines.)

The letter was beautifully composed.

Textbook perfect.

Boring!

I despaired and hesitated...

I hesitated a little longer.

Finally, I said to him, "May I suggest that you tear this up and write a new letter using exactly the same words you have just spoken?"

He had the courage to try this approach.

Less than a week later, he got the externship. I don't know who was happier, he or I!

The objective of a cover letter is to get an interview. A job offer comes later in the process. The cover letter initiates a conversation, in which you introduce yourself. It establishes the first connection between you and the recruiter, between the requirements for the job and your qualifications.

If you are responding to a blind ad, you may not know the name of the company. If you do know, try to make sure your letter is addressed to a real person and not to one who may simply toss your letter. If you don't know the name of the decision maker, try making a phone call and asking for this information.

To some degree, your cover letter will reveal your character. Don't grovel, brag, or lie—and check your spelling. Try to be as charming as you would on meeting your prospective in-laws for the first time.

A cover letter is not, or should not, be an abbreviated version of your résumé. It can include a personal anecdote describing how you heard about the job. Keep it short—not as short as Palladin's "Have gun, will travel"—but do confine it to one page of good stationery.

Don't end your letter with a wildly extravagant signature as though you were the Count of Transylvania. A simple, legible autograph is all that is required.

For more information about cover letters, and to see a sample, please visit FoodJobsBook.com.

RÉSUMÉ

What is a résumé? Like a passport, it states where you have been and when. If you hand your passport to the customs officer, you hope there will be no questions, just a stamp. This is the opposite of what you hope for your résumé. A résumé should provoke interest and prompt positive questions—a desire to know more about you.

Above all, state clearly what it is you want. If you say that you are willing to do anything, your application will be rejected, because no one will know exactly what to do with you. If you don't care, why should anyone else?

How will your résumé stand out if it looks exactly like many others? How can you make sure yours stands out from the crowd? Good graphic design immediately captures the attention of the reader. Spend time in the library learning the principles of résumé writing.

Ask a colleague to skim your résumé for twenty seconds. Ask her whether she knows what you want and whether she would hire you based on the strength of your résumé alone.

Have you convinced the recruiter of the skills you will be bringing to the table? Do you think the recruiter really cares that you were captain of the swim team when you were twelve or that you washed the floors and counted the money at a shop where you worked before you closed at the end of the day?

Your information should fit on one page. Don't use up space to say anything about references. The employer will ask for them—and check them—if you are seriously being considered for the position.

For more information, and for examples of how to format a résumé, please visit FoodJobsBook.com.

Don't Send a Résumé

Some experts suggest you send the cover letter without including your résumé. The theory is that the cover letter is a million times more likely to be read than a résumé. If the reader likes the sound of your "voice" you will be invited to come in for an interview. Bring several copies of your résumé with you.

Recommended Book

Don't Send a Résumé: And Other Contrarian Rules to Help Land a Great Job by Jeffrey J. Fox

THE INTERVIEW

An interview is like a dance: you have to learn the steps in order to be a good partner. Pay attention to the music and decide if you are the leader, the follower, or the colleague.

RSVP

As I've said, employers are in business to make money; they are not overly interested in your health or happiness, so don't waste their time declaring that you love people or that you think you will learn a lot if you are hired. They do not care what you want. They care about what they want.

Explore typical interview questions and rehearse your responses. Don't be astonished if the first thing you are asked is, "Tell me about yourself." What will you say? Note that your answers to such questions may be less important than the attitude you convey. Don't interrupt. Listen carefully. Don't make the interviewer struggle alone though the process. Volunteer pertinent information. Be nice, and be cheerful. Afterward, make notes as soon as possible. Always ask for a business card, and jot down something on it to which you can refer in your thank you letter (e.g., "I hope your cat came home," or "I hope your son's team won the game").

Shake Hands

Practice. Don't shake hands as though you were wet lettuce. A hand-to-elbow shake is for goofballs and would-be politicians. Receiving a stranger's hand in both of yours is ... tacky. Shake the hand of everyone in your orbit, and have a response ready in the event of a feeble fumble. Gazing is not the same thing as eye contact. Body language is remarkably eloquent.

> *The best way to persuade people is with your ears—by listening to them.*
>
> —Dean Rusk

The most important thing in communication is hearing what isn't said.

—Peter F. Drucker

References

You can be sure an employer will check your references. Be careful in asking people to vouch for you. Ask that any person providing you with a recommendation give you a copy of the letter to review *before* it is sent. He or she may have you confused with another person or may have subtly conveyed a negativity that will doom your application.

Thank You Notes

Always follow interviews with thank-you notes. As I've mentioned, use these to refer to your conversation, and if possible, offer a solution to a problem that was raised in it. Don't worry about "giving away" your ideas. A thoughtful thank you letter can tilt the scales in your favor when two or more candidates are equally qualified for the job. Adopt the position "What more can I give?" rather than "What more can I take?" Don't ask "What's in it for me?" even though this should be exactly what you are thinking.

JOB OFFER

Until you receive a job offer, you are in a buyer's market. You are trying to sell yourself. When you receive an offer, you are in a seller's market: you have momentarily gained your greatest strength. Now is the time to ask for what you want. You are in control of your destiny.

Resist the temptation to accept an offer on the spot. Ask if you can think about it overnight. When you get home, you may realize that there were a couple of things you forgot to ask. For example, can you work from home one day a week? Will the company pay the expenses for you to attend industry-related conferences and other work-related courses?

When negotiating your salary, you could ask if your employer would consider paying off your student loans; you never know what could happen. There may be a tax advantage for the employer, and it could be better for you to get rid of this interest-bearing obligation even if it means temporarily accepting a smaller salary.

Will the offer be withdrawn if you dare ask for what you want? This of course depends on the personality of the employer, but it is very unlikely. If you are wanted, you are desired. Show your strength and your ability to negotiate well. You will receive respect for trying and great satisfaction if you succeed.

My Word

If you decide to share your decision about accepting a specific job offer, you must also be willing to accept the opinion of another (possibly uninformed) person. Decide whether you are willing to risk such a person's wrath if you disagree with his or her opinion. What will happen should you decide to do what you had planned all along, before asking for an outside opinion. In other words, as English playwright Brian Clark asked, "Whose life is it anyway?"

Salary

One employer may offer a significantly heftier salary than another, but if the job requires a long commute, figure in the additional costs in time and money as well as the physical and emotional toll. What will the quality of your life be if you have to travel several hours a week? What matters most to you? Is it the money? Is it the hope for professional advancement? Do you anticipate making useful contacts? These are not frivolous questions. It is hugely important to take your time before making such a major life decision.

But also bear in mind, if you discover you have made a mistake, you have the ability to correct it. Don't agonize about five-year plans. Look back at the last five years, and notice how many incredible changes have occurred. Do what you think is the right thing—for you.

Life isn't fair yet. In general, women earn seventy-seven cents to every dollar earned by men, and when performing the same work for the same hours, women still make 9 percent less than men do. For example, then, where a man receives a job offer at $30,000, a woman is likely to be offered $27,300. Over the course of their working lives, this wage differential will add up to an astronomical figure. As Oliver Twist said (having first checked the going rate for the job, and having accounted for the fact that salaries vary by location): "Please sir, can I have some more."

CHAPTER 12

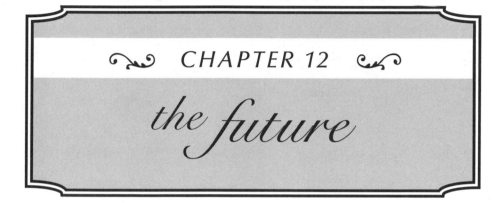

the future

Trend Tracker

EVERY DAY, WE stumble upon something else to worry about. We're concerned about global warming and the soaring price of gas. We're apprehensive about hurricanes, tornadoes, tsunamis, earthquakes, mud slides, red tides, snowstorms, hail, and hell.

I think we are fretting too much. We should get a life, and, in fact, we've got nearly two lives compared with those who lived in 1900. The life expectancy back then was 47.3 years. Maybe we're living longer because we have so many good things to eat and drink? I vote to put the butter back on the table. Bring back the salt too. And leave the pepper mill. Not many people will steal it. I'd put the Parmesan cheese on the table too so everyone can help himself or herself instead of having the server interrupt our conversation to ask if we want any.

WHAT IS A FAD?

Fads erupt in a tumbling profusion. Suddenly oats are in; tiramisu is in, then out; Caesar salad with grilled chicken is in, then out. Chocolate mousse has been out for ages. Fashions change as frequently in food as they do in clothing, but many conditions have to be right for a food fad to be accepted. This means the price must be right (cheap), it shouldn't contain any bones, the taste should be inoffensive though sweet, salty, and crispy are preferable. If it is to be hot, the "heat" must emanate from the microwave. Any new product launch has a greater rate of acceptance if it handheld, bite-sized, and wrapped in "noisy" paper.

Fiber and bran have been elevated to alimentary sainthood. We are allowing ourselves to be seduced by one product after another before abandoning it with the disillusionment of a failed love affair. But while the fad is hot, it is very hot, and some eat the food in fashion to such excess that they tire of it. By the time we are ready to relinquish it, its variations have become barely recognizable. Take croissants: a golden, flaky, buttery croissant, warm from the early-morning oven, was created by culinary angels to be savored slowly, with a frothless cup of coffee. This glory of French cuisine has no relationship to the doughy crescent made from fake fat and stuffed with tuna-fish salad. As usual, we are going overboard.

A Few Fads

Hot dogs are going haute. Several restaurants have crossed the bridge from "dirty water dogs" to all kinds of fancy variations: seafood, turkey, vegan, etc., with toppings ranging from fresh-grated organic horseradish to kimchee and carrageen seaweed.

Popcorn, too, has gone uptown. the *Baltimore Sun* reported sighting popcorn doused in duck fat, garnished with black truffles, and seasoned with truffle butter and *fleur de sel* (a sea salt from Brittany, France, costing close to two dollars for 1.5 ounces).

WHAT IS A TREND?

Dozens of trends occur simultaneously. We must be able to link them in order to stay ahead of the market. This means we must look at changing social and economic patterns. We must be fully aware of demographic shifts, employment projections, housing starts, new government regulations, corporate annual reports, global trade, and the circulation figures for vegetarian magazines.

Never since history began has any nation changed its diet as rapidly as we have done. In the blink of an eye, we have achieved the social equivalent of persuading an alcoholic carnivore to stop smoking three packs a day, stop drinking, stop eating red meat, and to start walking to work and start going to bed early (preferably alone).

The family meal is rapidly passing into history. Many of us are living in a kind of *Alice in Wonderland* world in which we are constantly looking for that little bottle that says DRINK ME on it, in the hope that, if we do, we will immediately, effortlessly become three sizes smaller.

FOOD JOB: *Trend Tracker*

The NPD Group, Inc., is a global leader in consumer and retail market research for a wide range of industries. NPD currently receives information from over 900 retailers representing 150,000 retail doors worldwide.

The company website reveals:

> Today, more than 2,000 manufacturers, retailers, and service companies rely on NPD to help them drive critical business decisions at the global, national, and local market levels. NPD helps our clients identify new business opportunities and guide product development, marketing, sales, merchandising, and other functions.

For more information about working in this ever-fascinating field, take a look at the company website at NPD.com.

FOOD IS FASHION

As Oscar Wilde observed, "Fashion is a form of ugliness so intolerable that we have to alter it every six months." The same can be said of food. We fall in and out of love with pastas, cod's cheeks, clams, frog's legs, and snails. We become mired in guacamole gridlock, and no matter what other choices are offered, we go for the fried calamari. Momentarily we adore minestrone, vichyssoise, borscht, and onion soup. We crave quiche and lobster thermidor, Szechwan food and Hunan cooking, Swiss fondue and Swedish meatballs, Russian chicken Kiev and blini, crêpes Suzettes, peach Melba, chocolate mousse, Neapolitan ice cream, canned fruit cocktail, maraschino cherries, and Cheez Whiz and Twinkies. Then, abruptly, we say good-bye to all that. Farewell Norman Rockwell. Hail to Danny Meyer's wildly popular Shake Shack, whose menu includes burgers, fries, hot dogs, cones, and shakes. The long lines wind their way slowly as salivating customers stand and wait for comfort food. The wheel turns from foreign foams and froths to the familiar; chicken pot pies are back in vogue.

• •

My (Last) Word: Brie, Bran, or Barbecue?

We have three political parties: Democrats, Republicans, and the maybe/maybe nots. Similarly, we can divide eaters into three groups: the Brie Brigade, the Bran Brigade, and the Barbecue Brigade.

The Brie group is populated with exuberant folk who live to eat something new. These are the explorers who flock to el Bulli, the French Laundry, Alinea, and the Fat Duck. Their heroes are Ferran Adria, Thomas Keller, Grant Achatz, and Heston Blumenthal. The Bries are the Cirque du Soleil of chefs, the high-fliers who soar to new heights on bended twigs and clouds of dry ice and liquid nitrogen, the Iron Chefs who continue to astonish and delight as they exhibit jaw-dropping expertise.

The Brie group hurries to every new restaurant, daring to savor novel tastes, marveling at the dazzling décor and freedom of choice. They are having a glorious time, shouting applause and spurring the chefs on to new creations with which to delight their fans, much as an encouraging audience might spur a group of jazz musicians to play set after set, variation after variation.

The Bries have a special regard for soaring creativity anchored in scientific principles. A new way to describe their work may be the phrase "Art is sense." More accurately, to this set, art is five senses, because their creations appeal not only to the senses of smell, sight, and taste, but also to touch and hearing.

As Bobby Flay observed, "In the end, your creativity—perhaps even your outrageousness—will determine the final result."

A characteristic of the Bran brigade is their tendency to treat themselves as outpatients. They study food labels as though they were reading prescriptions for life or death. Members of this group concern themselves with calories, cholesterol, fat, and gluten. The Brans medicate themselves with food supplements, rigorous exercise regimes, and diets of denial. They fret about fluorides in the water and salt (except for sea salt) in the soup. They do not lie in the sun. They worship Dr. Oz. And Saint Alice.

Many Brans are united in their devotion to slow food. They sing choruses of amens to the principles of sustainability and seasonality, as well as to farmers' markets. They believe that we should treat animals humanely so that we can eat them.

The Barbecue brotherhood is an entirely different kettle of fish. They are happiest when dressed in warm clothing and fortified with spirited drinks. They like to hunt and kill their own food—doves, ducks, and deer. The Barbecues may often be found striding around re-creations of ancient campfires in their backyards. They carry two things, a spear and a beer, and do the hunting while their mates do the entirety of the gathering—and the dish washing. The Barbecues regard a large steak with the same near-reverential awe reserved for the flag and the Constitution. Their hero is not the Jolly Green Giant.

It is interesting to note that all three of these disparate approaches to dining result in almost identical lifespans: three score years and ten.

• •

CONVENTIONS DIVIDE AND CONQUER

We can simultaneously enjoy fast and slow foods. If, in the olden days, we wanted a cup of tea, we would have had to pump the water from the well, build a fire, and worry about paying a tax on the tea. Now we can make an entire meal from store-bought, prepackaged food.

It costs $1,500 for dinner for two at Masa restaurant. Even so, the diners will be hungry for breakfast. The average cost of breakfast at IHOP ranges between five and ten dollars. No matter what we eat, our DNA remains the same.

> *Knowledge can be acquired: imagination changes everything. Success is limited only by the breadth and depth of your ideas and the degree of your dedication.*
>
> —Albert Einstein

recommended reading

Ad Hoc at Home Cookbook by Thomas Keller (Artisan, 2009)

A Feast for the Eyes: Evocative Recipes and Surprising Tales Inspired by Paintings in the National Gallery by Gillian Riley (National Gallery London, 1998)

Beaten, Seared, and Sauced: On Becoming a Chef at the Culinary Institute of America by Jonathan Dixon (Clarkson Potter, 2011)

Blood, Bones, and Butter: The Inadvertent Education of a Reluctant Chef by Gabrielle Hamilton (Random House, 2012)

Catching Fire: How Cooking Made Us Human by Richard W. Wrangham (Basic Books, 2010)

Cod: A Biography of the Fish That Changed the World by Mark Kurlansky (Penguin Books, 1998)

Consuming Passions: The Anthropology of Eating by Peter Farb and George Armelagos (Houghton Mifflin, 1980)

Don't Send a Résumé: And Other Contrarian Rules to Help Land a Great Job by Jeffrey J. Fox (Hyperion, 2001)

Eating History: Thirty Turning Points in the Making of American Cuisine by Andrew F. Smith (Columbia University Press, 2011)

Encyclopedia of Jewish Food by Rabbi Gil Marks (Wiley, 2010)

Fast Food Nation: The Dark Side of the All-American Meal by Eric Schlosser (Harper Perennial, 2005)

Food Landscapes by Carl Warner (Abrams Image, 2010)

Four Fish: The Future of the Last Wild Food by Paul Greenberg (Penguin, 2011)

How Carrots Won the Trojan War: Curious (but True) Stories of Common Vegetables by Rebecca Rupp

How's The Squid?: A Book of Food Cartoons by Jack Ziegler (Harry N. Abrams, 2004)

Imagine: How Creativity Works by Jonah Lehrer (Canongate Books, 2012)

Inventing the Truth: The Art and Craft of Memoir, edited by William Zinsser (Mariner Books, 1998)

Jean-Georges: Cooking at Home with a Four-Star Chef by Jean-Georges Vongerichten and Mark Bittman (Broadway Books, 1998)

Joan Nathan's Jewish Holiday Cookbook by Joan Nathan (Schocken, 2004)

Julia Child: A Life by Laura Shapiro (Penguin Books, 2009)

Kib (Brimming with Hope): Recipes and Stories from Japan's Tohoku by Elizabeth Andoh (Ten Speed Press, 2012)

Little Meals: A Great New Way to Eat and Cook by Rozanne Gold (Little, Brown 1999)

M.F.K. Fisher and Me: A Memoir of Food and Friendship by Jeannette Ferrary (St. Martin's Griffin, 1998)

Masters of American Cookery: M.F.K. Fisher, James Andrew Beard, Raymond Craig Claiborne, Julia McWilliams Child by Betty Fussell (Bison Books, 2006)

Menu Design in America: 1850–1985 by Steven Heller and John Mariani (Taschen, 2011)

Much Depends on Dinner: The Extraordinary History and Mythology, Allure and Obsessions, Perils and Taboos of an Ordinary Meal by Margaret Visser (Grove Press, 2010)

Onward: How Starbucks Fought for Its Life Without Losing Its Soul by Howard Schultz and Joanne Gordon (Rodale Books, 2011)

Pancake: A Global History by Ken Albala (Reaktion Books, 2008)

Salt: A World History by Mark Kurlansky (Penguin Books, 2003)

Season to Taste: How I Lost My Sense of Smell and Found My Way by Molly Birnbaum (Ecco, 2011)

Song for the Blue Ocean: Encounters Along the World's Coasts and Beneath the Seas by Carl Safina (Holt Paperbacks, 1999)

The Bread Bible by Rose Levy Beranbaum (Norton, 2003)

The Bread Bible: 300 Favorite Recipes by Beth Hensperger (Chronicle Books, 2004)

The Butler's Guide to Clothes Care, Managing the Table, Running the Home, and Other Graces, by Stanley Ager and Fiona St. Aubyn (Simon and Schuster, 1981)

The Cookbook Library: Four Centuries of the Cooks, Writers, and Recipes That Made the Modern Cookbook by Anne Willan, Mark Cherniavsky, and Kyri Claflin (University of California Press, 2012)

The Fat Duck Cookbook by Heston Blumenthal (Bloomsbury USA, 2009)

The Intolerant Gourmet: Glorious Food Without Gluten and Lactose by Barbara Kafka (Artisan, 2011)

The Magic Harvest: Food, Folklore, and Society by Piero Camporesi (Polity, 1998)

The Making of a Chef by Michael Ruhlman (Holt Paperbacks, 2009)

The Pleasures of Slow Food by Corby Kummer (Chronicle Books, 2002)

The Sacred Cow and the Abominable Pig: Riddles of Food and Culture by Marvin Harris (Touchstone Books, 1987)

The Sharper Your Knife, the Less You Cry by Kathleen Flinn (Penguin Group, 2008)

The Sociology of the Meal by Roy C. Wood (Edinburgh University Press, 1995)

The Solace of Food: A Life of James Beard by Robert Clark (Steerforth, 1998)

The Sorcerer's Apprentices: A Season in the Kitchen at Ferran Adrià's elBulli by Lisa Abend (Free Press, 2011)

The Splendid Table: Recipes from Emilia-Romagna, the Heartland of Northern Italian Food by Lynne Rossetto Kasper

The United States of Arugula: How We Became a Gourmet Nation by David Kamp (Broadway Books, 2006)

The Uses of Enchantment: The Meaning and Importance of Fairy Tales by Bruno Bettelheim (Vintage, 2010)

Tyler Florence Family Meal: Bringing People Together Never Tasted Better by Tyler Florence (Rodale Books, 2010)

Washoku: Recipes from the Japanese Home Kitchen by Elizabeth Andoh (Ten Speed Press, 2005)

Watching What We Eat: The Evolution of Television Cooking Shows by Kathleen Collins (Continuum, 2010)

What Now? by Ann Patchett (Harper, 2008)

Why We Eat What We Eat: How Columbus Changed the Way the World Eats by Raymond Sokolov (Touchstone, 1993)

Writing the Memoir: From Truth to Art by Judith Barrington (Eighth Mountain Press, 2002)

index

A

D

G

N

O

P

R